THE WILDLIFE OF THE ROYAL ESTATES

By the same author

THE BENEFITS RACKET
DOWN AMONG THE DOSSERS
THE DECLINE OF AN ENGLISH VILLAGE
THE HUNTER AND THE HUNTED
WEATHER-FORECASTING THE COUNTRY WAY
CURES AND REMEDIES THE COUNTRY WAY
ANIMAL CURES THE COUNTRY WAY
WEEDS THE COUNTRY WAY
THE JOURNAL OF A COUNTRY PARISH
JOURNEYS INTO BRITAIN
THE COUNTRY WAY OF LOVE

THE
WILDLIFE
OF THE
ROYAL ESTATES
ROBIN PAGE

HODDER AND STOUGHTON
LONDON   SYDNEY   AUCKLAND   TORONTO

BOOK DESIGN BY SHARYN TROUGHTON

British Library Cataloguing in Publication Data
Page, Robin
   The wildlife of the Royal Estates.
   1. Natural history—Great Britain   2. Crown
   lands—Great Britain
   I. Title
   574.941   QH137
   ISBN 0 340 32352 3

The wild life of today is not ours to
dispose of as we please.
We have it in trust.
We must account for it to those who
come after.

King George VI

It is obviously impossible for any one generation to create wildlife habitats from scratch. Conservation techniques have been practised on the Royal Estates for very many generations with each one attempting to limit damage and degradation and to make a useful contribution to the future.

I welcome this book by Robin Page as it is an expert assessment and therefore most valuable to those involved as an indication of what is right and what is wrong and what needs to be done. I hope it will also be valuable to the general reader as an insight into the stewardship which I believe all responsible land-owners feel for their estates. The will is there, as much of our landscape demonstrates, but the author points out the very serious economic pressures bearing on all those who are involved with the land, farmers and land-owners alike.

I am glad that the author makes the important point about the problems of erosion, litter and damage which are the inevitable consequence of greater public access to the countryside. The offenders are a minority but they do make difficulties for both the considerate visitors as well as for the conscientious land-owners.

Contents

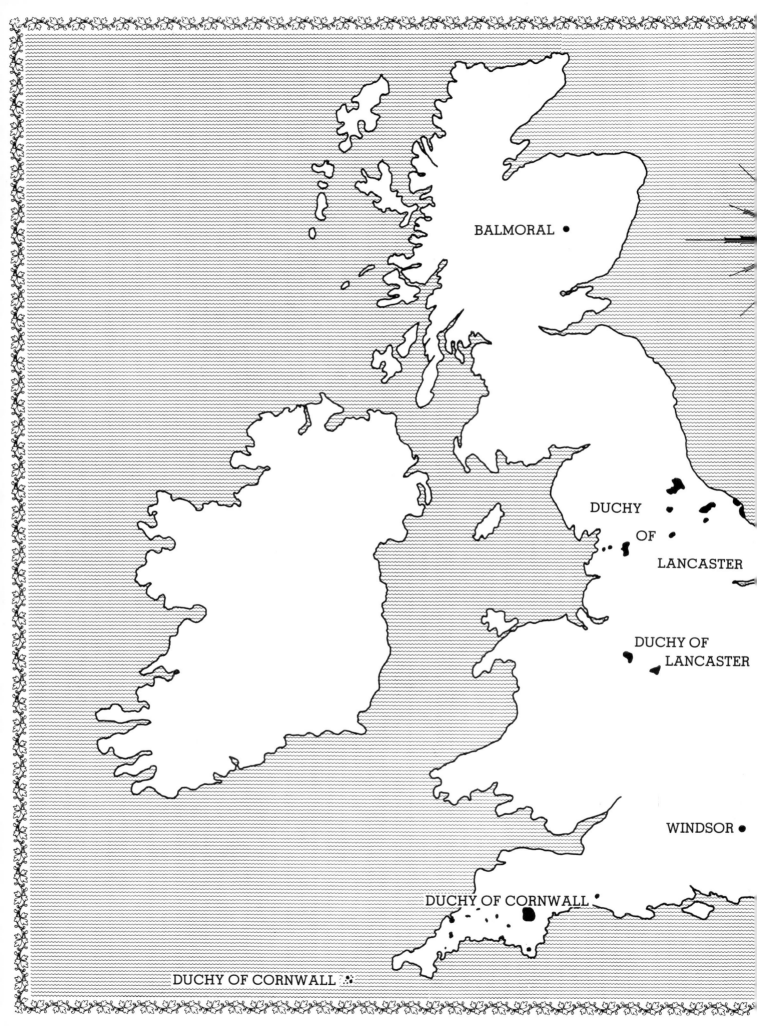

BALMORAL •

DUCHY
OF
LANCASTER

DUCHY OF
LANCASTER

WINDSOR •

DUCHY OF CORNWALL •

DUCHY OF CORNWALL

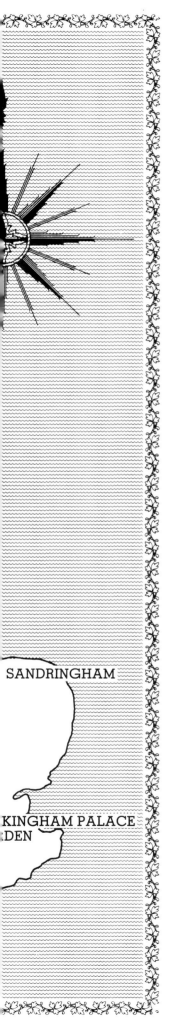

SANDRINGHAM

KINGHAM PALACE
DEN

Introduction

The birth of this book was a complete accident. Three years ago, two friends were busy producing a number of "package" books on members of the Royal Family. One day when I visited them, material was strewn all over the floor of their office, and each book seemed to be following well worn and familiar themes. My spontaneous reaction was: "There is only one really good book left to be written on the Royal Family, and that is 'The Wildlife of the Royal Estates'." The seed was sown and it began to germinate immediately. Its growth was helped by a coincidence, for at the same time, criticism was being directed against members of the Royal Family for allowing deerstalking to take place on the Balmoral Estate. The claim being that stalking was harmful to wildlife. It seemed to me a very misguided view, for if deerstalking took place, it meant that there were many red deer, and from its position in Scotland I assumed that there would also be roe deer, golden eagles, peregrine falcons, ptarmigan, crested tits, salmon, probably otters, and many other fine examples of our native fauna and flora. Far from threatening wildlife it suggested that the area could in fact be an important natural sanctuary.

The idea grew, for with just a slight knowledge of the locations of "royal land", it was clear that the Royal Estates covered a great variety of countryside. They included mountains, moorlands, islands, bogs, forests, fens, lowlands, sand dunes and the sea; an example of almost every type of landscape to be found in the British Isles. It was obvious therefore that the estates should hold birds, animals and plants as varied as the habitat.

Another great attraction was the fact that the estates really could be classified as refuges. Although large areas of the Royal Estates are open to the public, much of the land is still private where only estate employees and local people work and walk. Consequently in some areas the wildlife would not be suffering from the same degree of disturbance as in many parts of Britain where there is unrestricted public access.

Living as I do, on a small Cambridgeshire farm, one further reason made me keen to see the estates; for large landowners and those involved with small family farms have more in common than is at first obvious. Many care for their land because it has been handed down to them, and they in turn want to pass it on to their children; as a result landscape and continuity are important, and owners want to leave their land as attractive as the day it was inherited.

This is not always the case with the strictly commercial side of agriculture; much land is now owned by "agro-businessmen" and institutions, and most of them see their bank balances as the only important features; they do not understand the traditional farmer's feelings for his land, or his relationship with the plants and animals that share his fields and depend on his husbandry, and so wildlife and the whole principle of "conservation" suffer as a direct result. Consequently I wanted to see land that had been managed, preserved and enjoyed over several generations.

Surprisingly, I discovered that a book on the natural history of the Royal Estates had never been undertaken before. This was a genuine surprise, not only because of the contrasts and beauty of the areas involved, but also because of the long and active association that members of the Royal Family have had with conservation. There are numerous royal connections with wildlife organisations and schemes, and often it is not simply a passive interest. Among the many positions held, Her Majesty the Queen is Patron of the Royal Society for the Protection of Birds, His Royal Highness the Duke of Edinburgh has been President of the World Wildlife Fund for a number of years, and His Royal Highness the Prince of Wales is Patron of the Royal Society for Nature Conservation.

I assumed that three or four days on each estate would produce all the required information, and it seemed sensible to include only the most well-known estates as well as the Duchies of Cornwall and Lancaster; anything more would have been an intrusion, for members of the Royal Family enjoy, and earn, their small amount of privacy.

A visit to Buckingham Palace followed, for a meeting with His Royal Highness the Duke of Edinburgh, and his interest in conservation and the breadth and depth of his knowledge were immediately obvious. Prince Philip spoke of some of the rare species on the estates and of the problems involved if too many people became aware of their exact presence, but he approved of the idea in principle and the book was under way.

My estimate of the time required proved to be extremely naïve, for my "three or four" days on each estate turned, over eighteen months, into numerous treks from almost the top, to the very bottom of the British

Isles, and it made my last book, *Journeys into Britain*, seem very leisurely by comparison. In all, I spent over four months visiting and travelling, from Deeside, to the Isles of Scilly. I covered well over 30,000 miles by road and in excess of 200 miles on foot. I did see golden eagles, peregrine falcons, salmon and red deer, as expected, but the diversity and sheer beauty of the estates far exceeded my expectations. I saw clear flowing streams, wide valleys, raging seas, peaceful sunsets, harriers hunting, foxes scavenging, badger cubs playing and deer browsing. In addition there were ancient trees, fragrant flowers and the fragile beauty of a butterfly's wings. Strangely, almost the only thing missing was the crested tit, for although it flourishes along Speyside, it has not yet crossed in any numbers into Deeside, because of the great blocking mass of the Cairngorm mountains.

The book is very much a personal view of the wildlife to be found on the Royal Estates, and it is not meant to represent an exhaustive scientific study, or a complete natural history guide, as it quickly became clear that such works would require several volumes. It is a report of what I saw and found, as well as information from keepers, naturalists and local people, to whom the areas have been places of work, study, or home, over many years. Nevertheless I hope it will be of interest to both the serious naturalist and the general reader, giving information on a number of scarce and declining species, describing old landscapes that in other areas are under great pressure, as well as giving glimpses of places that, although well known, are essentially distant and private. I hope too that the book conveys some of the excitement, wonder and calm that can still be experienced in overcrowded Britain, and also the great sense of discovery that wildlife gives. My research and travels also taught me a very important lesson; that I still have a great deal to learn, appreciate and enjoy.

On many of the estates visitors are welcome and details of public access are given towards the end of the book. Because of the vulnerability of some birds, butterflies and flowers, caused by the activities of various collectors, irresponsible birdwatchers, and plant thieves, I have not been able to give the exact locations of several species. This has been necessary to protect them from harassment, disturbance and loss; if any of these things do occur, then my main aim, to encourage an interest in wildlife and conservation, will have been defeated.

I hope, however, that this does not diminish the interest or usefulness of the book. I hope too that visitors to the estates will respect the private areas, for even on royal land some wildlife needs every help and consideration. With the continuing active interest of members of the Royal Family, places such as Balmoral, Sandringham, Windsor and the Isles of Scilly should keep their wealth of wildlife for years to come; our royal heritage will be even richer because of it.

Balmoral

BALMORAL is probably the best known of the Royal Estates, and each year during the late summer and early autumn the Court is in residence. It is a custom started by Queen Victoria, for on her first visit to the Highlands in 1842 she became captivated by their wildness and beauty. Further visits followed and in February 1848 the lease for Balmoral was purchased, before she had even seen the property. Both the Queen and Prince Albert loved their Highland home, with Queen Victoria relaxing by walking and meeting the local people in their cottages, and Prince Albert enjoying the farming, forestry and sport offered by the estate.

Because of its appeal, Balmoral was bought outright in 1852, together with the neighbouring property of Birkhall, and they have both been popular with successive generations of the Royal Family ever since. In her diary Queen Victoria described Balmoral as: "A pretty little castle in the old Scotch style." Yet by 1855, as more room was needed, the present castle was built, under the direction of Prince Albert, and the old building, 100 yards away, was demolished.

Balmoral lies in the heart of the Highlands, with the attractive turreted castle overlooking the river Dee and the 50,000 acres of the estate covering some of the finest and most rugged mountain scenery in Britain. The land is dissected by fast flowing mountain streams, with waterfalls and deep cut valleys; there are areas of ancient forest, peat bogs, where even in the driest summer water oozes, great tracts of open heather moor, distant lochs, towering walls of vertical granite and an ever changing sky. The wildlife is as spectacular and varied as the physical features, moving through the seasons in an annual procession of birth, vitality and death. It has colour, beauty and suffering too, and each year it is renewed as the cycle of life revolves slowly within its ancient prospect. It represents one of the last and most precious areas of true wilderness in Britain, where the forces of nature can still be felt, penetrating beyond its physical reality and touching the innermost spirit of Man. This feeling is amplified by the summit of Lochnagar to the south that dominates the estate with its high, towering presence. It is a great intrusion of granite, often half hidden in cloud, but even in summer, under an open sky it looks mysterious, even foreboding, with its grey, bare rock contrasting sharply to the ridges and gulleys of lingering snow.

It is a mountain whose profile becomes etched in memory and inspired Lord Byron to write:

> England! thy beauties are tame and domestic,
> To one who has rov'd on the mountains afar:
> Oh! for the crags that are wild and majestic,
> The steep frowning glories of dark Loch na Garr.

The whole landscape exudes antiquity, with wild skies, the great amphitheatre of sheer and shattered rocks at the corrie of Lochnagar, and the steep, rounded sides of Glen Muick, with its loch and meandering stream, that as darkness falls and the air cools resembles a tributary and pool of pure liquid ice.

The great valleys and lochs of the Highlands were gouged out by glaciers over thousands of years, before being washed and worn by the meltwaters of receding snow. It is a landscape moulded and modified by the intense cold of an age of ice, and in winter that same force still tries to hold the land in its grip.

My first view of Balmoral was in complete contrast, on the last day of July, with the sun beating down from a cloudless sky. Even so Lochnagar still held patches of snow and immediately I was drawn towards its summit, approaching from the wide, winding beauty of Glen Muick.

From the Spittal of Muick, the floor of the valley is rough grassland, dotted with harebells, ''the bluebells of Scotland'', and the yellows of tormentil and bog asphodel. Foxgloves flowered at the roadside and a dipper flew low along the small river. Down the valley a plantation of fenced young trees shimmered in the heat; pines with a fringe of rowan and birch. The new woodland was at the beginning of a well established wildlife pattern; without the presence of deer a luxuriant growth of grass had encouraged a large vole population to build up within the enclosure, which had in turn attracted short-eared owls to settle for the summer to breed. The adults hunt even in daylight and when they have young the fledglings wheeze away in the undergrowth until food is brought and hunger is appeased. Whinchats too find it an ideal place to nest and rear their young, because of the abundance of insects and good vantage points from which to catch their food and sing their monotonous song or

Short-eared owl.

"chat". They like perching on the forestry fence posts, as well as the low gorse or "whin"; hence, "whinchat".

Later, when the trees of the new plantation become more dense and the grasses die back, the voles will go and the birds are replaced by pigeons, tawny owls and mistle thrushes. Finally, when the trees are large enough, the fences will be removed and the deer will move in for winter shelter. Red squirrels will also be attracted, as well as birds such as redpolls, crossbills, sparrow-hawks and capercaillie.

Across the valley older pines had already reached the final stage, and beyond them the climb to Lochnagar really began, upwards, through open heather. The heather was just coming on to early flower, as bees, wasps and flies all worked busily, with the scent hanging low in the heat. The cross-leaved heath and bell heathers are the first to bloom, followed by the more prolific ling, that continues well into September. Ling has the finest leaves and the most abundant flowers, while the flowers of the cross-leaved heath are larger, and more bell-like, than even those of the bell heather itself.

A stream tumbled and murmured with summer gentleness, while brilliant copper wings flew fast above the grasses by the water. The dark green fritillaries had a rapid flight between long glides, their wings almost translucent in the strong light. Although they are considered by some to be a woodland butterfly, they thrive in heather and moorland grasses and can fly in all but the strongest wind. The caterpillars feed on the leaves of violets, particularly marsh violets, while the butterflies themselves are fond of the flowers of thistles, and several briefly sipped nectar before continuing their rapid flight. Devil's bit scabious also flowered among the grasses, while the heather competed with the broader leaves of bearberry, cowberry and bilberry. Clumps of distinctive crowberry also flourished, with its heather-like leaves and dark berries, that, as its name suggests, are only fit for crows.

Along the valley of the small stream a mistle thrush sang from a lichen covered birch: with boulders and smoothly flowing water, butterflies and the heather covered hills, it was Highland life at its most benevolent. Higher, on a well worn path, small tortoiseshell butterflies flew and rested on rocks, taking in heat through their open, quivering wings. Other fliers were more erratic over the heather, for the male northern eggar moth flies frenetically by day, searching for the scent of unmated females; the females only begin to fly at dusk.

Approaching the stream's source, its flow gave way to a series of boggy pools, clear water surrounded by squelching peat. Pond skaters moved easily over the surface and then, even at this altitude, a large black and blue dragonfly, a common hawker, droned backwards and forwards, patrolling its territory. Several times another came too close and they engaged in brief aerial combat. They are ideally named for they do literally "hawk" for their food; they are winged marauders, flying

A ptarmigan in summer plumage.

strongly and plucking smaller insects, including damselflies, out of the air. The dragonfly nymphs live in the cold, dark pools to emerge and burn out their bright, brief, aggressive lives during the short highland summer.

Wading through heather, there were boulders and hidden streams covered by mosses and arches of granite, only sound betraying their presence. Where the rocks were mainly bare, with scant vegetation, a small covey of ptarmigan watched, with slight movement revealing both themselves and their apprehension. They are remarkable birds, members of the grouse family that prefer the tundra-like conditions of the high tops, rarely being found below 2,500 feet. In winter their plumage turns white to match the snow and they are the only British bird to have evolved this method of arctic protection. In summer their feathers are marbled and mottled, like the lichens, mosses and patterns of igneous rock that surround them. As I approached, the ptarmigan burst into rapid flight, immediately losing their camouflage as their white wings beat rapidly. They feed on the shoots of heather as well as the leaves and fruit of bilberry and crowberry and their young can fly just ten days after hatching.

Along the ridge of Lochnagar, hollows of snow remained hard and cold, and below, lochs shone a deep metallic blue, a darker, cooler shade than the colour of the sky. The great cracked and fissured walls of the corrie were impressive, with sheer rock faces and still streams of splintered scree. Beyond were ridges and mountains, an almost alpine scene; dark in a haze of heat. The alpine or arctic likeness did not result from a romantic imagination, for the corrie of Lochnagar has plants that are also found in far colder climes; Alpine sowthistle, Norwegian cudweed, roseroot, mountain sorrel, Alpine lady fern, Alpine scurvy-grass, globe flower, Alpine speedwell, Alpine mouse-ear, chickweed willow-herb, downy willow and various others.

The exposed tops are also arctic by nature, because of the bitter winds and intense cold that are not always restricted to winter. Consequently, above 3,000 feet heather is replaced by carpets of a low mat-like vegetation, consisting of stiff sedge, least willow, hair moss and three-leaved rush. The lichens also reflect the conditions, with plenty of reindeer moss "Cladonia rangiferina", and another "Cladonia belli-diflora", which still only has a Latin name. Why that should be is strange, for it is an attractive little lichen, with spores produced on small stalks with bright scarlet caps.

Once at the top, 3,784, 3,786, or 3,789 feet high, depending on which map or book is consulted, I rested, with a panorama of ridges and mountain tops in every direction. Compass bearings carved in stone showed Cairngorm to be 18½ miles away to the north-west. Incredibly, at this height, a small tortoiseshell butterfly flew over me, oblivious to the summit's altitude or arctic reputation, and miles away from the

Loch Muick from the head of the valley.

stinging nettles on which it fed as a caterpillar. In more exotic climes we would pay much more attention to its extravagant beauty. On a far valley side a small group of red deer hinds quietly grazed; spending high summer up in the hills to reduce the temperature and the number of flies.

I began to descend away from the well worn path. Back into heather a grouse erupted into flight, its red eye stripe clearly visible, and its laughing call fading as it fell back into concealment. On damper ground several cloudberries were ripe, each plant with a single orange fruit, rather like a large solid raspberry, with a tart refreshing taste. Patches of Alpine lady's mantle were on flower, its small frond-like leaves making it one of the most attractive cold-loving plants.

Several lochs and lochans dotted the moorland below, one fed by a falling stream, with water shooting, not tumbling, down great slabs of smooth, flat rock. A larger loch had a beach of pure white sand and was overlooked by a sheer rock wall hundreds of feet high. From a distant place, high pitched mewing came in on the breeze; the ''begging'' calls of young peregrine falcons, fledged, but still depending on their parents for food.

I walked in a wide circle over ridges, boulders and through heather

back to the valley of the Glas Allt, another falling stream with water
shooting along sheets of rock. It gave music to the hillsides and the
meadow pipits added to the feelings of peace. They were false of course,
for human sentiment can be dangerous and misleading; further along, a
few feathers, caught up in flowering bell heather showed where a less
fortunate pipit had met its end. Whether it had been killed by a bird or
beast was not clear, but nearby a fox "scat" indicated that one hunter was
present. The dropping contained pips from berries, as well as fur or
feather, showing that the fox was living well on a varied diet. There were
hare droppings too, but the mountain hares remained well hidden from
view.

A pair of wheatears called in alarm and one flew, its white rump
showing clearly. They always give me great pleasure, for they pass
through Cambridgeshire and the farm every March and April, and we
usually see them as we are sowing spring corn. Then, they are heading
north to breed, away from the warm wintering grounds of tropical
Africa. In some regions they are actually known as "white rumps",
although the vulgar call them "white highland flash farts".

The volume of the stream increased with cataracts of white-topped
water tumbling into swirling, bubbling pools. Gnarled birch and rowan
grew, with tufts of lichen and twisted limbs, and then the stream fell
vertically, as spectacular falls hastened its flow towards Loch Muick and
its smooth, curved valley. The flowers of rosebay willow-herb added
height to those of the heather and a clump of brilliant yellow mountain
saxifrage flourished where spray dampened its roots.

Loch Muick was still, reflecting the mountains with absolute clarity.
Suddenly, from its far off surface came a familiar call, gooselike and
ghostlike, a haunting, evocative sound, that I had last heard in the
Shetland Isles. Two distant red-throated divers were riding low in the
water, and another flew in with fast wingbeats, its neck outstretched. It
splashed down by them and the noises became even more ethereal as
they beat the water with their wings in display. The red-throated diver is
one of our most beautiful and primitive birds and could well breed in
some of the small lochans around Lochnagar. If seen in the spring and
early summer, away from the main loch, they should never be
approached, for they are shy and easily leave their eggs, which then cool
or can become easy prey for crows.

Well over nine hours had passed before I returned to the "Spittal of
Glenmuick". It is ideally named for "spittal" means "resting place". In
the past it served as a stopping and watering point for drovers as they
moved their cattle to the lowland markets. The old track passes alongside
Loch Muick, over the Capel Mount and into the wide splendour of Glen
Clova.

The appeal of Balmoral goes beyond its high peaks, heather moors and
lochs however, for the valley of the Dee itself contains two ancient

elements, rare and natural, that have so far, in part, resisted the passing of time. At first glance the Dee is simply another river, winding through a mixture of forest and farmland. But it is much more, for the flow is still determined by the melting snow, and not by the dams and sluices of hydro-electricity. The water is cold and fresh having seeped through peat or washed over bare rock, far away from agricultural drainage channels and the filtration beds of industry. Each year since the ice retreated salmon have "run" up from the sea to lay their eggs in the headwaters, and otters breed in the quieter reaches of the Dee valley.

Along the banks there are regimented blocks of alien, commercial pines, but again there is more, for Deeside retains remnants of an ancient world – areas of old Caledonian pine forest, that with its wildlife forms a direct and living link with the time when the Ice Age slowly melted away.

It was another day of summer heat when I walked by the Dee for the first time, upstream from the castle. The river flowed quietly, its water pushing lazily over shelves of rock, squeezing by boulders and gliding into silent pools. It was clear and clean, with small fish, salmon parr, darting for cover. A high heron glided erratically in steep descent, its wings tucked in and its legs hanging loosely; it landed clumsily on a boulder to fish. A large salmon jumped, or rather flopped, languidly, only just clearing the water; it matched the weather and the mood. Many insects flew above the surface and wagtails, pied and grey, pursued them. By the boulder-strewn river were flowers and then ancient forest, rising to high mountains. It almost had the look of the Canadian Rockies.

On the bank, movement drew my attention; it was a stoat hunting. I sucked the back of my hand loudly; it stopped, stood up and ran towards me, thinking of a young rabbit or a bird in distress. It stood up again on its hind legs, but then my scent caused it to scurry away.

There were many wild flowers: yarrow, knapweed, harebells, Devil's bit scabious, heartsease – the small wild pansy associated with love, zigzag clover, bird's foot trefoil, eyebright, pignut, hogweed, meadowsweet, lady's bedstraw, yellow rattle, ragwort, ox-eye daisies, melancholy thistle and angelica; such descriptive and attractive names. They are appropriate too, for the seed pods of bird's foot trefoil look just like a bird's foot; dried lady's bedstraw was once used to stuff pillows because of its pleasant aroma and the melancholy thistle was so called because its head droops down until the flower finally opens. They are so much better than the Latin names given by scientists, who in their enthusiasm to classify and standardise have managed to frighten many people away from the appeal of wild flowers.

Between birches, with lichens growing on their bark, grasses had been left to flower and seed. Among knapweed, harebells and yarrow, butterflies flew; the large white, small white and green-veined white were all familiar to me, although until I came to know Gordon Beningfield the

Alpine lady's mantle.

butterfly artist I called them all "cabbage whites". It was Gordon who first made me aware of their ephemeral beauty and the changing butterfly cycle throughout the summer.

He showed me the importance of wild flowers and grasses as food plants for caterpillars, with each type requiring a different diet, and how the butterflies themselves have their own favourite flowers. More importantly, butterflies are not just insects to give pleasure, for they can also indicate changes around us caused by pollution, destruction and even the long-term trends in the weather. Consequently, the disappearance of a butterfly usually means that its food plant has gone because of sprays, chemical emissions or development. The reverse is also true, and an abundance of butterflies indicates a diversity of wild plants, a healthy environment and sympathy for the land.

A new butterfly flew by with a flopping flight; it was a Scotch argus, a mountain butterfly with a liking for the grassy fringes of high woodland. Several more were active; their wings varied from brown to velvet black, with dark red spots and pin-points of white that looked like minute sunlit holes. The caterpillars feed on the plentiful purple moor grass and the butterflies are usually on the wing from the middle of July until the end of August. The smaller wings and faster flight of a solitary Northern brown argus caught my attention; although it is called an "argus", it is not related to the Scotch argus, and despite its colour, a dark chocolate brown, it is a member of the "blue" family. It looks like a rich female blue, with dark, white-edged wings and a row of small orange dots. It differs from the English brown argus by having a tiny white speck on each forewing, giving it the alternative name of "Scotch white spot".

Where the river flowed through an enclosure of pine, a common sandpiper called and flew low over the water. It was a comparatively new plantation with older pines beyond. A doe roe deer tip-toed delicately, browsing as she went, while larger slot marks (footprints) showed that red deer were in the block too, having crossed cattle grids when they were full of snow. More dark green fritillaries flew through glades in the warm sun and the small mauve flowers of bitter vetch grew where water glistened.

Walking into natural pine forest is like seeing and breathing a part of our primeval past. The Scots pine is one of only three native conifers, the others being the yew and juniper; after the Ice Age it grew over most of Britain. Gradually the climate became warmer and wetter and in much of England the pine was replaced by woodlands of oak, ash, lime and alder, with the natural pinewoods being restricted to Scotland, and a few heaths and fens. Then in the eighteenth century large scale felling took place for timber and firewood as well as to clear the hillsides for sheep. As a result the Scottish forests dwindled almost into extinction. When the Forestry Commission was created in 1919, to undertake massive re-planting as an acknowledgment of Britain's great shortage of wood, it did not fall back on the Scots pine, despite the quality of its timber, preferring instead to use faster growing foreign conifers.

Consequently only a few thousand acres of the indigenous pine forests are left and even some of those are under threat. Although large Scots pines can legitimately be felled for timber, a few owners continue to "clear fell", to replace the native trees with Sitka spruce and lodgepole pine. The other problem is caused by deer; in the past old forest renewed itself naturally; the mature trees seeding and young saplings growing up beneath them. The deers' search for winter food did not prevent this process as they were controlled by large predators and the needs of man. Now, with almost no natural enemies, a higher deer population with surprisingly efficient browsing patterns has meant that few trees survive.

The Royal Family is appreciative of the old forest and aware of the problems threatening its future. Indeed this awareness goes right back to Queen Victoria herself who walked and rode for hours through the woods. Her love and concern was shown when she sold a small part of the old Caledonian forest to a neighbouring estate to make the boundaries more rational. Shortly after the sale, as she was driving in her carriage, she heard the sound of an axe. She was horrified and the new owner was told: "I sold you the land, not the trees," and the felling was stopped.

Scotch argus.

Since then the pressures have increased, for estates are costly to run and have to pay their way; consequently the threats from felling and deer remain very great. Because of this an area of fifty acres in the centre of Balmoral's forest has been fenced off to allow natural regeneration to take place, and strangely, this began with the help of the deer. The Duke of Edinburgh explained this process to me: "Few of the remaining areas of old Caledonian pine forest regenerate naturally and so it is much better to allow the deer in to 'poach'* the area. We did this with a very small piece in 1972 which was then fenced off. As a result young rowan and Scots pine quickly appeared. We then organised an area of about fifty acres for a longer study and fenced it in. We shut in thirty to forty hinds and they stirred up the whole enclosure, with their hooves ploughing the ground. This worked, for now, with the deer driven out, many seedlings are coming up, but they have to get well established before the heather gets back and smothers them."

The Prince of Wales is particularly fond of Balmoral and in 1980 published a delightful children's story, *The Old Man of Lochnagar*, written for Prince Andrew and Prince Edward, when they were nine and five. He is glad that the natural succession of the forest has been restored: "The old Caledonian pine forest is enormously special to me. The Scots pines are almost magical with their different shapes and the noise of the wind through their needles. I like to walk through it alone, away from people, or sit and draw. It is what Scotland looked like three or four hundred years ago and we have an obligation to future generations,

* over-graze

Red squirrel.

as well as to ourselves, to keep it as it is. We must create, not destroy habitat.''

To see, hear, and smell an area of ancient Caledonian pine forest is to understand and feel why it is so special. It has a quality of almost ecclesiastical magnificence; a natural cathedral of sanity, sanctuary and beauty, set in stone. The Scots pines themselves can grow to a height of 120 feet, with a girth of eighteen feet, and wafting through them is the aroma of pine needles and damp places, as well as the sounds of water, wind, bird song, and silence.

It was in such a place that Queen Victoria had an arched iron bridge erected over a steeply falling stream. I walked up the valley away from it and sat by a large old tree, to watch and reflect on what Scotland had already lost. From one of the tall, flat-topped trees, probably 250 years old, a stream of debris slowly fell. I scanned and strained my eyes to see the cause and it took several minutes to focus and identify the head of a red squirrel at the very top of the tree. Later, another, with a lump of moss in its mouth travelled from tree to tree on its way to add comfort to its drey.

Where the valley briefly opened out there were lush green hummocks; boulders covered with mosses, lichens and bilberry. Each solid core was encased in thick peat and vegetation, showing its great untouched antiquity. As I moved on, coal tits, chaffinches and blue tits could be seen in the trees and a sparrow-hawk perched briefly on a dead branch. Around a damp flush, heath spotted orchids still flowered and there were patches of wavy hare-grass and hairy woodrush. Away from the stream, I still passed through old pines, as well as birches with lichens and fungi feeding on their bark. Juniper grew with spreading twisted limbs, and appropriately for Scotland, there were clumps of stagshorn moss.

Movement came from an area of deep shade; it was the flickering ears of a roe doe trying to keep off flies. She was lying down and periodically rolled her head in clumps of long grass to gain temporary respite. It should have been ideal for blackcock and capercaillie, two gamebirds of the ancient forest, but I caught no glimpse of them. In earlier years I had walked many times through the woods of Speyside in the hope of seeing them. I met with no success and I began to think that they were mythical creations of inventive highland minds.

Again, from a winding path there were fine views, through trees, of the whole valley, with forest, the meandering Dee and the high crumbling walls of well worn rock. Closer at hand a red deer calf, still with its ''Bambi'' spots, drank from its mother, head-butting her udder to increase the flow of milk, oblivious to the gaze of an intruder. As I walked down to a small lake, with a log cabin at the water's edge, to watch the lengthening shadows and the changing light, a buzzard circled effortlessly above. It seemed remarkable that in just two days of high summer, in Britain, I had still been able to see and experience so much.

With a mixture of patience, good fortune and physical endeavour Scotland's wildlife can be seen at any season, but it is best to see it in sequence, through a highland year. Strangely, the wildlife year at Balmoral does not start in the spring, but in the autumn.

Autumn is a time normally associated with the decline of the year, when the life and vibrance of summer slows and dies, leaving behind it the drab dormant landscape of winter. Such a concept is wrong, for autumn in the Highlands is when life begins, a season of passion, struggle and hot blood, made manifest by the roaring of the red deer stags and the hostile clash of antlers in the still night air.

It is breathtakingly beautiful, and, ironically, it comes when the tourist season is almost over. I arrived after days of October rain and the morning broke with a brilliant dawn. Shafts of light illuminated the valley, catching the fields of fresh green, as pasture held its final flush of autumn, and the leaves of the trees reflected shades of gold, russet, yellow and copper. The river itself was in spate with the roar of its white-topped water and its never-ending echo filling the whole valley. Beyond, even the dark blocks of planted pines were broken by the burnished bronze of sun-fired larch. The sun gave an intensity of colour and crispness of definition that through the cool limpid air painted a patchwork of light and shade on the rich mellow tones of a season in transition. The duns and browns of heather and bracken on the high moors absorbed bronze, while as the sun rose higher the lambent rays caught Lochnagar, picking out its distant rocks and gulleys with perfect clarity.

Birch, beech and sycamore wore their final splendour of the year and the golden leaves of rowan exaggerated its clusters of crimson-orange berries. Rowan berries are bitter to human taste, but birds enjoy them and migrating redwings, fieldfares and mistle thrushes were feeding greedily.

The castle, granite grey, seemed warmer surrounded by the gentle shades of autumn. In the old forest the scent of pine was rich, cool, and damp as light mirrored from countless drops of grass-held dew. Despite the rush of water, pounding and foaming beneath the iron bridge, the level had fallen, for soil and rock had been washed from the roots of overhanging rowan, alder and pine, leaving them mapped out in air.

Through trees, three roe quietly browsed, their coats already dark brown for winter. They merged easily with the rocks and the trunks of trees, until they turned, showing their rumps of brilliant white. But it was the red deer that dominated the scene, on grass below the forest, and it was clear that the annual rut was well under way. Large mature stags were roaring in paroxysms of agonised passion, their heads and antlers held high, warning intruders to keep their distance and to keep away from their harems of in-season hinds. It was a fine sight, for a red deer stag with a good set of antlers is our largest and most magnificent animal.

Red deer stag.

The Scottish red deer come mainly from native stock as they have been in Scotland for almost a million years. Then, they were forest animals and spread over most of Britain, and even now the country's largest red deer live in the forests of East Anglia. With the disappearance of vast tracts of woodland the deer were pushed back into the Scottish highlands and when the forests disappeared there too, they took to the open moorlands. Numbers fell, and there is no doubt that it was only the sporting interest that enabled the red deer to survive. In the rest of Britain they were hunted down and pursued into oblivion for the sake of arable agriculture and raising sheep.

Since then, the number of "deer forests" on the large estates has increased and the population has risen to over 260,000, with an aimed for annual cull of about a sixth. Without control the population would soar and much damage would be done to forestry plantations and farm crops. In addition many would die a slow, painful death during the long northern winter because of starvation and cold. Apart from the weather the only natural enemies of the deer are foxes and eagles, and they may take a few small calves during the summer; their overall effect on deer numbers is virtually nil. Those deer shot are not wasted, for venison is a tasty, lean meat and venison with redcurrant jelly and vegetables makes a far superior meal to traditional roast beef. Despite this, it is a peculiar fact that a high proportion of Scottish venison is exported to Germany, although efforts are now in progress to increase the British market. Without the deer the hillsides would be planted with conifers or stocked with high density sheep and the heather moors and the distinctive wildlife associated with them would soon disappear.

Now in Britain the red deer is nearly always associated with heather moors and mountainsides, showing how well it has adapted to life away from its most suitable habitat. It is the head of the stag that gives it the look of nobility and grandeur, and a good set of antlers can have as many as sixteen "points" (tines), although the better forest diets of Europe can produce even more. The antlers themselves are made of a bony substance covered with "velvet", a living skin much valued in the Orient as an aphrodisiac. The old antlers are cast mainly in March and April, and the new growth usually finishes in July. The velvet is cleaned away in August, allowing the antlers to harden, ready for the battles of the rut. Oliver Goldsmith, the eighteenth-century poet, was much better at poetry than he was at describing deer, for in his *History of the Earth and Animated Nature* he wrote: "Thus the horns may, in every respect, be resembled to a vegetable substance, grafted upon the head of an animal. Like a vegetable, they grow from the extremities; like a vegetable, they are for a while covered with a bark that nourishes them; like a vegetable, they have their annual production and decay; and a strong imagination might suppose that the leafy productions on which the animal feeds, go once more to vegetate in his horns."

A red deer stag roaring during the rut.

For most of the year the deer live in single sex herds, but then in late August the mature stags begin to get restless, thrashing young saplings and clumps of heather to rid their antlers of the now dead velvet. By the middle of September they move to the traditional rutting areas where the hinds also arrive and the rut slowly gets under way. The large stags show their masculinity by roaring, a deep guttural roar, and each one will attempt to hold a harem of hinds. At this time they appear darker than usual and have a rank smell, for although deer normally like to wallow, during the rut it becomes part of the ritual and they become covered with peat, mud and mire, made worse by the addition of their own urine.

Often the roar is enough to intimidate a rival, but fights do occur and injuries are common. While a large stag is busy with a rival or a responsive hind, an unsuccessful old or young male will attempt to secure a mate for itself unobserved. At the climax of passion, the back legs of the stag actually leave the ground.

Normally a stag will spend up to half his day eating, but during the rut this will decrease to just five per cent of his time and an animal with many hinds, and would-be intruders, can lose a fifth of its body weight. Indeed, some of them go into winter on the point of exhaustion and leave the rut early, allowing the weaker stags to meet with success at last.

Undoubtedly the best place to see the rut is in Glen Muick, where wide, uninterrupted views show many groups of deer. As darkness falls and the moon rises, the roaring intensifies and the sound seems to be magnified by the valley walls. It comes from all parts of the valley, and when a stag bellows out his challenge, the roar evaporates into a cloud of steam, as the year's first frost lays a carpet of glistening white. With head outstretched and a number of short sharp coughs, young stags will be seen off, and the clash of antlers will resound only where a more determined challenger has stood his ground. The clashes are usually brief and finish with the loser fleeing from the rutting ground. If a hind is in season the stag will become besotted with lust, and the "monarch of the glen", will pursue her, tongue hanging out and eyes rolling, as if demented by his own passion.

When Loch Muick reflects the moon and the river turns to a stream of silver, so the valley slowly drifts into a starlit night. A grouse calls, and the roaring is all around; it is an autumn scene that has been re-lived for thousands of years, and again new life has been assured for another generation.

In the swollen rivers another struggle for life reaches its climax as the salmon strive to reach their breeding grounds, and theirs is a story almost unrivalled in the natural world. It is in September and October that they move upstream, to the headwaters of small mountain streams, where the eggs are laid in gravel beds from November until January. Each "hen" fish lays about 3,000 eggs, and it is essential for at least two survivors to return as adult fish. The life cycle of the Atlantic salmon is a romantic one, summed up by the salmon's Latin name "salar" – the leaper. But Scotland's salmon, including the fish of the Dee and those that start and finish their lives in the streams of Balmoral, are under threat.

The eggs hatch by the end of March, and for the first year they are known as "fry" and each small fish becomes very territorial. Those that do not find a territory may starve or become the victim of a predator – a brown trout, sea trout, heron or goosander. In that first year the population loss may be as high as ninety to ninety-five per cent.

After a year the fry become parr, and incredibly some male parr become sexually mature and capable of fertilising the eggs of an adult female. It could be nature's way of safeguarding the cycle of the species. Parr remain in fresh water for two to three years, feeding on insects, before becoming "smolts" and moving down to the sea, where they make for their traditional feeding grounds, rich in herrings, sand eels and sprats. For years it was not known where they fed, but then adult salmon were caught in the seas around Greenland and the Faeroes and so sadly, and possibly disastrously, some of the secret areas became known to man.

The fully grown adult salmon are beautifully streamlined silver fish, equally at home in the sea's tidal races or a fast flowing stream. After three to four years at sea they return to their river of origin, although some "grilse" return after only one year away. What guides them back is unknown; perhaps the stars, moon, position of the sun, the smell of

Leaping salmon.

fresh water, or simply the rhythms and currents of the sea.

In his fine book *Salar the Salmon*, Henry Williamson wrote of the salmon as they again met fresh water: "The returning salmon are excited and confused. Under broken waters the moon's glimmer is opalescent: the fish swim up from the ocean's bed and leap to meet the sparkling silver which lures and ever eludes them, and which startles them by its strange shape as they curve in the air and see, during the moment of rest before falling, a thrilling liquescence of light on the waves beneath." They are the ones that have survived the threats from nets, seals, and traps to leap again in their home rivers. But even then they are not safe, for they have another gauntlet to run; more nets, fishermen, poachers, mink and the occasional otter.

Some salmon enter fresh water as early as January and move upstream slowly, resting in pools during the summer, and, according to accepted belief, not eating in fresh water. Again, the steady arrival of fish throughout the year could be nature's way of avoiding catastrophe. As time passes, so the passage to the headwaters becomes more urgent and the sight of running salmon jumping falls and walls of white water, in the final stages of their journey, is both exciting and emotional.

From Balmoral I made the short journey to the Falls of Feugh, on a small tributary of the Dee, to watch the salmon jump. At that time the water was not quite high enough and they were failing in their leaps. There, in a cauldron of white, foaming water, salmon were trying to jump the first and highest of a series of natural barriers. It was pitiful, for each one crashed into rocks and was immediately swept back. Some hit head first, while others landed on their sides with a sickening thud, before bouncing back into the water. There must have been many casualties and an injured fish would have been easy prey for an otter. There were large and small fish, some a deep red, showing that they had been in fresh water for some time. A small Scotswoman told me that she often watched the fish jump: "When the water's right and they manage to move up the falls you feel like cheering when they get to the top."

The River Muick also has falls and there too in the autumn the salmon jump. Without help their efforts would be in vain, but now a salmon ladder of pools and concrete jumps enables them to reach the quieter waters of Loch Muick. It is an amazing sight that in memory leaves a mural of spray, light, rocks, foam and leaping fish.

Sadly fewer and fewer salmon are jumping the falls. Earlier the decline was caused by "ulcerative dermal necrosis" (UDN), a fungal disease that seems to run in cycles. It attacked fish in rivers throughout Britain, then, when the worst was over the Atlantic feeding grounds were discovered and Faeroese fishermen, anxious to make easy money, plundered the stock. The situation has been worsened by an increase of illegal netting at sea by some British boats, as well as netting in the estuaries as the fish return. The scale of poaching has also changed; instead of taking the odd fish for the pot, or to sell at the back door of the local pub, the poachers now work commercially with nets, gaffs and cyanide, clearing out whole pools, with little regard or care for the future survival of the fish. All these activities, based on human greed, make the fisherman with a rod and line seem a complete irrelevance.

But even those fish that complete their cycle in the safety of Loch Muick may have made a wasted journey; for increasingly, although the water looks clean and pure, it contains the poison of "acid rain". This can lead to poor hatches of both young salmon and trout, and to eggs turning rotten. It also causes a decline in other life, and so even those fish that do hatch have insufficient food to allow them to survive. This invisible pollution is created after sulphur and nitric oxides have been thrown into the atmosphere by fossil-fuel power stations, to return in rainfall as dilute solutions of sulphuric and nitric acid. For years pollution from Britain and Western Europe has drifted, with the prevailing winds, to Scandinavia, where thousands of lakes and rivers have died as a result. Nothing has been done, except the instigation of "long-term studies" to buy time and save the expense of modifying power stations. Now, as Scottish rivers and lochs begin to die it is being realised that when the wind is from the north and west, the rain is good, but when it comes from the south and south-east, it is "acid", and the problems and death associated with it are gradually building up. This means that Britain is actually poisoning itself, and the Dubh Loch, above Loch Muick, is already almost dead. The politicians complain of cost and public expenditure when excusing this pollution, yet the long-term cost to ourselves and to the environment may be impossible to measure. What cost can be put on Royal Deeside, if eventually it dies?

Charlie, a retired keeper of thirty-five years' experience at Balmoral, has witnessed the decline with great sadness: "I have seen the best of salmon, and now the worst. You no longer see the great numbers of small fish in the summer. I'm sure it's all this acid rain." Snow retains a particularly high proportion of acid rain and it is melting snow that feeds the headwaters and lochs of the Dee. Another old keeper is also worried: "It is very strange, now some of the heather appears to be burnt in the spring, after it emerges from long lying snow."

The autumn is a season for other great journeys, in addition to that of the salmon, for as the swallows and warblers of summer move to warmer climes, so birds that have bred further north, move south, and many choose the comparative warmth of Britain in which to spend their winters. The redwings and fieldfares feeding on rowan berries were part of that great southerly flow of birds, renewing strength after arriving from northern Europe and Scandinavia. They are attractive members of the thrush family, with an undulating flight and chuckling call. For much of the winter they wander through lowland Britain, feeding on the hips and haws of the hedgerows, as well as windfall apples in gardens and orchards.

Opposite page: The Linn of Muick.

Migration is a dangerous time for birds, depending on favourable winds and fine weather for success, as well as on plentiful food at the beginning and end of the journey. It was on a still day that the fieldfares encountered another unexpected hazard. Loch Muick and Lochnagar have been made into a nature reserve, watched over by a countryside ranger; he is a very good naturalist, with patience and a fine sense of humour, barbed with cynicism. He had taken me to a high, wide valley, in the hope of seeing mountain hares. Several were present, their coats patched with white, starting to change colour for winter protection. An old stag rested in a dip, out of the wind; he was already exhausted by the rut, and rose to his feet slowly, stiffly, and reluctantly. As we walked, steady streams of birds were moving up the valley and thousands must have passed during the course of the day. One small flock flew close to a high rocky outcrop: "That's not very clever," the ranger observed ruefully, "the peregrines won't be able to resist the temptation even if they've already fed." No sooner had he spoken than the birds scattered in alarm as a male peregrine took to the air and pursued them over a ridge. The female too left her ledge and followed as if out of interest. Soon she returned, gaining height as she flew, before gliding straight and true, from one side of the valley to the other, without the slightest flicker of a wingbeat.

The female is the actual peregrine "falcon", while the smaller male is known as the "tiercel". The ranger was not impressed at the effort: "They weren't really interested. If they mean business they get up high and hit them from above." A female meant business later in the afternoon in an adjoining valley. Again fieldfares and redwings were moving through in loose-linked flocks, and our first sight of her came when birds veered away in alarm as she closed in on them in a tremendous "stoop". The pursued passed over the brow of a hillock, with the pursuer gaining; she missed however, for soon she reappeared soaring and circling, higher and higher. She was little more than a speck, drifting on the wind, when another group of fieldfares came slowly along the valley. Suddenly, the peregrine began to fall like a stone, accelerating in a headlong stoop of amazing speed, her wings tucked in to gain extra velocity. The birds again scattered, but in her aerial view the peregrine had isolated one straggling, struggling bird, and she locked in on it like a missile of destruction. Just as contact was about to be made they passed over a ridge and out of sight. The peregrine stayed down, suggesting a kill and I breathed deeply, aware that the drama, beauty and tension had literally taken my breath away. The peregrines must live well in the autumn as inexperienced birds make their first migration; waiting, perched on rocks, for the young birds to fly innocently and exposed along the valleys. It seems a hard end for fieldfares that have just struggled across the North Sea at the start of life; but their death allows the peregrines to face winter in peak condition.

Peregrines nest successfully most years at Balmoral and Prince Philip takes a personal interest in them. The head keeper also likes to see them: "If there aren't enough grouse to keep a pair of peregrines, then it's not worth the bother of shooting," he says realistically.

Although birds of prey were persecuted in Scotland for many years, to "protect" grouse and lambs, more enlightened attitudes are gradually gaining ground. There is no doubt that peregrines take grouse, but their diet will include a wide range of highland birds as well as rabbits and young mountain hares.

It was while we were looking for mountain hares that another group of winter migrants flew by in a perfect V formation. We heard them first to the north, calling as they flew, almost as if in conversation. The arrival of autumn geese is a moving, memorable experience and one of the most evocative in nature; it conjures up the image of wild remote places and the spirit of freedom. Their loyalty also inspires, for geese pair for life and each flock is made up of just a few family parties making their great journey together. To see the slightly undulating formations of flying birds above the wide valleys, calling quietly as if to reassure, is matched only by the arrival of swans; for the gentle whooper and Bewick's swans also pass south along the valleys. Their annual, aerial trek brings them from their Siberian breeding grounds, and they occasionally pause to rest on the waters of Loch Muick.

Every year the southerly movement through the valleys of the greylag geese is taken as a sure sign of the onset of winter. If they arrive early it is said to forecast a cold winter, while if they arrive late then the winter will be mild. They try to leave the north with a tail wind and if conditions are right they can fly at well over forty miles an hour. A few pairs of greylags breed in northern Scotland and the Western Isles each year, as Britain's only resident native geese. The familiar farmyard goose was bred from them, and the name greylag comes from the fact that when the other grey geese – the pink-footed and white-fronted – head northwards in spring, the greylags are the grey geese that lag behind.

All day, with an open sky, flocks of geese were moving south, some flying as high as 5,000 feet, well above the summit of Lochnagar. Late in the afternoon another V suddenly broke formation and fell into a ragged skein, calling loudly as the birds lost height. The ranger thought an eagle could have stooped at them, not to gain a meal, for a greylag goose is the same size as a golden eagle, but simply for the enjoyment of seeing chaos and panic.

Eagles have been seen to take geese, but it is a far from common occurrence. It seems strange to refer to "enjoyment", for a bird as wild and primitive as an eagle, but their liking for flight and for deliberate near misses has been noticed by generations of Scottish shepherds and naturalists.

The Duke of Edinburgh has seen it too:

Birds of prey are not much of a problem. The hen harriers and peregrines take some young grouse during the breeding season and buzzards and eagles are a nuisance during the shooting season. Not because of the birds they kill, but when they get over a moor they clear the whole area of birds. I've seen it many times. It's almost like a game, with the eagles getting the grouse to react even when there's no danger to the grouse, they fly in all directions and the shooting's finished. But now both owners and keepers are aware of what is going on. They care more about the wildlife on their estates and understand more about them.

For years there has been speculation as to the guiding mechanism for migration. How does the greylag find its way from Iceland to Scotland? Some say that navigation is by the stars or the position of the sun, while others believe it to be innate; an awareness of magnetic fields or a deep, inborn instinct, beyond the experience or understanding of man. To further their studies scientists have even fitted gadgets to pigeons to limit their vision, but still many of the questions remain unanswered. On the last day of my autumn visit the weather closed in, with rain and low cloud hiding the tops of the mountains. Even so a large flock of geese flew up Glen Muick, to the Loch, where their passage was blocked by the valley as it merged with the mist. Instead of settling on the water, waiting for the weather to clear, they flew, circling the valley, calling impatiently. It seemed to suggest that, at least in the final stages of migration, greylags depend almost entirely on vision and communal memory.

Autumn is also the best time to see wildcats, as they spend much time hunting, particularly for voles and rabbits, to build themselves up for the winter. The wildcat is one of Europe's rarest animals, although it still flourishes in the Highlands. It is a creature that I have wished to see in the wild for many years, and in addition to walking miles, in the hope of a sighting, I took the advice of the head keeper and drove along several country roads at night, wanting to pick out real ''cats' eyes'' in the car's headlights. I had no luck; I saw tawny owls and rabbits but encountered no wildcats and had to be satisfied with a visit to a wildlife park to see wildcats in captivity.

The wildcat is larger than the household cat and is recognised from domestic or feral tabbies by its tail, which is shorter and bushier, with up to five black rings and a black, blunt tip. It is a very shy animal and is most often seen at dawn, dusk, and during the night, on farm land, in forests, and on moorland close to coniferous plantations. They eat anything they can catch, with small rodents providing the largest part of their diet. Live mice are not taken back to their dens, to be played with, as

Wild cat.

is the habit of domestic cats, but they will breed with tame cats, and as a result there are many feral cats in Scotland that, although living in the "wild", are not true "wildcats".

The female wildcat will vigorously defend her kittens, and even if the young are taken into captivity, they rarely lose their wildness – a characteristic shared with most fox cubs. The last wildcats vanished from England well over a hundred years ago, and from Wales at the end of the last century. Their decline was caused by persecution from gamekeepers and poultry owners, as well as through the loss of suitable habitat. After the First World War pressure on wildcats eased slightly, and the population is now increasing and expanding from its Scottish strong-holds, particularly on Forestry Commission land. The Forestry Commission has several plantations on royal land along the Dee. If young plantations become over-run with voles and mice, then wildcats and pine martens can be beneficial.

Wildcats were not my only failure, for I again walked through ancient pine forest in the hope of seeing capercaillie and blackcock. Old Charlie knew a path, where, according to him, an encounter was almost certain; once more it was a place of old Scots pines and twisted birches, but there were no large birds. Perhaps they had disappeared, for the ranger asked me in an exaggerated southern English accent: "What's a capercaillie?" – the Scots pronounce it "*capper*caillie" and claim to have seen or heard "a capperr".

Lochnagar in snow.

Winter arrives quickly in the Highlands, with the first frosts cutting the leaves and the wind bringing them down in fluttering showers of drifting gold. Apart from the dark blocks of pines, the landscape is bare, with early powderings of snow high up, slowly becoming a brittle white as the cold returns and the gulleys fill with accumulated snow. The Dee roars, and some of the grass meadows meandering by it become black with rooks, prodding and probing the ground for "leather-jackets". The rooks give warmth and reassurance to the scene, for in my region of East Anglia great flocks are no longer a part of the landscape; just small gangs calling and flying raggedly in the wind. In lowland Britain their numbers have fallen dramatically over recent years due to the increase in arable agriculture as well as the loss of nesting sites through Dutch elm disease. Rooks are still common, but as with so many things, it is Scotland where conditions remain most favourable and where memory and modern experience can still meet in harmony.

The cold makes winter a difficult time; the red deer move down into the valleys for food and shelter, and after snow they dig down with their front feet to feed. Food becomes all important and with few hours of daylight available in which to hunt, it is the season when eagles and buzzards can be seen most often on the wing. In the valleys flocks of small white birds are sometimes encountered, as snow buntings pass through. They are delightful birds and a recent visitor to Scotland described how he had seen a flock of about 200 in February: "It was like seeing a little shower of wind-whipped snowflakes," he recalled with pleasure. At this time the mountain hare is white, to match its surroundings, as is the stoat, apart from the black tip of its tail, that gives it value as "ermine". Hedgehogs are the most sensible, for during the worst of the weather they will be in the deep sleep of hibernation. Red squirrels do not hibernate, but they do spend longer each day in the warmth of their dreys, which are usually built high up, close to the trunk of a pine. For all wildlife winter becomes the season of hanging on for survival.

I was disappointed with my first view of winter, for I had wanted an arctic scene, instead it was damp and drab. The early morning sky was wild, dark and streaked with crimson, and the hills were covered by light snow, with the high tops lost in white. It was a cold landscape, dark and leafless except for the green blocks of pines. On the farms, sheep were feeding in fields of "neeps" (turnips), and cattle were being given plenty of hay. The birch trees had a rusty tinge to them and with the leaves gone, their bent and lichen-covered limbs seemed to gain in age, as they could be seen in their entirety.

At the Linn of Muick the ice cold water foamed, with no signs of fish; the salmon having finished spawning, to drift downstream in death. High up a golden eagle circled, the light patches beneath its wings showing its immaturity. Deep in the wood a solitary roe stood motionless, its coat as dark as the season. At Glen Muick red deer were out on brown grassland, which offered little nourishment, and a small group of hinds and calves plunged into the river to wade across with the water well up to their shoulders. On reaching the far bank they shook themselves, shedding a spray of fine, freezing droplets. The valley sides held small patches of snow and ice; as we approached one, it moved. It was a mountain hare in full white camouflage. It ran thirty yards before stopping and sitting up; it looked most attractive in its long white fur, and larger than in summer. There were several hares, but it was difficult to detect them from real snow. When there is no snow they are distinct and obvious, but even then they are not easy prey as they run and seek refuge among the rocks. With patches of snow, granite and brown heather, the ranger has never seen hares run to snow for deliberate concealment. One day, however, he saw a woodcock fly to a clump of brown bracken on a snowy hillside; its plumage immediately mingled with the tangle of autumn colours.

Loch Muick was rough in the wind, with white-topped waves breaking on a small beach of fine white sand. Among pines, cone fragments showed that red squirrels had recently been busy and high up in the branches a group of redpolls were looking for food. Along a small valley the sides were streaked with snow, but beyond, the higher white slopes of Lochnagar were lost in cloud. Despite having the ranger with me,

A mountain hare in winter coat.

there would be no attempt to get to the summit for fear of a "white-out", which even with the experienced can lead to danger. It is where fallen and falling snow merge into a single dense blanket of glaring white. In every direction, up, down and across it is the same; white with a visibility of nil. I have been in a white-out once when folly overcame reason, and the full dangers only asserted themselves later. It is something I do not want to face again.

The ranger's dogs were also with us, for we wanted to see ptarmigan in their winter plumage, and in high snow, a dog's nose is often more efficient than human eyes. The Glas Allt falls were spectacular in winter flow, and across the stream a group of hinds and their well grown calves were sheltering; it was surprisingly warm out of the wind. Where water oozed the ranger called the developing trickles by their descriptive Scottish name of "rimlets", and when I mentioned "mountain ash" he was horrified: "It's a rowan; there is no such tree as a mountain ash in Scotland."

Higher, the snow fields were larger, frost was still in the ground and a cold wind whistled over the ridges. Without warning a grouse flew over us, high and fast, with the wind. The ranger had no hesitation: "There must be an eagle about for a grouse to do that. Or even two, for sometimes they hunt in pairs." Sure enough a golden eagle soon appeared, circling over the horizon, its fingered wing tips and its seven foot wingspan making an impressive sight. It saw us, and instead of taking fright it glided with the wind, closer and lower; it was so close that we could see every detail. It wheeled and on seeing the dogs it dropped lower still as if wanting a better look. I was glad that I had left Bramble, my little lurcher, at home, for he would have been in danger of becoming eagle food.

In the early days of falconry, kestrels were the birds of the common people, peregrines of the aristocracy, but eagles were for kings. I could never understand why, for in my earlier experiences of golden eagles I had been impressed by their size but not by their flight. After seeing the dogs, this eagle tucked in its wings and arched them close to its body, and then, without a wingbeat, it accelerated into the gale-force wind and glided back over the ridge. It was a demonstration of flight that I would have found difficult to believe if I had not seen it myself.

With altitude the snow became compacted, almost into sheets of solid ice and the wind was bitter. One of the dogs "pointed" where rocks protruded and three ptarmigan burst into flight, their plumage now a vivid white. They landed on a sheet of frozen snow and their bodies merged instantly into ice. Through binoculars they could be seen stationary and concerned; their red eye stripes standing out clearly, as well as their feathered feet. It is remarkable how they thrive in such a cold, hostile world.

Returning we crossed deep ridges and folds of snow where the tracks of

A golden eagle with a mountain hare.

foxes and hares passed over gradients impossible for people. Recent fox droppings were full of hair, as if the fox had taken voles. Again grouse flew over us and another eagle appeared above a distant ridge. It had been a good day, and once back, below the snow, we decided to look for blackcock and capercaillie, with the usual result. The head keeper also tried, taking me to an old birch wood, by a stream along a valley floor, where blackcock "lek" in the spring. Apart from a brambling perching high up, the wood was empty, although it glowed a deep mauve in the afternoon light.

As I passed the ranger's house at dusk, he waved me down: "Come and see this." A bird as big as a hen pheasant had gone up to roost in a tree at the back of his cottage. It was a magnificent bird with a rufus-chestnut breast, changing to white and tawny, striped and mottled, suiting either the snow of winter or the lichens of summer. "There you are," he said with a smile, "a capperrr." It is the male capercaillie that is usually praised for its appearance, but the female was beautiful in her own right. The bird had resulted from a clutch of eggs that the ranger had managed to hatch and rear, before releasing them back into the wild. Because of their specialised diet and the fact that they are prone to disease when kept in artificial surroundings, he is one of the few people to have achieved success. After release the birds continued to stay in the vicinity and visit his garden. So at last, part of the "capper" myth had been revealed, but could it be called a truly "wild" bird? As night fell the temperature dropped and the stars shone brightly between heavy clouds rolling in from the north.

The following day was January 13th, St Hilary's Day, according to tradition the coldest day of the year. By coincidence the morning broke with frost on the windows, a bright blue sky and a carpet of snow. The scene was transformed into a wilderness of white and I was able to travel into deepest winter. Snow was frozen to the trunks of pines and held aloft in their branches, although squalls of wind sucked plumes of white from their tops like columns of smoke: "This is nothing," Charlie commented, stamping his feet, "sometimes it happens on Lochnagar itself, with a great sheet of snow being blown from its top. One year we even had young pines with so much snow on them that they bent over and the tops were stripped by rabbits."

I walked into an old plantation with Charlie, the snow crunching underfoot, to feed the deer. Each winter when they are down in the woods they are given hay. They do not need the same amount of food as in the summer, as their whole metabolic rate slows down, but the extra hay helps them to get through, especially when there is prolonged snow cover. As we walked, stags approached through the trees, recognising the kindly old keeper and realising there would soon be hay. Although the rut was well over, two briefly clashed antlers. Charlie spoke to them as he spread the bales and they went very close to him. He treated "Old

Spiker'', with one second rate antler, as a friend, and it took hay from his hand: "I love these deer; to tell you the truth I don't like killing them any more, but it has to be done."

We went on through the old Caledonian pine forest; it had taken on a new soft aspect and still the pines along the valley sent out great showers of snow. The trees out of the wind were silver white; there were slot marks of deer; streams with icicles and sheets of ice; the carcass of a hind picked clean by foxes, and goldcrests and coal tits – which Charlie called "tomtits" – searching for food among the pine needles. It was good to hear him use "tomtit", a name close to the "titmouse" used by Thomas Bewick, the famous eighteenth-century wood engraver. The sculptured shapes of juniper bushes stood out dark against the snow, with their oily leaves having the same taste as gin. Scotland seems to have a fixation for alcohol, as juniper is still used to flavour gin, and the water of Lochnagar itself can be sampled as a twelve-year-old malt whisky of the same name. The fresher water of the Dee threaded a line of silver meanders through the valley and the mountains beyond were a dazzling white.

Glen Muick too had adopted a new and frozen, arctic beauty. In the valley, pillars of snow were being drawn up into whirlwinds of icy air. It was strange; they reminded me of the dust devils of the African plains – both caused by extremes of temperature. Where stags fed, their antlers and heads were encrusted with snow, but the mountain hares were hidden as nature intended. Two hinds briefly stood up and boxed, and above, a golden eagle looked truly golden as it planed high towards the setting sun. Loch Muick was calm and reflected the cold and depth of real winter.

The harshness of winter is felt most as winter drags on into spring; when the season should be turning and new growth beginning, but still it is cold, damp and unchanging. This was shown to me during the first week of May. On the farm there were spring flowers and fresh foliage, yet returning to Balmoral was like travelling backwards into winter. The trees were bare, with droplets of water shining on the birch buds instead of newly sprung leaves. Only the larches had moved, showing a slight haze of green and small flowers of rich scarlet.

On arrival I drove towards the old forest along a narrow track. A group of stags watched. They looked weary, their coats dishevelled and weather-worn, totally lacking in the lustre of good health. But although they were finding the season long, they too indicated that change was on the way, for already new antlers were visible, covered in velvet.

Looking down into a small valley, there was a movement – strange movement. It was Charlie, running round his van, being pursued by a large black creature; I assumed he was playing with a dog. On drawing closer I halted and seized my binoculars; it was not a dog but a large black bird. Charlie was being chased by a superb cock "capperrr"; a "rogue".

The rogue cock capercaillie in the spring.

At last he had managed to produce evidence to shatter the myth. Tired, he dangled his deerstalker in front of the bird. It tore it from his hand, pecked it and hit it with its wing, so claiming another victory.

It was magnificent, the size of a small turkey and like a turkey it had its tail feathers fanned out in display. It was the time of the "lek" when cock capercaillie assemble to impress the hens and this rogue had decided to see off anybody or anything that trespassed into his territory. The appearance of "rogue" cappers is a strange phenomenon, as normally they are shy and retiring, yet when love and lust are in the spring air they are transformed and odd ones turn up throughout the Highlands, chasing off dogs, fighting their own reflections in car wheels, and they have even been known to knock postmen from their bikes.

The previous year this cock had set up his territory near some cottages, attacking the occupants, their dogs and cats, at every opportunity; consequently he was moved deep into the old forest. His reappearance a year later at his place of release suggested that he had found plenty of wild hens to keep him happy.

With the arrival of a new interloper he turned his attention to me; advancing slowly, his head held high, and making an indescribable noise – a series of gobbles, wheezes and belches all mixed into one. His feathers, black, white and grey, were immaculate, and when he puffed out his chest it shone with the same green sheen as a mallard drake. Above his eyes were vivid red stripes, his beak was slightly hooked and beneath it was a fine feathery beard. His legs were also feathered, right down to his scaly reptilian feet. He advanced between old pines and a small loch, with mountains behind; I felt peculiarly privileged to be part of such an ancient scene.

I expected him to peck, which at the height of his beak, was an embarrassing and painful prospect, but suddenly, when I least expected it, he struck me a stinging blow on the knee with a wing. It was not a gentle flap to visually impress; it carried all his weight and was meant to injure. It had the desired effect, as I backed off and fled he chased, ignoring Charlie completely. When I stopped, the slow advance began again and when I held my thumb-stick between us he kept his distance. The next day he had thought the problem through, for he attacked the hand holding the stick with beak and wings, and when I picked him up he was so enraged he stuck his beak into my shoulder, drawing blood. Sadly, some rogue cappers get killed, because people fail to understand that they are just temporary springtime aberrations; fortunately, the Balmoral "rogue" is understood and treated as a friend, albeit a ferocious one.

The story of the capercaillie is interesting, as the capper is one of Scotland's indigenous birds. The name probably has Gaelic origins; the most attractive suggestion linking it with two words, "gabur" – goat, and "coillie" – wood, making "gaburcoillie", or "goat of the wood", because of its fine beard. Other names include "cock of the woods", "horse of the wood", "wood grouse", and "great grouse".

Once cappers were common throughout Scotland, but they declined rapidly in the eighteenth century because of the destruction of habitat and the activities of sportsmen, for like all members of the grouse family, they are strong fliers. They are large too, with the cock bird weighing as much as seventeen pounds. Although an isolated bird may have hung on, deep in a remote wood, it is generally accepted that the last two indigenous cappers were shot in 1785, and the capercaillie was then extinct in Britain.

Fortunately there were landowners who mourned the loss and several attempts at reintroduction were made with birds from Scandinavia, but they all ended in failure. Success came at last in 1837 when Lord Breadalbane released Swedish birds at his home, Taymouth Castle, in Perthshire. Gradually the population expanded and spread, and they were helped by several more reintroductions. Now the capper can be found in many parts of the central and eastern Highlands, being particularly strong in the valleys of the Dee, Don, Spey and Tay, and its future seems secure. It is reassuring to have the return of such a bird, for it shows that reintroduction can be carried out successfully. Because of this, zoos and wildlife collections take on a new importance, as they could supply stock for possible reintroductions in the event of any future wildlife catastrophe.

The capercaillie is now sufficiently numerous to allow shooting as a sporting bird, but there are differing views as to its taste. The head keeper has no doubt: "They're revolting to eat. They contain so much turpentine they're only good if you've got worms. There's just one way to eat them; you take out the crop, as it will be full of pine needles, and put in an onion. Then skin the breast and wrap an old boot around it and bury it. A month later dig it up and eat the boot." Another keeper had a slight variation: "You bury a brick and the capperrr in the same hole. When the brick's soft the capperrr's ready."

Charlie disagreed however: "They're delicious. It all depends on the cooking."

Capercaillie live mainly on the buds and shoots of pines, although in the summer and autumn, berries and insects are included in their diet. Because of this, in the early days of economic forestry they were disliked by foresters who saw damage to their "crop". But as is so often the case, the problem was usually exaggerated, and the capper is now welcomed as part of the natural forest scene. It was ironic, for I had wanted to see a wild capercaillie for years, yet after my encounter with the rogue cock I saw several, throughout the Balmoral estate, including the Glen Muick and Lochnagar Wildlife Reserve.

Leaving the cock capper strutting in self-admiration I walked through the old pine forest to see fleeting signs of spring; a male redstart and a

Goosander.

willow warbler, recently arrived for the summer, and at the base of a large pine, a small arch of rock, covered with mosses and bilberry. From inside came a strange hissing sound; it was a female goosander already incubating eggs. She puffed out her chest to add to the intimidation and opened her long saw-edged bill in threat. Sometimes goosanders nest in trees and the young chicks have to tumble down before following their mother to water. The beak is serrated to hold fish more efficiently, and their diet is almost entirely fish, frogs and various aquatic creatures. As a result, although they do not take many young salmon and trout, they are not liked by salmon fishermen. I left her in peace and later Charlie saw a mother and eight youngsters on the main river Dee.

Across the stream a roe buck stood watching; his antlers full grown and out of velvet. It is peculiar how the cycles of red deer and roe have few things in common. A woodcock flew over, slowly, making the strange croaking call and high pitched whistle of its "roding" display. Fox scats warned of the presence of a fox; if it was a vixen she would already have given birth to her litter of cubs in a rocky den, and her nose would be the main threat to the safety of the goosander.

A wide, green valley, with a gentle gradient branched out from a stream, with heather and more pine, attracting many meadow pipits and chaffinches. Large birches sprawled, some split by age and the force of the wind and from the trunks large razor-strop fungi grew, some old and hard, looking like the feet of elephants. Above the tree line a small group of deer were browsing on the scant rations of old winter heather; with altitude the temperature dropped sharply and the high pools were still lifeless; large patches of snow told of the delay in the changing seasons.

Lower down there were more promising signs, for where "rimlets" flowed into miniature streams, there were several clumps of frog spawn; some milky white and lifeless, where they had been frosted. A pair of toads were actually mating among the silver strands of freshly laid eggs. The "capperrr" was still waiting for me when I returned, and once I was safely inside the car he perched on the wipers and attacked the windscreen.

"Lek" is the name for the traditional site where cock birds meet to swagger and display, and the other bird to partake in this springtime ritual is the blackgrouse. It was just before dawn that I approached the birch wood lek and immediately I saw a blackcock, not displaying to his own kind but to three red grouse. He too fanned his tail revealing distinctive short white feathers as well as long black outer-feathers shaped like a lyre. As he tried to impress he made a noise almost as eccentric as that of the capper; a series of coos, followed by a hiss, rather like a pigeon with air-brakes. The red grouse were not impressed and soon flew away.

At the bottom of the birch wood, with wood anemones underfoot, several cocks had assembled, taking an almost ostentatious delight in

Balmoral Castle in the snow.

Black cocks at the lek.

their own beauty; admiring, sometimes threatening and occasionally fighting, to the accompaniment of coos and hisses. In foggy weather, fearing that their performance may go unobserved, they make even more noise to attract the females. As I walked quietly towards them, a hen got up just in front of me, alarming the cocks, who flew away fast and straight, their long tail feathers streaming out behind. Although "black-cock" is a simple and accurate name, the female is known as the "grey hen" despite the fact that she is more of a chestnut brown.

Once out of the wood and on open moor there was a more harmonious blend of sounds and feelings; curlews bubbling, meadow pipits parachuting, water tumbling and a cuckoo calling; all amplified by the deep silence of high mountains. It seemed strange to hear a cuckoo in conditions so bleak and bare. Soon it was joined by more pleasant calls, as a large V of 500 greylags passed overhead, this time flying north. Some of the locals say that when the geese leave it is a sign of good weather; hence the saying:

> Wild geese, wild geese ganging to the sea,
> Good weather it will be;
> Wild geese, wild geese ganging to the hill,
> The weather it will spill.

Listening to the local people can have its problems, particularly after an early morning watching blackcock. If breakfast is arranged for "half-eight", to most people that means "half-past-eight", or "eight-thirty". To the people of Ballater and Balmoral "half-eight" is "seven-thirty": "It must be, because seven-thirty IS half-eight, and half-past-eight is half-nine." The logic is difficult to follow but the language must be learnt or it can lead to a plateful of cold porridge.

Another peculiar habit of some of the locals is to wear their deer-stalkers with the flaps up, even in the coldest weather; they never have them tied over their ears. This seems to be a typically Scottish habit; it is to make sure that whenever they are offered a "wee dram", they hear the invitation and can accept.

Despite the cold and damp, spring could be seen by the Dee and its tributary streams, and the river Muick was typical. Along the banks, under alders and birches wood anemones flowered and a dipper stood "dipping" on a boulder in midstream. Suddenly it dived, head first, to reappear in swirling water before emerging on another rock. Upstream where meanders wound through open moor there were several common sandpipers, summer wading birds of upland streams, many of whom wisely spend their winters in southern Africa. They are delightful, loving little waders with a high whickering call and a flight that takes them low over the water. There were several pairs and on a sheltered bend one fluttered briefly over its partner in the act of mating. A pair of mallards flew, and at a shingle bank two oyster-catchers called out in alarm. In Scotland it is common for oyster-catchers to breed well away from the sea. Somehow, I became aware of speed, as wings cut through the air and a bird flew fast over a ridge. It was a merlin, and most years this small, attractive bird of prey breeds on the estate.

There were several deer carcasses along the valley, showing the cost of the long drawn out winter. Some had been pecked at by crows, carrion and hooded, for the line dividing the two species, north and south, passes almost through Balmoral. They are so closely related that they inter-breed quite freely. "Hoodies" are hated by gamekeepers and local people alike, because of their ruthless destruction of nests and young life. It is a dislike matched only by that for mink, which regularly work the streams and lochs for food. The keepers maintain that dipper and sandpiper numbers have been reduced by mink, and otters are also less common since the arrival of this American alien. The wild mink population grew from fur-farm escapees and it is unlikely that it will ever be reduced. Shortly after my winter visit a keeper trapped a mink, but, more promisingly he also saw otter tracks in the snow. At about the same time a great grey shrike was resident in the area for several days.

Higher up the valley several pairs of common gulls were resting, for a few pairs breed by the river, and at Loch Muick itself. A cock red grouse flew in display; rising rapidly, to glide over the apex of its climb before sinking back into heather. Loch Muick was as still as a mill pool, reflecting the washed out landscape of late winter; all memory of autumn colour had been leached and lashed away by the waters of melting snow and wind driven rain. The wind had even changed the loch itself, pushing out a sand bar into the cold clear water.

Once it starts, spring moves quickly into a full highland summer, and by mid-June a complete transformation has taken place, with the whole area throbbing with life. The trees have created a revitalised country of fresh, melting greens; the growing tips of pines, the renewed needles of larch, the luminous young leaves of birch, and even the grasses and bracken

Loch Muick with its new sand bar.

look lush. It is a season almost too rich to absorb, leaving a succession of vivid images, soothing sounds and sweet scents.

Patches of snow were still on Lochnagar, but from the loch at the base of its corrie it showed an unfamiliar gentleness. A valley of stones and rocks where solitary hinds were searching for sheltered and secluded peat hags to drop their calves. It had a pure silence, bearing a quality and depth that allowed sound to move freely and easily through it; drifting, wavering and fading away – a grouse, the snorting call of ptarmigan, and then a deep and resonant quiescence.

Loch Muick had been restored, as if touched by an artist's brush; its sides splashed with bilberry and unfurling bracken, and common gulls floating in tranquillity. The heather was dotted with small white flowers, the bright starred heads of chickweed wintergreen, and a narrow stream blazed with the vivid yellow flowers of marsh marigolds. They were a fraction of the size of southern plants, being the "dwarf montane" variety; kept small by the harsh conditions. Where water dripped through mosses and liverworts more white flowers shone on plants of starry saxifrage, their roots digging deep into rock. Because of their hold, seeking out the smallest joints and fissures, they were once believed to actually crack rocks; a property that made them popular in early medicine to combat gall stones. Higher still dwarf birch stood, just above the ling; another plant of the true arctic.

A hen grouse and her chicks crossed the path and vanished into heather. On some parts of the estate the heather is "managed", to

Flowering chickweed wintergreen.

Adder on the path near Loch Muick.

encourage the grouse. It is burnt in strips, in rotation, to provide young shoots for food, as well as old plants for cover. Scottish grouse have not fared well over recent years. Charlie dates their decline to the production of the Land Rover in the fifties: "It meant that more drives could take place in the course of a day, and even the remotest places could be reached by the guns." This is not the whole story for, despite the Land Rover, grouse have continued to thrive in parts of northern England, and they are notorious for the great explosions and slumps in population. They are also very susceptible to disease, one of which is carried by ticks, and the sheep tick is a common parasite in Scottish heather.

Returning towards the lake, I started at the sound of a hiss. It was a dark adder, beautiful but malevolent. I would never kill one, but I cannot pretend to like them. The following day, walking along a different path, with heather brushing against my legs, I was on the verge of saying to the ranger: "This looks a good place for adders," when an even louder hiss literally made me leave the ground. They eat small mammals, mice, voles and shrews, as well as lizards. One of their victims is the pygmy shrew, for Balmoral has Britain's smallest mammal, as well as its largest, the red deer. It is a wonder that the keepers do not get struck by adders when stalking through the heather. The keeper at Glen Muick has actually crawled over one, without being bitten; he was told the good news afterwards by a companion, who saw the surprised snake slithering away. Charlie's grandson was not so lucky, for he received a bite by the river Dee, without seeing the aggressor. The two small holes on his leg were immediately sucked out, but he was still required to stay in hospital for a week.

Adders do not have it all their own way, however, for buzzards sometimes prey on them and the ranger once saw a hedgehog shaking a body. Whether the hedgehog had killed it is not known, but there is an old rural belief suggesting that hedgehogs are immune to snake bites. Another tradition claims that adder skins bring luck and that they should be hung in cottage roofs or over the hearth.

Two enclosures totalling thirty acres had recently been fenced off in the valley; it was another experiment in natural regeneration. Like the old Caledonian pine forests, the birch woods are under threat, and the areas had been set aside for new growth. Most of the woods contain both the silver and the downy birch. The birch wood of the blackcock lek was quieter than in the spring, although a few cocks were still present, looking distinctly tatty and uninterested after their earlier exertions. The wood anemones had been replaced by a variety of flowers, wild pansies, milkwort, lousewort, violets, heath spotted orchids, and many more stars of chickweed wintergreen. By the stream, bog myrtle was made more conspicuous by the scent from its sun warmed leaves. Coal tits and redpolls were busy in the branches and in addition to giving good sites for nests, the birches would provide catkins for winter food. The older trees are favoured by great spotted woodpeckers, for they develop areas of rotting wood, ideal for both insects and the excavation of nesting holes.

The open moorland beyond still carried the bubbling call of curlews, as well as the spiralling songs of meadow pipits as they parachuted downwards in territorial display. Twites also nest on the moorland and several pairs of wheatears had returned to breed. The mountain hares were in their summer coats, grey-brown with a darker, bluer tinge, giving them the alternative name of "blue hare", and already the year's first leverets were almost full grown. Fox moths flew and among the heather were the violet-blue flowers of butterwort, rising from leaves resembling the arms of green starfish. Starfish have suckers on the underside of their arms, whereas the leaves of butterwort are sticky at the top, for it is an insect eating plant. When an insect lands on a leaf it becomes stuck, and the leaf curls around to trap and digest its victim. After its meal the leaf opens and the few remains of legs and wings blow away in the wind. The leaves of the plant were once rubbed into cows' udders to improve the milk and butter, and they were also added to milk to make it curdle. Because of its attractive appearance and liking for damp places it is also called in some areas the "bog violet".

One morning the head keeper took me on to open moor where the mournful warning whistles of golden plovers accompanied us. They had nests and were in their full and striking summer plumage, speckled gold with ink black breasts. I enjoyed seeing them, for previously I had only come across them looking plain and ordinary on our farm fields in winter.

Dunlin can also be found breeding on moors chosen by golden plovers, but their nests are usually harder to find. Unlike the plover they remain silent, but if a golden plover flies up to call at an intruder, the smaller dunlin will often fly close to it, giving it the local Scottish name of "plover's page".

Approaching a tree in a steep valley we stopped. Near its top was a large heap of sticks lined with fresh twigs of green pine. It was the nest of a golden eagle. Most years they breed successfully, nesting on a high rocky ledge or in a tree. Eagles nest as early as March, with the female occasionally sitting surrounded by snow, and only the crossbill is earlier. When young are in the nest the full range of an eagle's diet is revealed, from grouse and mountain hares to foxes and their cubs.

One early writer, the Reverend Samuel Ward, vicar of "Cotterstock", in Northamptonshire, gave eagles an even wider diet in his *A Modern System of Natural History* in 1775. He wrote: "They are not contented with the larger birds, as hens, geese, and cranes, but pursue rabbits, hares, lambs and kids, which they lift from the ground and carry off. Nay some tell us of their attacking even bulls." If no bulls were available then babies could be included on the menu: "It is dangerous to leave infants in places where eagles frequent, an instance being recorded in Scotland of two being carried off by them; but fortunately the theft was discovered in time and the children restored unhurt out of the eagle's nest to the affrighted parents.''

The flight of eagles also inspired him, so much so that it encouraged him to mix his natural history with Biblical interpretation. The wonders of flight start, according to him, when the adult eagles teach the young to fly:

> He takes them afterwards upon his back, in such a manner, that the fowler cannot hurt the young, without piercing through the body of the old one: quits them in the middle of his course in order to prove them; and if he perceives that they cannot as yet support themselves along, and that they are in danger of falling, he darts himself below them with great rapidity, and receives them between his wings. He is the only bird into which nature has instilled this kind of instinct; which the scripture has chosen as an expressive symbol of the tenderness with which God protected his people in the wilderness. ''I bare you,'' says he, ''on eagles' wings, and brought you unto myself.''

For old eagles the good reverend had a novel way of restoring their strength:

> It is certain that the eagle rises to a prodigious height. To this instinct he owes the renewal of his strength and youth, in which the learned, and even the critics themselves are agreed; every ten years his feathers become heavy and less proper for flight: he then makes an effort and approaches nearer the sun than usual, and after being excessively heated, he plunges immediately into the sea: his feathers fall off, and new ones supply their place, which restore him to his pristine strength. It is this particular, perhaps, which David intended to express in the following words: ''Thy youth shall be renewed like that of the eagle''. Psalm 103:5. And perhaps to this total loss of his feathers the passage in Micah 1:16 may refer: ''Enlarge they thy baldness as the eagle.''

I saw the wonders of flight with the ranger on a hot day, high up where we had a commanding view of several valleys. It was the ideal place for peregrines to nest, as it gave uninterrupted views of approaching food in most directions. The ranger wanted to check the nest to ensure that the eggs had safely hatched, but the falcon did not appreciate his care for she wheeled high above screaming in agitation. I was not watching her when I heard a rush of air, and by the time I looked up she was pulling out of a warning stoop. Again she rose high to drop at us like a stone, with the same uprush of air, before she pulled out and glided away. It is estimated

Golden plover in summer plumage.

that peregrines can reach 180 mph during a stoop, and after my views of them at Balmoral, it is easy to believe.

The three chicks had white down, with dark streaks showing where feathers were forming. They were being fed well, for the nest contained the legs of several birds that had been eaten; a grouse, a lapwing, a sandpiper, a common tern, one that could not be identified, and several racing pigeons, including some from Wales. Peregrines must find racing pigeons easy prey for they are birds that have lost their sense of fear; a vital requirement for survival, and they are simply let loose, or become lost, to fly along wild, open valleys. Pigeon fanciers have been known to persecute peregrines, but losses are their own fault; releasing birds to pass through peregrine country is unfair to pigeons and falcons and simply invites trouble. Although domestic pigeons make easy prey, a stoop to catch a sandpiper or a common tern fishing along the Dee would require amazing speed and accuracy.

We searched for another eyrie, where peregrines had been seen, without success. Astonishingly, high up and close to a rocky ledge we found a frog. It seemed an incredible place for a frog to be. In a good frog year herons will follow the streams up to their source and can be seen at quite high altitudes. Nearby was a hummock of reddish-brown sphagnum moss; on one occasion a keeper shot a clump in mistake for a sleeping fox.

Across a valley we went higher still: where snow had recently melted the small dwarf cornel flowered. Although to the layman it looks like a normal flower, the experts claim that it is related to dogwood. Even the apparent single flower is misleading, for it is in fact a number of tiny purple flowers, all surrounded by four white petal-like bracts. In the hollows there was still plenty of snow and the cold surface had killed numerous insects. They had been pushed up by the wind, or carried on thermals, to be deposited on their cold grave. Snow buntings occasionally breed and the insects form an important part of their diet. Wheatears and meadow pipits are also attracted to summer snow in the hope of deep-frozen food.

Once near the top there was another surprise, beds of dwarf mountain azalea, with small flowers, bright pink and blood-red against the background of snow. Fir clubmoss grew, upright, like miniature desert cacti in a desert of cold, alongside the equally attractive Alpine clubmoss. A plover-like bird ran slowly forward; it had a conspicuous white eye-stripe and a chestnut breast. It was a dotterel, one of the rarest breeding birds in Britain, and sadly, one that is still in decline. They are tame, almost confiding birds, and so, although they only nest in wild, desolate terrain, above 2,500 feet, they are vulnerable to the activities of egg collectors. They are summer visitors and have traditional resting sites where they stop while on their journey, and each spring they are seen along the East Anglian coast. In the past they were regarded as a great

Opposite page: Dwarf mountain azalea near the summit of Lochnagar.

delicacy, which acted as an added drain on their numbers. In courtship the female is the dominant bird, leaving the male to incubate the eggs and rear the young. Perhaps the bird's decline could even be attributed to the effects of long established "women's liberation". We approached no further in case the bird had a nest and eggs.

Balmoral is fortunate to have eagles, peregrines, buzzards, merlins, sparrow-hawks and kestrels among its breeding birds. Other birds of prey are also occasionally seen: hen harriers quartering the moors for grouse; goshawks flying fast and low through old pines, and ospreys fishing in the lochs. An osprey was seen fishing at Loch Muick in the early fifties, and they have visited the area quite regularly ever since. With an expanding population on the Spey it should be only a matter of time before they start to breed on Deeside. One loch on the estate is perfect, quiet and fringed with trees; it is ideal for other birds too and nest boxes have been erected in the hope of attracting goldeneye.

Some of the most pleasant images of summer were left by salmon, for I wanted to see if they were already moving up river. Charlie was not too hopeful, for the season had been the worst he could remember and his fishermen were having little success. By the falls it was peaceful with no signs of fish; just grey wagtails, pied wagtails and dippers gathering beaks full of insects for their young. Flowers were in full bloom, bugle and dandelion, their nectar attracting butterflies, including the small pearl bordered fritillary. Between the birches and alders, bird cherry was flowering, with its hanging bunches of blossom adding a sweet almond fragrance to the air. It is one of our most picturesque native trees, but again it is called "bird" cherry because its fruit is bitter and only fit for birds.

The main river was perfect too, with patches of blue wood cranesbill along its bank. A pool, much loved by the Queen Mother, looked ideal for salmon; white water narrowing over rocks before broadening into swirling currents of greens and blues. Wearing a face-mask and flippers, but without a wet-suit, I decided to see for myself whether fish were present. The water was cold as I waded and swam towards the white water, but soon temperature was forgotten. In the middle it was deep, the current pulled, and I let it take me. It was a new world of waves, eddies, countless bubbles, bright refracted light, boulders with flowing weed and the sun glowing through brilliant ripples, making even the smallest translucent aerations shine. Suddenly, below me, were salmon, large and small, facing upstream with little effort. They seemed even more beautiful in their own element and quite unafraid. One swam to the side as I passed and I went directly over two, between large boulders, no more than three feet away. The water was clear, with a milky-blue tinge from the bubbles and the sky. There were at least eight salmon lying easily in the water, the current caressing their streamlined bodies. In seconds it was over and the pool was behind me, but the memory has remained indelible. I went in again with an underwater camera, but the strong current, collisions with boulders and the desire to stay alive ruled photography impossible. Once I was out of the water several salmon jumped, as if trying to glimpse beyond the fringes of their world.

At another wider pool, with a slower current, there were more fish; six in line abreast facing the flow, six others and a sea trout. It was where Charlie had taken fishermen regularly during the week and they had caught nothing. They all looked in superb condition and it seems incredible that salmon can stay in fresh water for months on end without taking food. Charlie does not completely agree with the experts, for although a salmon's stomach is always empty, he thinks that they can take food. When they are caught on a fly the hook is always in the lip. But when they go for a worm they are usually hooked in the throat, which suggests that they do eat worms. The usual theory is that salmon seize flies out of boredom and then spit them out, but Charlie believes that with worms and some insects the salmon sucks out the juices before ejecting the debris. He could be right. Again it may be nature's way of helping the salmon, for if it had its sea appetite in fresh water then young salmon parr would be in danger from their own kind.

On the river bank I met another species of Scotland's flourishing wildlife, the biting midge. Which of Britain's 130 species were attracted by my blood I did not bother to find out, but in the best traditions of eighteenth-century natural historians, I swatted them enthusiastically. A local way of dispersing midges is to light a smoky fire. During my visits to Balmoral I stayed on a small farm overlooking the Dee, where Mrs Fraser ran a few sheep. The shepherd from a nearby estate arrived in the midge season to help her with the shearing, and they made a smoky fire from old sacks and pieces of carpet to reduce the bites. When she returned to the house a visitor greeted her with: "How nice of you to light a fire to keep the sheep warm after losing their wool." Mrs Fraser was not surprised: "She came from England and lived in a toon."

The spirits and moods of summer are concentrated best in the areas of ancient forest. The lace-like wings of insects caught by the sun; shafts of light; sprawling ferns, and the rich scent of pines made aromatic by warmth and growth. Even the birch trees radiated a beauty that I had never seen before, shimmering and shining with reflected light, their brilliance amplified by the dark pines behind. Whether the angle of the sun or the intensity of the light caused the leaves to blaze so brightly was not clear, but those in sunlight could only be described as "silver birches". Beneath them the new leaves of bilberry glowed a brilliant green and another smaller tree sparkled as light glanced from its ever quaking leaves. The aspen is a member of the poplar family and legend has it that the wood was used to make the cross on which Jesus was crucified; the leaves of the tree have trembled ever since.

A hind trotted over a track, with her new calf trying to keep up on

Male redstart.

unsteady legs, and a hen capercaillie slunk in the heather with her seven young, just able to fly. Three blackcock flew, and the peeling bark on ancient pines glowed bronze. Chaffinches, tits and spotted flycatchers busied themselves feeding young, as a willow warbler sang. Young coal tits were being fed in the safety of a narrow crevice in the damaged trunk of a pine and a blue tit's nest was carefully lined with the hair of red deer. Two buzzards were thermalling in warm air over the river, while a common lizard scuttled over rocks. I saw what I thought was a sparrow-hawk sitting in a tree; its hooked beak clearly visible. It jerked its head and the beak straightened. The cuckoo had simply been holding a long caterpillar in its bill before swallowing. As the bird flew, the alarm call of a chaffinch followed. Again I was wrong; for a flickering tail of rufous red revealed a redstart; both male and female were taking insects to their nest hole in a tree. To some rural Scots the redstart is known as the "firetail"; a most suitable name. There could be other birds nesting inconspicuously in this priceless area of Caledonian forest, as fieldfares, redwings and greenshanks are all colonising from the north, and several pairs now stay on to breed during the summer.

As I left, bracken moved by the side of the track and a young roe kid emerged, unhurried and beautiful, having recently lost its spots. It looked around before trotting back into concealment. It was as if the forest had briefly wanted to show one more of its secrets.

Harebells in the early morning.

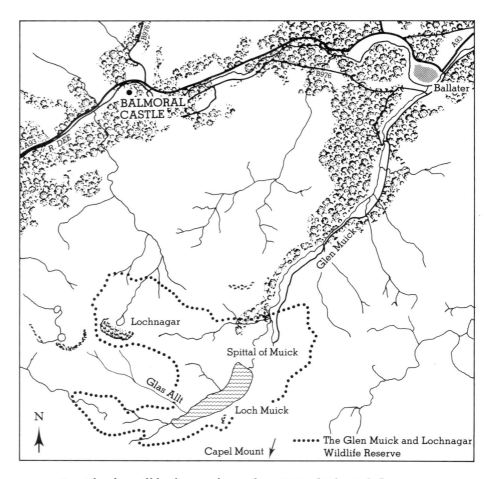

But Charlie still had something else: "It's a little pink flower, so pretty and delicate. It grows in just a few secret places in the old forest. We keep them secret to stop people stealing them for their gardens." As we drove back among tall pines, Charlie asked me to stop. Below, in a small dip, close to the roadway, were several stags, lying among bilberry and moss. Most had well developed antlers in velvet, except one, Old Spiker. Charlie got out, holding an apple; the other stags made off, but Spiker remained, looking apprehensive. Charlie called out: "Spiker . . . Hallo Spiker . . . Come on." Slowly the old stag approached in recognition; he stopped ten yards away and Charlie threw him the apple. It was touching to watch the old man and his stag, for there is a place for sentiment in man's relationship with wildlife, as long as it is tempered with knowledge and reality.

The place of the flowers was so secret that at first Charlie could not find it. It was not his fault, for eventually, when he came across the plants they were not yet on flower. They were beneath tall pines with large girths: "Look at them," he said, "if only these old trees could talk, what a story they could tell."

The Queen out riding at Balmoral.

The ranger knew of another more sheltered area where the twin-flowers grew, and they were already flowering. They were far more attractive than I had expected. Each plant had long stems trailing over the ground, from which grew small, fragile, upright stalks; at the top of each stalk were the delicate "twinflowers". They seemed so small and finely formed compared with the large trees towering above. The only sad thing about the twinflower (*Linnaea borealis*), is that it is named after Linnaeus, the man who organised wild flowers into "botany" and Latin confusion. Another small flowering plant can also be found in the area; its name, "creeping lady's tresses", is as attractive as the actual flower itself; botanists call it *Goodyera repens*.

Mid-summer gradually moves into high summer, with colours mellowing; the small deer growing in confidence and many young birds on the wing. It is also the time of damsel and dragonflies. In addition to the large common hawker, of my first visit, there are large red damselflies, and in some pools and bogs there could be the rarer azure hawker and northern emerald dragonflies, as well as the northern damsel. It is the pause before the mountains and moorland blaze with the colour of flowering heather. Then bumble bees with rufous rumps compete with honey bees to make heather-scented honey and the yellow striped caterpillars of the broom moth eat hungrily on broom and bracken. The rowan berries begin to ripen and bilberries can be picked and baked in pies. Dew lingers on harebells and fading grass and ring ouzels leave their high territories and begin to head south. The red deer become restless and the evenings cool. The year has run full circle and soon it will be signalled by the roaring of stags.

Sandringham

THE SANDRINGHAM ESTATE makes a complete contrast to the inland highland wilderness of Balmoral, being low-lying and intensively farmed, with its fenland so low that the fields are protected from storms and tides by a long sea wall. It is situated in one of the most attractive parts of East Anglia, spreading eastwards from the southern end of the Wash into north-west Norfolk. From pre-Roman times it was favoured as a place in which to live, with sheltered sites for villages, heathland for grazing cattle, fertile soils for primitive arable agriculture and abundant wildfowl in the marshes.

The Romans left a long straight road, Peddars Way, that now forms a farm track, marking part of the eastern boundary of the estate, and even the name "Sandringham" is a link with the past. It was first mentioned in the Domesday Book as "Sant Dersingham", a mixture of Celtic and Anglo-Saxon words: "Sant" meaning sand, and the nearby village of "Dersingham" – "the dwelling of the water-meadow". From this Sandringham was accurately described as "the sandy place by the dwelling of the water-meadow".

From its earliest days Sandringham would have possessed a variety of natural features: stretches of lush grass and scrub – liable to flood, sandy heaths with heather, bracken, birch and pine, salt-marsh, bog and forest, and to these man soon added areas of cleared land for cultivation. As husbandry improved, so the landscape changed through the clearance of woodland, the grazing of livestock and the patterns cut by the plough. But although planned farming grew, the old natural influences continued to dominate, and by 1862, when the Sandringham estate was purchased by the Royal Family, it was still noted for its mixture of heaths, marshes and fertile soils.

It was 1861 when Prince Albert decided that his eldest son, Albert

Edward, the Prince of Wales, should have a home of his own, away from his official residence in London. Unfortunately, before a purchase could be made, Prince Albert died, but typically, Queen Victoria insisted that her husband's wishes should proceed. It was then that the Hon. Charles Spencer Cowper, a stepson of Lord Palmerston, the Prime Minister, decided to sell his Norfolk estate before settling permanently in France. The Prince of Wales liked Sandringham and within a few days of his visit the sale was completed.

Prince Albert Edward enjoyed Sandringham for forty-nine years, latterly as King Edward VII, and it has been a well loved home of every monarch since, with the exception of Edward VIII whose intention to sell was interrupted by his abdication. Sandringham became the centre for family gatherings at Christmas, and it was from there that George V made the first Christmas radio broadcast in 1932. He described it as: "Dear old Sandringham, the place I love better than anywhere else in the world." King George VI also had a deep affection for it, developing both its shooting and its farming sides, and the feelings for Sandringham have continued with the present Queen and Prince Philip. Although Christmas is now celebrated at Windsor, Sandringham becomes "home" for the New Year and January, and in addition, several members of the Royal Family spend occasional days and weekends on the estate throughout the year.

Partly because of this love for the house and its surroundings the Queen, in 1968, decided to turn part of the nearby woodland into Britain's first privately owned Country Park. Now everyone can enjoy some of Sandringham's pleasures: 600 acres of mature trees of pine, oak, and sweet chestnut, and beneath them, flowering banks of summer rhododendrons. Small areas of heathland add to its appeal, while along the paths and rides it is possible to catch glimpses of its wildlife: woodland birds, pheasants, flowers, fungi and even deer.

Through the years the estate has grown to over 20,000 acres with the Wash to the west, the Babingley river in the south and sections of Peddars Way in the east, forming three distinct boundaries. Some 14,000 acres are let to tenants with the remainder split between arable farming (3,000 acres), forestry (2,000 acres) and soft fruit (144 acres). The ever changing fashions of farming have continued to alter the landscape; fields have grown larger, marshes have been drained to bring fertile land into production and woodland has been planted. The whole ethos is one of fertility, with the land yielding high quality wheat, malting barley, potatoes, carrots, sugar beet and apples, as well as timber, beef, brussels sprouts, lavender, and blackcurrants for Ribena.

Yet despite its agricultural emphasis Sandringham has not become the typical "prairie farm" of the agro-businessman's dream. Elsewhere in East Anglia a huge acreage of countryside has been sacrificed without feeling or soul on the altar of agricultural efficiency. The traditional

Cock pheasant crowing.

scenes of lowland England have been transformed into treeless tracts of arable mono-culture, as aesthetically sterile as the minds that helped to create them. But Sandringham has managed to retain an attractive gently rolling unity of farm fields, avenues of trees, hedgerows, spinneys and belts of woodland. Small clean villages nestle around country roads and the songs of yellow hammers and skylarks still accompany those who work the land. The flavour of the area is captured accurately by the places within it; Blacksmith's Covert, Wild Wood, Folly Hang, Field Farm, Further Back Wood, Fox Covert, Eleven Acres, Woodcock Wood, Gypsy Lane, Wild Boar Wood and Cat's Bottom — names from the past, still suiting the rural present. Just as the old names survive, so do parts of the ancient landscape; small areas of heathland, water-meadows, reed-beds, bog and woodland. More significantly, pockets of long established wildlife live on as well.

The survival here of wild areas and hedgerows is no accident. Like so much of lowland Britain Sandringham became caught up in the agri-cultural changes of the fifties and sixties; it was an agricultural revolu-tion more complete and devastating than anything that had gone before, based not on biological improvement, selective breeding and enclosure, but on agro-chemicals and mechanical power. Prince Philip was greatly affected by what he saw:

One of the reasons that I became so closely involved with conservation and the threat to wildlife was my first-hand experience at Sandringham. I saw the devastating effects of poisonous chemicals that were introduced to agriculture during the fifties, and that was matched by the tremendous power of modern machinery in the reclamation of marginal land. In a few years the improved drainage on the marshland has completely changed the character and the wild populations of the area. It was not difficult to imagine what this meant when translated into national and world terms. Wildfowl numbers on the washes halved, through drainage and disturbance, and because of this I created a small sanctuary. We left thirty acres of reclaimed salt-marsh as grassland, with pools, away from people. Unfortunately it has only been partially successful so far.

Although Prince Philip expresses disappointment, his reserve regularly attracts a variety of wildfowl and waders, including shelducks, shovelers, gadwall, snipe and redshank, as well as rarer visitors such as black-tailed godwits, avocets, greenshank and goldeneye.

Prince Philip has also been saddened by the disappearance of hedgerows as a mark of agricultural progress, and he has attempted to reverse the trend by planting both hedges and hedgerow trees. In just two planting seasons at Sandringham, in 1982–3, some 400 chains of hedgerow were replanted or gapped as well as sixty chains of entirely new hedge. The work involved 10,000 quickthorns and 400 young trees, including wild cherry, rowan, red thorn, oak, field maple, ash, blackthorn, hazel and hornbeam. To Prince Philip the need was obvious:

We planted new hedges because the old ones were getting gap-toothed and needed regenerating. Very few large fields are all one crop and are divided up and so why not do it with hedges?

Hedges and hedgerow trees provide a land and treescape that is attractive. One of the problems now is the flail mower. When hedges were cut by hand, if the men found a sapling of oak or ash they would leave it. Now the flail mower takes the lot. We have tried to overcome the problem by marking trees so the tractor driver leaves them. A good, well run, profitable farm looks better with trees and hedges; it looks well cared for, not like the awful prairie landscapes. There is a place for prairies – that is in the Prairies, not here. Without consideration it is difficult for anything to survive. I have seen farms designed for maximum production only. They are dead, they certainly have no game on them, let alone wildlife.

If Prince Philip's philosophy was accepted by other large landowners and institutions, then the countryside would be renewed. Sadly, tree planting has no immediate reward; it is undertaken only for the benefit of

Common snipe.

future generations. But justification does come, as can be appreciated when walking through the magnificent woodland of the Country Park. There the mature trees confirm perfectly the old proverb:

He that plants trees loves others besides himself.

The wildlife of Sandringham is an unexpected mixture of the familiar and the precious; the commonplace and the extremely rare. Again it fluctuates with the ebbing and flowing of the tides of the Wash and the rhythms of the seasons. It is this never failing annual cycle that creates a number of surprising links with Balmoral, for birds seen in Scotland also pass through or settle at Sandringham, according to the time of year.

At Sandringham the wildlife year starts even earlier than in the Highlands, for it is caught up inexorably with work on the land, and this work has almost reversed the farming calendar. Once, "seed-time and harvest" meant sowing in the spring, and cutting the corn in late summer. But now, as the evenings begin to shorten and autumn can be felt in the air, so the seasons have joined to become a single period of frenetic activity. Immediately the combines have harvested the cereals, heavy ploughs and cultivators rip into the land and by the end of September many fields are already green with the new shoots of next year's wheat. The old "Plough Monday", in January, when all ploughing should be completed, is obsolete and indicates how modern agriculture has changed.

It was mid-September that I went to see the start of the year, with light mists lingering in meadows and the first hints of autumn tinting the landscape. Russets, browns, bronzes fired the edges of the hawthorn leaves and burnt deep into the horse chestnuts. As the sun warmed, the drone of working tractors filled the mellow air. They were carving long straight swathes of soil from the shrinking area of stubble and clouds of black-headed gulls followed, circling, wheeling and falling to feed. The gulls were already losing their black heads, showing the approach of winter. The soil was being gently turned by the plough before crumbling into the furrows, almost ready for drilling. Those who farm such land are fortunate and would find it hard to cope with the heavy clay of our Cambridgeshire farm, which, if the season is unhelpful can blunt the implements and break the heart. But not all the arable land was being worked; on some the harvest had still to come, for sugar beet and carrots had yet to be lifted, and brussels sprouts would not be ready until well into winter.

Around grass meadows the natural harvest was reaching its peak, and one small overgrown field was particularly appealing, hemmed in by large old hedges, ripe with abundant autumn fruit; hawthorns heavy with scarlet haws, the briars of wild roses bending under the weight of their bright orange hips, strings of crimson bryony, the keys of ash, blackberries and clusters of sloes in clumps of blackthorn.

Black bryony berries.

Goldfinch on a thistle head.

The field comprises fifteen acres of old water-meadow, almost untouched, apart from grazing cattle in late summer. Its hollows and depressions fill with water after rain and a pond flowers, lives and dies during the course of each year. As I walked through summer-bleached grasses the sun shone between white clouds, illuminating countless thistle heads with a bright, incandescent light. Some hung on bent and broken stems, while others still stood upright with candelabra arms; all were transformed, with their soft white down glowing like flame.

Where goldfinches fed, thistle down drifted gently until the birds flew, startled by a bolting hare. There were hundreds of them, the sun striking their gold streaked wings and the breeze carrying their quiet metallic calls; it was clear why a flock of goldfinches is known as a ''charm''. A male chaffinch sang in an old ash tree and pigeons clattered into flight. Some late thistles still flowered, together with pink hemp agrimony, attracting the year's last butterflies; red admirals and painted ladies in perfect condition, together with a few peacocks and tattered large whites. A cock and two hen pheasants flew, catching the top of the hedge as they climbed, for the old meadow provides good food and cover for pheasants. At Sandringham the pheasants are all wild birds and make the estate one of the best shoots in the country. Some people consider shooting and conservation to be diametrically opposed, but carried out with understanding and sympathy they are complementary; as Prince Philip says: ''Conservation and shooting are the same thing. You won't get wild pheasants unless you get good habitat and that is good for conserving all forms of wildlife.'' Without an interest in pheasants the old water-meadow would probably have been drained and ploughed years ago, but now with its sprawling hedges, grasses, pond and pools it forms a small, but rich wildlife haven. Many of the copses, coverts and shelter belts, adding beech, oak and pine to the landscape have also been planted, or retained, as pheasant cover.

Although the pheasant is often regarded as a native British bird, it is in fact an alien, having been introduced for its splendid appearance and taste. The common pheasant originated near the Black Sea and is thought to have been present during Norman times, while the ring-necked pheasant was brought in much later from China. Both types can be seen at Sandringham and they interbreed freely; the ring-necked has a distinctive white collar around the neck of the cock. A small number of brilliantly coloured golden pheasants from central China also breed, but are few in number. The cock is quite unmistakable, with a golden crest, long tail, and bright scarlet breast. Unlike other pheasants they skulk in dense cover and are very difficult to see. As they are ground nesting birds, large pheasant populations can only be obtained by controlling some of their predators; those that kill adults, or steal their eggs and young. Consequently foxes, stoats, weasels and crows are not welcome in large numbers. Indeed, without this protection and the preservation of habitat, the pheasant would become extremely rare in areas of intense arable agriculture. Its loss would be sad, for it is a fine bird and a welcome addition to the rural scene. There is also no doubt that the mild game flavour of roast pheasant makes a delicious meal.

From the water-meadow, a farm track led close to a wood of planted pine where the now retired head gamekeeper, Mont Christopher, wanted to show me another natural harvest. He is a fine, upright man, whose interest spreads beyond the welfare of game and into many other aspects of natural history and country life. He appreciates wild flowers, understands birds, accurately mimicking their calls, and makes much home-made wine. His eyes sparkle with mischief as he talks, as they do when he sings traditional songs and plays the mandolin.

As we walked through the woodland enjoying the smell of pine and long-fallen leaves, a more unpleasant odour gradually fouled the air. It grew stronger and heavier, until we came across some fungi that looked as disgusting as their smell. They were stinkhorns, which for once have an accurate Latin name – *Phallus impudicus* – ''the unashamed phallus''. The old English name is even more exact – ''pricke mushroom''. Because of its remarkably rude resemblance to an erect male organ it was once used as an aphrodisiac, although how anybody could handle or eat a fungus with such a revolting smell is hard to understand. The smell is so strong and thick that it catches the back of the throat and made me feel quite sick. When ripe the stinkhorn is black and sticky, and flies are attracted by its rankness. The spores stick to their legs and so the awful effigy is spread. The Victorians had the best idea; they sought stink-horns out to destroy them, to prevent the corruption of young girls walking in the woods. Mont had a different view: ''I think it would be interesting to have one of those in your handkerchief at a dinner party. It would certainly be an aid to conversation if it fell on to the table when you went to blow your nose.'' Even the young fungus is strange, with the horn growing from a base with the texture of a ''lush'' egg.

There were other fungi with names to suit their shape or character: shaggy ink cap, poison pie, deathcap, the charcoal burner, fairies' bonnet and King Alfred's cakes. But then, along a ditch, we found Mont's speciality, the cep, or ''penny bun''. Although penny buns are popular and considered to be a delicacy in Europe and Scandinavia, because of the dubious reputation of fungi in Britain, few people bother to pick them. I was at first apprehensive, but Mont picked some for his own use, and fried in butter they were excellent. There were other edible fungi too, the parasol mushroom and the giant puffball. The parasol gets its name from its attractive shape and the puffball from the millions of brown spores that can be puffed out when ripe. Once it was used to drive out bees so that honey could be taken from their hives; it is also an antiseptic and used to be put on cuts to stop bleeding. I had never eaten parasol mushrooms before, but they were large and tasty, not unlike horse

Fly agaric in the autumn.

mushrooms, and certainly far better than the small button mushrooms grown commercially. The puffball is best eaten when it is firm and white; it should be sliced, like a loaf of bread, and again, fried in butter.

Below birch trees stood a group of the strikingly attractive fly agaric. But its appearance should not be allowed to mislead for it is poisonous; at best it causes hallucinations, at worst, death. Before the age of fly sprays it was chopped up and put into saucers of milk to stupefy flies.

As we returned with our penny buns and parasols, the slot marks of deer crossed the winding path. Not roe as I expected, but fallow. Occasionally too, small groups of red pass through, usually pushed out during the rut from Thetford Forest; 50,000 acres of Forestry Commission land thirty-five miles to the south-east. Strangely, in all his eighteen years at Sandringham, Mont had only seen one roe, a few weeks before my first visit. There is a flourishing and expanding roe population at Thetford, however, and it can only be a matter of time before they become another regular feature of the wildlife in the Country Park. In addition to fallow the other resident deer is the small and secretive muntjac.

''Follow me,'' Mont said quietly, and we branched away from the main path, to a large pool surrounded by dense rhododendrons. It was peaceful; bright water, mallard and teal quietly dabbling, and a heron hunting, motionless in mid-stride. One duck saw us and flew and the whole pool erupted in wings and cascades of sparkling water, the sun catching the metallic green wing flashes of the teal as well as the green eye-stripes of the drakes. Once more the collective name seemed most appropriate, for it is a "spring" of teal. They are delightful little ducks, some breed locally, but numbers had already been boosted by autumn immigrants. They circled several times, gliding down in unison before accelerating upwards again. Each time they rose, fell and wheeled away, they acted as one, in the same way as a flock of waders.

During my visits to Sandringham, Mont showed me several more places special to him; pools surrounded by willows and alders and fringed with reeds – a haven for summer warblers and breeding wildfowl; sandy heathland with gorse and rabbit-grazed grass where green woodpeckers like to feed on ants, and a wood where wild lily of the valley flowers and woodcock rear their young.

Mont left with his hoard of fungi and I moved on to visit an area of self-set Scots pines, with the Country Park ranger. A great-spotted woodpecker pecked busily above and goldcrests flitted daintily among the branches. On the edge of a steep escarpment the pine trees stopped, revealing an expanse of heathland, with heather and browning bracken descending into bog. The whole area covers nearly 400 acres and is one of the most important areas of heath and acid bog in East Anglia. Two large birds of prey drifted over birches and reeds; they were marsh harriers, the male being smaller than the female with slimmer wings. They gained height before parting, the male gliding away and the female descending to hunt. Soon they would be moving south to spend the winter as far away as Africa.

As we walked down into the bog, a common lizard ran across the path. It is the most common lizard in Britain, as its name suggests, growing up to 6 inches in length, half of which is made up by the tail. The common lizard has an uncommon habit for a reptile, as the female gives birth to live young instead of laying eggs. Slow worms have also been seen in the bog, but although they resemble small, smooth snakes, they, too, are classified as lizards. It is a peculiarity of the Sandringham bog that despite its sandy soils, bracken and heather looking ideal for adders, so far they are absent, although they are plentiful in other parts of Norfolk.

The area itself has an interesting mixture of plants; sphagnum mosses that squelch underfoot, ferns, cotton grass, liverworts and sundews, those attractive insect-eating little plants with sticky leaves. As the bog is so rich and rare much work has to be carried out to stop the encroach-ment of birch and even pine. If birch trees were allowed to throw up a canopy of light-excluding leaves, with their roots sucking the bog dry, then the communities of damp-loving plants would disappear, as would birds that each spring arrive to breed.

Some of the pools were of bottomless bog, but others were shallow pans caused by beds of ironstone. Locally the stone is known as "carstone" and has been used for generations to make roadways, walls and houses. The ranger took me to a nearby quarry where the carstone is still excavated; it is a strange substance caused by iron in solution percolating upwards into sand. Where the sand escaped the liquid it is still loose and crumbles, but where it came into full contact, they fused together as solid rock. In places the carstone has formed attractive metallic shapes, almost like sculptured clinker from a great subterranean furnace. The houses built of carstone are extremely picturesque and sometimes local flint has been applied for additional decoration.

Many garden and churchyard walls are also of carstone, which provides excellent conditions for attractive rock-loving plants; the sprawling but delicate ivy-leaved toadflax, clusters of yellow fumitory, polypody ferns, and wallpepper, well named because of its hot taste.

The ranger is a sensitive, appreciative man, fascinated by shape and texture. He sees beauty in the form of rocks and the same qualities attract him to trees; he has a wide selection in the Country Park, from towering Douglas firs to once coppiced hazel. In his spare time he works in wood; turning bowls, plates, lamps and vases on his lathe. His favourite woods both grow in the Country Park; yew, because of its fine grain, and beech.

On the fenland, drilling was in progress, with gulls, rooks, lapwings and starlings all being drawn in by the drone of tractors and the promises of insects and worms in the freshly disturbed soil. Pheasants too were numerous and had obviously enjoyed a successful summer. Another female marsh harrier hunted above the tasselled reed heads of a ditch, with her gold-streaked head bright as it caught the light. Suddenly she stalled and rose in the air, her long yellow legs descended and she fell; she stayed hidden from view and a small mammal or bird had become one of her last victims before migration.

As the sun sank lower it seemed to draw up moisture from the land to hang in a fine glaring mist; it made Prince Philip's sanctuary seem larger. With its main pool, flat grassland and grazing cattle, it had the same feel as the Ouse Washes, or even the Camargue. Thistle heads were breaking up in the breeze without the aid of goldfinches; a pintail flew over, its white wing bar showing distinctively and a pair of gadwall floated without purpose. They are much under-rated and overlooked ducks, yet the drake in particular has a fine dark marbled plumage. Redshank and spotted redshank prodded and probed in the mud and a snipe dropped down to feed. Behind them a kestrel hovered expertly.

Along the overgrown sea wall small tortoiseshells and red admirals still fluttered and beyond them were the plants and twisting creeks of salt-marsh, extending far out to the waters of the Wash. Theoretically the foreshore belongs to the Crown Commissioners, yet it cannot be separated from the estate, as part of the Wash's great bird population

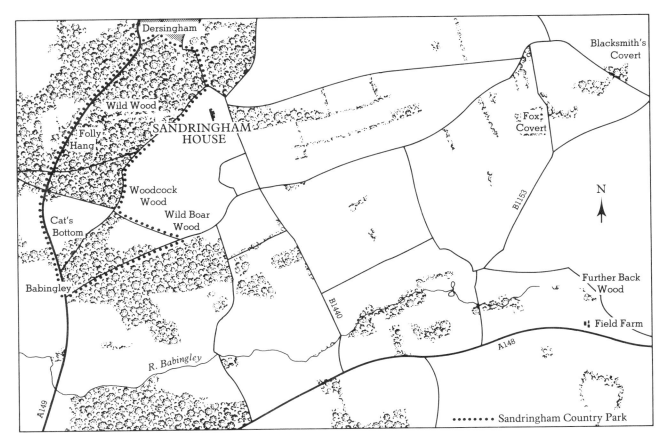

depends on the adjoining land, and thousands of birds spill over the sea wall to feed, and for shelter during storms and very high tides.

Several kestrels were also hunting the marsh, where numerous vole runs criss-crossed through grasses. The sea asters were flowering and there were several plants that seem to thrive on salt, spiky clusters of sea arrow grass, sea purslane, of cacti appearance, and the reed-like flowering heads of marram grass.

At one time the tracks of otters were often seen in the mud of the marshes and along the Babingley river, but now they rarely visit, with only an occasional animal passing through. Their numbers have fallen drastically throughout East Anglia and just a few places in Norfolk give them refuge. One of the possible reasons for the otter's decline could be seen at the Babingley, where its uniform flow and smooth, even sides suggested more of an engineer's theory, than natural flow. Unfortunately, throughout lowland Britain, water authorities have turned once appealing, varied and living rivers and streams into mere drainage channels, efficient, uniform and almost dead. Each time the drag lines gouge out the beds, disturbance drives any remaining otters away, and suitable sites for breeding are destroyed.

Butterbur by the River Babingley.

Fortunately the character of the Babingley has not been completely changed, and as I walked along its banks at the end of the day I saw the remnants of its once rich fauna and flora. A trout darted below the surface of the water and a moorhen dived, leaving a trail of rising bubbles to mark its progress. Water mint, purple loosestrife, horse mint, water forget-me-not, hemp agrimony, rosebay and great-hairy willow-herbs and ragwort all still flowered. The large rhubarb-like leaves of butterbur were also plentiful; it won its name quite simply, for in days gone by it made an ideal wrapping for freshly made butter. John Gerard the sixteenth-century herbalist reported other uses: ''The leaf is of such a widenesse, as that of itselfe it is bigge and large inough to keep a mans head from raine, and from the heate of the sunne.'' Culpeper too had uses for butterbur: ''The decoction of the root, in wine, is singular good for those that wheeze much, or are short-winded. It provoketh urine also, and women's courses, and killeth the flat and broad worms in the belly.'' He finishes with a request: ''It were well if gentlewomen would keep this root preserved to help their poor neighbours. It is fit the rich should help the poor, for the poor cannot help themselves.''

At the little river's source was another untouched water-meadow, where the tenant grazes cattle, but refuses to use weedkillers. Each spring, because of his care, the field bursts into bloom and continues well into late summer. The pleasure it gives him far exceeds the value of wheat or Italian rye grass that drainage or chemical sprays would give. At the back of his farmhouse a small lake attracts many wildfowl, and it is during late summer and early autumn that scarce early migrants briefly drop in at the local pools and streams; greenshank, curlew sandpipers and green sandpipers, moving south from their arctic breeding grounds. The tenant farmer has had other rare visitors too, in 1981 a little egret and in 1977 a pair of stone curlews successfully bred in a field of sugar beet. At one time stone curlews were so common that they were known as "Norfolk plovers", but the ploughing and planting of heathland has removed many of their favourite Norfolk nesting sites.

As the light faded, white wings flew above the river bank before turning and floating silently along the side of a hedge. The barn owl was the same colour as the mist that was slowly engulfing the land.

With autumn moving well into October, so the colours intensified and leaves began to fall. The larches of the Country Park looked as if they had been set in polished copper and beneath them the dying bracken fell into broken patterns of yellows, browns and gold. The lighter leaves of ash and hawthorn along the hedges of the water-meadow had fluttered down, leaving bramble, streaked with stains of crimson, and dogwood turning deep mauve. Ivy supplied the last flowers of the year, where bees and wasps worked busily and the sunlit colours of birch, beech, larch, oak and bramble perfectly matched the feathers of a cock pheasant's breast.

The year seemed to be slowly dying, yet within the woodland there were signs of urgent action; scrapes of disturbed soil and frayed saplings, barkless because of batterings by antlers. For just as in Scotland, autumn brings the red deer rut, so from mid-October until early November, the woods of Sandringham see the mating of the fallow.

I have a deep affection for fallow deer. They are smaller than red, but larger than roe, and have a remarkably wide colour range from white to almost black. In summer the most beautiful have a coat of light chestnut-brown dappled with fresh white spots. The mature bucks grow wide palmated antlers that give them a look of arrogance and assurance; it is misleading, however, for they are shy and retiring, except during the rut. The origin of the fallow deer is not really known; some say it was brought over by the Romans, others by the Normans, and it has even been suggested that it is indigenous. Whatever the truth, there is no doubt that any early stock has been greatly supplemented by animals brought in for deer parks. It is these deer that form the bulk of today's population, for feral herds formed when deer escaped and when the parks themselves were allowed to fall into decay. Fallow deer in Norfolk were mentioned in the Domesday Book and there have been several parks with deer since, all contributing to present numbers.

Dusk and dawn are the best times to see deer and Mont was anxious to show me the rut. Towards the end of the day we made for a traditional rutting area, and as we passed a small conifer plantation a young buck was crossing, thrashing at saplings as he went. There were slot marks clearly showing in the fallen pine needles and disturbed oak leaves, but the wood was unusually quiet. We waited just inside a block of pines overlooking a glade, rows of poplars and wind-tangled grasses. Leaves rustled in the wind, which carried the distant cries of lapwings and gulls; pheasant called as they went up to roost. Without warning there was movement in the long grasses and a small fawn moved along a concealed path towards us, unhurried and quite unaware of our presence. It was followed by its mother and a young immature buck, probably her son from the previous year. They were all very light in colour and they stopped just a few yards away to browse. The fawn made the best of the pause and began to suckle, its tail working much faster than its tongue in contentment. Then, just as quietly as they arrived, they slowly made off along a forest ride.

It was a beautiful but unexpected scene, for I had never imagined seeing a six-week-old fawn in October. Fawns are usually born singly in June, but this one must have been as late as August or even early September. The doe could have missed pregnancy during the normal rut, and come into season again, or she could just have been late, briefly re-firing a buck into activity.

Dawn was misty and dripping, with water spilling from the trees. It muffled sound and gave the scents of early morning a delicious dampness; spiders' webs were strung out in long spangled threads among meadowsweet, grasses and rose hips. Where we crossed a ditch Mont pointed out wild crab apple trees, now scarce, but once encouraged, not only for their fruit, which makes excellent crab apple jelly, but their wood which is strong, heavy and hard, ideal for mallet heads and the cog-wheels of wind and water mills.

Deer had been active during the night, especially under oak trees where they had been feeding on fallen acorns. During the summer they have their own favourite areas, away from people, but when the number of visitors declines and the acorns fall, they spread further across the estate. Again all was quiet, with the groaning of an amorous buck completely absent.

The noise of a rutting fallow buck is memorable, resembling a deep, loud and often repeated snore, resounding through the wood. It obviously bears an erotic message, for sometimes the does bleat excitedly in reply. With care and luck it is possible to approach quite near, as long as outlying young bucks or groups of does are not startled, putting all the deer to flight. On one occasion I approached to within a few feet of a large groaning buck and could hear him breathing deeply after each bout of passion; unfortunately, by the time we were close, it was so dark that I could see nothing.

There are other animals that are attracted to acorns, for Sandringham still has a small population of red squirrels, who bury and store them in hollow trees for later use. They are also fond of fungi which they wedge into branches before eating, either to improve the taste or to prevent them from being stolen by other animals. As at Balmoral the squirrel's main source of food comes from pine seeds, extracted from cones, and the Scots pine is again their favourite.

Unfortunately the Sandringham red squirrels appear to be doomed, for a combination of competition with grey squirrels and virus diseases seems certain to send them slowly into extinction. Numbers have been hit by several epidemics, the worst being caused by a parapoxvirus infection which gives symptoms similar to those of myxomatosis in rabbits. If the worst happens it will probably leave Thetford Forest and Rendlesham with the only remaining red squirrels in East Anglia. Numbers of red squirrels have declined and recovered before, even in Scotland, but the present trend seems irreversible.

But although the plight of the red squirrel is sad, each autumn brings a more successful story, with the arrival of brent geese for the winter. Until quite recently they too were thought to be in state of sharp decline; their main winter diet was eel grass, a plant of salt-marshes and salt water which was also hit by disease. As the eel grass declined, so did the geese. But agricultural change has unwittingly come to their aid, for brent geese have discovered the tender shoots of winter wheat. Consequently the increasing acreage of winter-sown cereals could not have come at a better time and now the population is rapidly increasing. Although some farmers are horrified to see flocks of grazing geese, they do little damage and the wheat quickly recovers in the spring. At one time winter wheat was actually grazed by sheep, as a part of normal husbandry, and geese only cause problems during exceptionally wet weather, when their feet push the young plants deep into the water-logged soil.

Brents are beautiful dark birds, seen at their best flying in ragged skeins from the Wash, to feed on the marshes and farm fields. Every autumn they fly in from their breeding grounds in Arctic Russia and Siberia and local people welcome their return. During the year of my visits to Sandringham I was on the east coat when migrating brent geese were arriving. It was an unforgettable day, for gale-force winds were blowing, icy rain was sluicing down so hard that it stung my cheeks and the sea was cold, grey, and rough. A flock of dunlin flew by, and then out of the haze came a straggling line of geese flying low, beating into the wind. They were "coasting", travelling just off the shore, skimming the waves and sometimes disappearing from view in the deep troughs of moving water. Several groups flew by, totalling more than 400 birds in just over an hour. A few flocks arrived high, from directly over the sea; as soon as they saw land they lost height to follow the coastline. Birds choose fine weather for their long distance flights, but the geese had obviously been caught out by the sudden arrival of storms and the last stage of their journey had been hard. When the weather calmed and migration had stopped, over 1,400 birds had settled in the vicinity of Sandringham for the winter.

Once it starts, the fall of leaves quickly turns autumn into winter and on a grey, late November day the landscape had changed to one of dull browns, greens and naked trees. The farm fields were a mixture of growing winter wheat and unharvested brussels sprouts, sugar beet and carrots, as well as bare soil. Along Peddars Way many fieldfares and redwings flew from hedgerows; it was pleasing to see that they had arrived safely. Over ploughed land a much larger bird approached; a bird of prey with long, slender, pointed wings. It flew with the easy buoyant flight of a harrier, and its conspicuous white rump confirmed it as a female hen harrier. Just as the marsh harrier moves south and away in winter, so the hen harrier arrives at Sandringham from its northern moorland haunts. Even in a strong wind it flew easily, in complete control, and went down for a "kill" in sugar beet. The beet and carrot fields must have high populations of small birds and rodents to attract the harrier away from its more traditional hunting grounds.

On "bolted" carrots other birds with white rumps fed, as bullfinches pulled out seeds. Flocks of linnets and finches flew from field to field and a hare loped through a hedge as pheasants fed. There were partridges too, both French and English, and a large covey of English flew over with whirring wings; in many areas of the country they have almost disappeared. On more winter wheat a flock of curlews stood, preening and resting, and behind them were much larger birds; a flock of about 500 pink-footed geese, some grazing and others just standing, watching. Another great flock came in, calling as they did so, gliding into their descent and spiralling down. They are slightly smaller than greylags, with much darker heads and higher pitched calls. Like the brents, Mont has seen their habits change over recent years. In his early days at Sandringham they would roost on the marshes and mud of the Wash, before feeding on the low fenland fields. Now they fly much further inland on to the higher ground and have developed a liking for left-over sugar beet, carrots and potatoes, as well as winter corn. As many as 10,500 "honkers" arrive during the winter, amounting to ten per cent of the world pink-feet population.

All over the farm land there were gangs of rooks and flocks of lapwings. As one large group of lapwings flew overhead, with their pleasant "lapping" wingbeats, smaller, faster birds went with them,

whistling, and flying in the manner of true waders. They were golden plovers, set to spend the winter away from the hard weather of the Highlands. They are very responsive to cold, so during a prolonged freeze-up they continue to move south, sometimes travelling as far as Spain and North Africa.

The bog too had withdrawn into winter; the birches leafless, the heather dormant and dark brown and the bracken dead, and flattened by wind and rain. Only the stems of cotton grass gave colour, in pools of deep mauve. Another female hen harrier began to hunt and a sparrow-hawk flew over with quick wingbeats, flying high. On marshy ground, tall grasses and reeds concealed pools, and soon the air was full of ducks. Slot marks showed that deer also used that corner for winter food and shelter. Oyster-catchers, redshank and snipe fed at the sanctuary, where the Queen and Prince Philip like to use an old shepherd's hut as a hide.

Beyond the sea wall it was bleak, with the cold wind increasing and blowing in from the sea; during the winter locals claim that it arrives direct from the frozen Ural mountains of Russia, with nothing in between to soften or warm its blast. In the distance a large group of brent geese were roosting on mud and further back still, huge groups of waders were flying in dense clouds, like locusts.

Returning, I was surprised but pleased to see a flock of sixteen feeding swans, for Bewick's swans are more regular visitors of winter. They are beautiful, gentle birds and when they fly their wings are silent, without the sibilations of the mute. Their call, however, is a wild and distant sound evocative of the far off tundra marshes, where they breed during the brief arctic summer. Each autumn and spring they make the journey; 2,600 miles over seas, mountains and political systems. When swimming they are distinguished from the mute by their necks, which they hold straighter, and the patches of vivid yellow on their bills. It is a surprising fact that swans have more vertebrae in their necks than any other creature, including the ostrich and giraffe.

The Bewick's swan is named after Thomas Bewick, the kindly and gifted wood-engraver. Ironically, it is highly unlikely that Bewick ever saw one of the birds now bearing his name, and in his work he only depicted the mute. The population of Bewick's has almost doubled in the last ten years, to about 12,000 in north-west Europe, of which 4,000 winter in Britain. Of these up to 100 spent time at Sandringham and sometimes they are joined by as many as fifty of the larger whooper swans. When airborne they must see the Ouse Washes about thirty miles to the south; 5,000 acres of land which in winter holds much of the water drained from the area of old fenland. It attracts up to 3,000 Bewick's and over 200 whooper swans, from November until early spring. It was Sir Peter Scott, at the Wildfowl Trust at Slimbridge in Gloucestershire, who discovered that each bird could be individually recognised by the varying yellow patterns on the beak. Since then many

Bewick's swans.

birds have been identified and seen to return for several winters; the most famous being named ''Lancelot'' and, in November 1983, Lancelot returned to Slimbridge for his twenty-first consecutive year.

Watching wildlife always provides interest, but it is unpredictable; some days are quite unexceptional, while others contain variety and incident that ensure a permanent place in memory. I had one of those days at Sandringham in winter, starting at dawn. As daylight broke, with an open sky, the temperature plummeted, frosting the grass with glistening ice. Even in the half light of early morning the barn owl was hunting, ghostlike over the fields of the Babingley. There was a high tide as I made for the marshes and the full moon was bright and being reflected in a shimmering path of silver over the Wash. From the far side it would have been the sun transforming the waves and ripples into gold. There were many gulls and shelducks riding on the water, their brilliant white being more than matched by each small wavelet which reflected concentrations of jewelled light from every side.

Oyster-catchers piped and teal whistled as a male hen harrier hunted over rough grassland; steel grey with ink black tips to his wings. He was flying low with three or four relaxed wingbeats followed by a glide, on half-raised wings. It was the more normal country for a hen harrier with plenty of mammals and small birds on which to feed; reed buntings, with their smart hirsute heads would be particularly at risk. He flew off towards gravel pits, startling the roosting birds. The pits are just off the estate and during very high tides knot and oyster-catchers roost in tens of thousands, standing in tight regimented rows. They can be so dense that when another bird flies in to land it sends ripples of movement through the assembled ranks. The disturbed knot flew in great masses, dark against the bright sky, with the unity of their changing shapes bearing the same symmetry in air as moving oil on water.

Over 220,000 waders visit the Wash during the winter and spring, as well as more than 25,000 wildfowl. In the eastern Wash, close to Sandringham, they include 35,000 knot, 12,000 oyster-catchers, 8,000 dunlin, 5,000 bar-tailed godwits, 3,000 grey plovers, 2,500 redshanks, 1,000 sanderling, 800 turnstone, 200 ringed plovers, 1,500 curlew, 7,000 shelducks, 5,000 wigeon, 2,500 mallard, and 2,500 pintail. It is difficult to give an accurate total for teal, as they are widely dispersed on pools and along ditches, but there is usually a minimum of 500.

As the moonlight evaporated under the brilliant sun, the cold air became full of geese. Two flocks of brents moved inland to feed, while a great V of high flying pink-feet flew in the opposite direction, out on to the Wash, calling as they went. They were followed by a long ragged skein at "hedge-hopping" height; as if some had been left behind by the first movement of birds. They had been feeding by the light of the full moon and were intending to roost during the day. A large group of wigeon were in the Duke's sanctuary, some grazing and others resting on the water. Redshank too were feeding, and another flew in calling melodically; their call in the wind is the music of wetland, marsh and muddy creeks. It is the sound of solitude, wild places and freedom, and it strikes a distant chord, gently stirring, soothing and releasing those emotions normally locked deep within the soul.

Leaving this still semi-natural wilderness I returned to the car park of the Country Park to search with the ranger for hibernating bats. As we spoke a family party of long-tailed tits moved through the treetops and a nuthatch began working on the trunk of a tree. It looked like a cartoon character, stretching up on tiptoe, while upside-down, to strike with all its might into the bark with its beak.

Suddenly a male crossbill landed on a low branch of larch; its rose-pink plumage was stunningly beautiful, intensifying to vivid orange on its back. I had never before been so close, and had previously regarded them as very ordinary birds. Crossbills are particularly fond of larch and its large crossed-over mandibles were clearly visible; ideal for cracking cones to get at the seeds. It flew down to drink from a gutter close to the souvenir shop, before flying high up into the larches where several more had begun to feed on cones; distance again restored it to anonymity.

Not only are the crossbills' beaks astonishing, but so are their habits, for they are the earliest birds to mate and nest. Some actually begin in January, but the usual months for egg-laying and incubation are February and March. As a result the crossbill's eggs are remarkably resistant to cold, as are the young. Once hatched, they become torpid when the adults are away foraging for food, but they quickly recover when brooded.

A Daubenton's bat.

We found hibernating bats in an old lime-kiln. They too were torpid, wedged tightly and comfortably between bricks. They were probably Daubenton's, and we were careful not to disturb them; for hibernating bats take several minutes to wake, and in so doing they use up valuable energy needed to get them through the winter. There are four other species in the area; Naterer's, long-eared, noctule, and pipistrelle. In the country as a whole bat numbers are decreasing rapidly because of the loss of ancient trees, with numerous holes and hollows, and through the destruction of hedgerows and grassland which has removed much insect life on which the bats depend for food.

As the tide ebbed we returned to the salt-marshes; shelducks were still feeding in mud and salty water and a mass of brent geese rose, their feeding finished, to fly noisily to open mud. They lived up to their country name of "clattergeese". The tide line was a depressing sight, with numerous sea-birds – guillemots, razorbills, and a few young puffins, all dead. They looked undamaged, with no signs of oil and the cause of the calamity was a mystery. Later it was estimated that over 30,000 seabirds had died, after gales, along the east coasts of England and Scotland. Many of the bodies were underweight and it is thought that birds already weak through poor feeding conditions, were blown away from their normal feeding grounds and starved. The same winds blew in many healthy little auks, a bird normally rare to British waters; they were seen along the coast and inland on numerous gravel pits.

Other natural disasters occasionally occur; in January 1978 geese were found dead in the area, mainly pink-footed, but also brent. They appeared to have simply fallen out of the sky, again in good condition. Post-mortems revealed internal ruptures and haemorrhages, as well as broken bones; it seems that they were sucked high up into a thunderstorm and then released to plunge, out of control, back to earth.

The pools of the water-meadow were all full, confirming "February fill dyke", and the branches of dogwood had adopted the deep reddish-mauve of its autumn leaves. Pheasants flew as a female harrier floated over the hedge and began to quarter the ground. The Babingley meadows had similar attractions and were squelching with water. Wigeon and teal whistled from the lake and Egyptian geese grazed. I was surprised to see the geese, having only previously encountered them wild, on the Tana river, in the Northern Frontier District of Kenya. There, in semi-desert I had been astonished by their capacity to survive the heat, and the threat of predators; crocodiles, lions, civets, snakes and eagles. In Norfolk, in winter, it amazed me still more that they could survive the damp and cold of an English winter. They are large, handsome geese, a mixture of browns, fawns and greys, with crimson legs, and they too now flourish in the wild after being imported originally as ornamental wildfowl.

Dusk came as the sun set in a great glowing fire, flooding the western horizon and the Wash with its glare. It promised an even sharper frost, as if to reaffirm the warning "As the days lengthen, so the cold strengthens". Again with the fading light the barn owl appeared, following the bends in the river, falling and rising, on silent wings.

Spring arrives slowly and falteringly, but much earlier than at Balmoral. The catkins of hazel and alder give false hope and the dawn chorus begins. But confirmation of the new season is gained by the arrival of wild daffodils in Woodcock wood, and two attractive wild flowers, butterbur and coltsfoot, both appearing before their leaves.

The peculiar mauve flowers of butterbur push up through bare ground on the banks of the Babingley. In southern England nearly all the flowers are male, with just the occasional female plant appearing. This causes no great problem, for they can spread through their creeping root systems, as well as from seeds.

At first glance the bright yellow flowers of coltsfoot can be mistaken for dandelions, but the flowers are smaller and denser, and there is a complete absence of leaves. After pollination has taken place the flowers droop until the heads of white down ripen; then the stalks stiffen once more to offer their seeds to the wind. The leaves appear later and can grow up to 9 inches across; the name coltsfoot comes from their shape. Another name is "coughwort", for dried coltsfoot leaves are used in herbal tobacco and are said to soothe coughs and wheezes.

Common frog.

A brown hare.

The white blossom of blackthorn also shows the gradual build-up towards spring, but a cold wind often accompanies it, reminding of the "blackthorn winter". It is strange how winter temperatures often return when the blackthorn is on flower.

Spring at the water-meadows starts with the dull flowers of dog's mercury in the hedgerows and on a cold blustery day I went to look for signs of new growth. In the pond among the ripples was a sight I had not seen for many years, clumps of frog spawn containing thousands of eggs. Many of the temporary pools also held spawn; despite the chill it was a heart-warming sight, for in so many places, through drainage schemes and the use of sprays, the common frog has become extremely uncommon. Around the edges of the pond several frogs had recently died, with their stomachs ripped open. It could not have been the work of ducks or herons; they would have swallowed them whole. Mont had noticed it in previous springs and assumed it to be the work of rats.

Then came a new, trembling sound; beautiful and wavering like pan pipes played in the wind. It was a snipe "drumming", flying fast and high before gliding to create a rush through its extended tail feathers. The air hummed as if blown over a specially cut reed, and the vibrations flowed far beyond the limits of its territory.

More exhibitions of aerial display were taking place over fields where lapwings called and tumbled. The large flocks had dispersed, with some birds staying to breed, while others had also paired but moved away. Buck hares walked stiff-legged before running and jumping in their "madness", as a doe sat watching impassively. Although hares breed throughout the summer it is only in the early spring that their behaviour calls for a psychiatrist's couch. Seeing them so wild, wide-eyed and besotted, is to understand how superstitions grew linking the hare with witchcraft and bad luck. These beliefs were aided by the fact that when a hare is injured, wounded or frightened it screams like a child.

Again it was a pleasure to see hares, for where over-intensive monoculture has replaced "farming", their numbers have declined dramatically. The population at Sandringham has declined too, but at present there is no cause for alarm. Elsewhere it is the continuous growing of winter wheat and the use of sprays that have caused the fall, coupled with an explosion in the fox population on non keepered land. Although we have kept our field hedges, and some grass, we have not seen a hare for two harvests; a loss not thought possible a few years ago. Unfortunately our small farm, and the hares, have been lost in an ocean of wheat.

Hares like a varied diet with plenty of places for shelter and concealment, and at Sandringham they still have them. On prairie farms, after stubble burning, they have little food to eat, and in the spring, when they crouch down, tractors with wide spray booms cover them with poison. Their demise is a tragedy, for the hare has been a well loved part of

A dotterel on migration in the spring.

Water avens.

country life for many generations. It has attracted the lurchers and long-dogs of poachers and sporting men; it has been pursued by hounds; caught in nets and been served up as delicious "jugged hare" in cottage kitchens, but it still managed to thrive. Now many of these activities are described as "uncivilised", yet ironically, it is "progress" that is actually killing the hare, often slowly and painfully.

Through the old pines many tits were active, and some would have already started to nest. The bog still looked bleak, but a few shelducks had gathered around a pool and two short-eared owls were hunting. They were flying so lightly that with every undulation of the wind they lifted and fell as if floating on an invisible sea. When they approached each other they climbed higher with faster wingbeats, before parting again to hunt. Some years they also breed on the estate, thriving on the abundant summer voles.

At this time too, many birds pass through Sandringham, for the movement of migration reverses; the geese and swans leave and new waders pause before continuing on their way. Occasionally a few dotterel are seen as they rest before resuming their journey north, and several traditional stopping sites are to be found close by.

As the season advances so the buds swell and burst on the hawthorns and birches, and the spears of bracken begin to uncurl. Willow warblers and chiff-chaffs sing, as does the cuckoo; rejuvenation and growth can be felt in the sweetening air. Along the roadsides cow parsley and Jack-by-the-hedge shoot quickly and even ground ivy becomes attractive with its many violet flowers. Brimstone butterflies and orange tips fly and the growing warmth of the season is reflected in their wings. Red admirals appear, vivid and finely coloured; it is difficult to believe that they are immigrants, unable to get through a British winter.

The orange tip is one of my favourite butterflies; each year I find myself looking for it on the first warm days of May, and when white wings flash orange I know that spring has really come. Orange tips choose Jack-by-the-hedge and cuckoo flower on which to lay their eggs and Sandringham has plenty of both. Jack-by-the-hedge is also known as hedge garlic because of its mild garlic taste, and when the leaves are young they make a fine addition to salads.

Cuckoo flowers, or lady's smocks, were scattered throughout the water-meadows, and they remain on flower for as long as the cuckoo can be heard. There were clumps of marsh marigolds, cowslips and water avens – deep mauve flowers with nodding heads on slender stems. In some areas they are known as Granny's bonnets or fairies' baths.

Even the pond had burst into bloom, with a mass of water violets standing clear of the water; they looked more like aquatic cuckoo flowers than violets, with fine feathery leaves submerged by water and many small tadpoles. Close to one bank the soft white flowers of meadow saxifrage grew in waving clumps. Once it could be found in meadowland

A young marsh harrier.

throughout Britain, but it has gradually been sprayed away and is becoming increasingly scarce. A snipe flew from rushes and circled in agitation, worried about the safety of her nest. Earlier her concern would have been far more basic, for the eggs of snipe are remarkably large for the size of the bird.

On the farm fields of Peddars Way, partridges had paired and cock pheasants "crowed", flapping their wings as they did so. Two advanced as if to fight, but their aggression quickly left as larger wings floated over a hedge to hunt the spring barley – the marsh harriers were back from their African winter.

The return of the marsh harrier as a breeding bird to Britain is one of the most remarkable events in recent years. For centuries the Fens formed an undrained land of rivers, pools, willows and reedbeds; the wilderness spread right into the salt-marshes of the Wash and each summer thousands of harriers would have hunted and bred in its vastness. Drainage came, marsh land shrank, and wildlife retreated. At the same time game interests joined in the attack and marsh harriers fell victim to dried out land and hard lead shot. In addition, many nests were lost to egg collectors who still carried out their fashionable and respectable pursuit, and by 1878 marsh harriers were extinct in Britain. Occasional birds were seen during the following years, but it was not until 1911 that breeding resumed. Numbers slowly increased until the late fifties, when inexplicably the population crashed again and by 1971, Minsmere in Suffolk provided the only breeding pair. Since then a minor recovery has taken place, with birds breeding at several traditional sites in Norfolk and Suffolk. Their future continues to hang in the balance, however, and there are still fewer breeding marsh harriers in Britain than ospreys or red kites.

Their arrival at several sites in Norfolk has been exciting and unexpected, for much of their favoured habitat has disappeared; it is as if deep ancestral memory has guided them back. The springtime display of the male, immediately after its return, is a most spectacular sight and sadly I have only seen it once. The male, slightly smaller than the female and with grey patches on his wings, soared effortlessly above the marsh, before suddenly tumbling down at great speed, almost somersaulting and flipping over on to its back. It righted itself just before disappearing into the reeds. The female must have been impressed, for the pair bred successfully.

At an old sand pit, once dug out to send silver sand to Java for glass-blowing, more summer visitors had returned. Sand martins are smaller and browner than swallows, with their tails only slightly forked and they often fly in small packs. Nest holes in the sheer quarry sides were being inspected and tunnelled out and one bird was starting a completely new hole; clinging to the wall with its feet and wings and pecking sand away with its beak.

A pair of shelduck.

The pool in the bog had attracted many shelducks, almost gaudy in their summer plumage. Some fed, others displayed, and several argued with heads working backwards and forwards, puffing out air as they did so; they reminded me of farmyard Muscovies. Before myxomatosis, most of the shelducks nested in rabbit holes, and they were even called ''burrow ducks''; now there are not enough holes to go round and so many nest in bracken, heather and occasionally hay bales. To feed, they fly to the Wash, following the retreat of the tide to puddle in mud.

At the Duke's sanctuary there were well over 100 shelducks, aggressive and loud in display. One, with neck outstretched, chased off several teal and mallard for no particular reason. A pair of mute swans preened and several breed successfully on the estate; they are beautiful, peaceful birds, but due to the activities of tourists and fishermen, their numbers are declining in Norfolk. Part of that decline is distressing, being long drawn out, painful and tragic, involving anglers' discarded nylon line, lead weights and hooks. Fortunately, those on the estate are safe from harassment. In the mud a lapwing searched for food; several times it stamped its foot quickly to encourage insects to move.

Over the sea wall hundreds of grey plovers were roosting; they looked far from grey in their full summer plumage, with the sun exaggerating their jet black breasts and wings of shining white. If they did not leave soon their arctic summer would be made even shorter.

The arrival of true summer is marked by flowers; the hedgerows of hawthorn laden with white ''may'', and when they fade the rhododendrons burst into pinks, reds, blues, purple and mauve. They form great banks of colour, humming with hover flies and working bees. In the water-meadows more delicate flowers emerge – orchids, finely shaped with matching petals. The deep mauve of the southern marsh with large flowering heads and the smaller early marsh, creamy white and spotted with pale pink.

There are pastoral scenes with grazing cattle in fields of lush grass and the leaves of the trees dripping with fresh colour. Wheat pushes ear and the buds of wild roses swell. It is a season of images, sounds and warm scents, when those who pause can make time stand still.

Peddars Way was rolling and rich in the greens of new growth, with its wide open sky full of birdsong; yellowhammers, corn buntings, thrushes, blackbirds, chaffinches, the call of pheasants, the cooing of pigeons and the comforting purring of turtle doves. High above came another independent symphony of falling sound as skylarks sang. The hedgerows were as varied in their leaves as the notes of the air – ash, oak, sycamore, buckthorn, blackthorn and hawthorn, as well as climbing plants, black bryony, the only British member of the yam family, and the unrelated white bryony, which is in the same family as cucumbers and marrows.

A stoat, and later a weasel, darted from one side of the track to the other, setting off the scalding cries of a blackbird. Peddars Way and the farm tracks that join with it, and branch from it, create an important network for birds and animals. They form a refuge for wild flowers too, allowing them to spread away from sprays. A hen pheasant and her brood were bathing in dust, for the roadways have become vital for game birds, providing insects for the young chicks, and also giving them open ground in which to dry off after rain. Partridges in particular need insects and clear areas. Mont considers that a simple change in farming practice could save them. "If headlands* were left without sprays and fertilisers the crops would be thinner with many wild plants and insects." They would be similar to the "hunting headlands" of the shires, which are kept to allow huntsmen access, without their horses damaging corn. As a consequence they leave great pathways of summer flowers when hunting has ceased. To a young chick, fully cultivated fields of wheat are dark, insects are few and after rain, water continues to drip, making them damp long after the sun has dried open ground. At one time rabbits helped to create thin headlands of grazed corn, but with larger fields their numbers will never return to pre-myxomatosis levels.

A skylark ceased to sing as new, narrower wings began hunting over wheat, with the light buoyant flight of a harrier. It was one of Britain's rarest birds, a Montagu's harrier, the smallest and most graceful harrier, as well as being the most scarce. Named after a Devon army officer and naturalist, Colonel George Montagu, who lived between 1751 and 1815 and was the first man to differentiate between the bird named after him and the hen harrier; it winters as far away as the tip of southern Africa, but returns in small numbers to breed. They nest erratically, with no set pattern, sometimes on moorlands as well as in farm crops.

Marsh harrier hunting.

This particular harrier drifted low over the field before quartering along an overgrown track; suddenly it rose, held its wings high above its head, lowered its long legs and fell. Its movement and grace held such beauty that it was easy to forget that such a climax usually means death. There was good hunting, with signs of voles and many small birds. Nearby a marsh harrier crossed on to wheat, but as it entered the Montagu's hunting area, the male, a much smaller bird, was immediately in pursuit. It flew high above, before stooping at the marsh harrier, lunging with its talons as it passed. The larger bird evaded skilfully, but the Montagu had immediately regained height through its own momentum and was already falling again in anger. A female flew to join in and the marsh harrier turned to fly off and hunt elsewhere. Other rare birds of prey occasionally pass over the estate, and rough-legged and honey buzzards have both been seen, but very infrequently.

Mont is fond of the area of Peddars Way, not only because of its wildlife, but also for the archaeology that surrounds it, with signs of Roman, Saxon and even earlier settlement. He has left his mark on the

* The headland is the strip of land around the edge of a field on which the tractor turns when ploughing is taking place.

landscape too, in the form of two large reed fringed pools surrounded by willows and alders. On a hot day they also formed a haven of birdsong, together with the alarm calls of reed and sedge warblers feeding their young. In this area they are both at risk, not from birds of prey, but from cuckoos wanting nests in which to lay their eggs. As one flew over in full voice Mont answered so accurately that the bird faltered in flight as if shocked by the presence of a rival.

The rhyme I learnt as a child about the cuckoo was an easy and accurate lesson in natural history:

> The cuckoo comes in April,
> He sings his song in May,
> In the middle of June he changes tune,
> And in July he flies away.

After sampling Mont's home-made wine, another old verse becomes appropriate:

> Heard in September,
> A thing to remember.
> Heard in October,
> You're not sober.

Unfortunately the cuckoo saw us and continued on his way.

Pairs of shelducks, tufted ducks and Egyptian geese already had young, with the small ducklings of the shelducks diving almost dizzily, to the concern of their parents. As soon as they are able, the parent ducks move with their broods towards the Wash. In the past, once there, most of the adults flew to the Baltic coast of north-west Germany to moult, but over recent years, an increasing number have stayed behind and now up to 1,500 remain to become flightless as new feathers replace the old.

A new day began in the company of Mont; walking near reeds we started, as large wings and long yellow legs lifted up close. A marsh harrier had left her nest leaving two grey, downy chicks, with black eyes and beaks. The mother called out in alarm and we left in haste, not wanting to leave the young at risk; the hen bird soon returned and both young fledged successfully. The male was trying to hunt over grassland but was being mobbed by several lapwings; they are courageous birds and when dive-bombing the harrier, surprisingly mobile. They soon forced him to give up and move away over wheat.

The feeding habits of the harriers are varied; when they first arrive they eat whatever is available, small birds, rats, rabbits, moorhens, coots and water-voles, as well as frogs. In the first half of June, they include young pheasants which are plentiful, but then they switch to young starlings. Flocks of immature birds come in from the Continent and

A reed warbler feeding young.

make easy pickings. Then the shelducks begin to move their broods along the dykes and ditches to get to the Wash, and the preference again changes – to duckling. By the time the ducks have moved through, the menu once again broadens out, but by then most of the pheasants are too big to be taken. When the birds are feeding young, spectacular mid-air food passes take place, with the male dropping its victims for the female to catch on the wing. The sequence of food is a fascinating one, and although the harriers take some pheasants, their overall impact on the pheasant "crop" is negligible. Although a keeper's neurosis is easy to understand when he sees a young pheasant taken, his fears are ill-founded, for he rarely sees the other victims taken in reeds or long grass. Harriers are also territorial and so the density of birds in a certain area is strictly limited.

Mont and I moved on to a wood where among bugle and red and white campion, lily of the valley flowered. It was smaller, with fewer blooms than cultivated varieties. Woodcock breed here, but in all his years of keepering, Mont has never seen them carrying young. Many people claim to have witnessed this unusual behaviour, but he disagrees: "I think it's accidental. When they have young and the hen takes off, she tucks in her tail as part of the distraction display. Sometimes a chick may be trapped and lifted off the ground, but it soon drops out. It might even be nature's way of dispersing the brood to beat predators."

For Mont odd corners are a pleasure, including one with gorse and broom where both stonechats and whinchats have bred and where ragwort was covered with the yellow and black striped caterpillars of the cinnabar moth. Ragwort is mildly poisonous and it makes the caterpillars unpalatable to birds. It is a greatly under-rated flower and every time I see it I think of the words of John Clare:

> Ragwort thou humble flower with tattered leaves
> I love to see thee come and litter gold.

There were clumps of viper's bugloss with its flowers of deep blue. Once it was used as an antidote for adders' bites, but the measure of success is not recorded. Another of Mont's delights was a roadside ditch which had sprung to life with tall, tapering yellow flowers. Its sides were covered with both common mullein, or Aaron's rod, and the rare hoary mullein, with lovelier, looser flowers on small individual stems. Both plants not only have pleasing flowers, but also large, soft, hairy leaves, giving the additional names of donkey's ear, old man's flannel and flannel jacket. On some of the leaves were the feeding, well camouflaged caterpillars of the mullein moth, emphasising once more nature's cycles and inter-dependence. Other rare plants in the locality include the round prickly-headed poppy, the long prickly-headed poppy and the long-stalked cranesbill.

Returning to the Country Park other summer visitors could be seen in large numbers, they were "grockles", a West Country name now widely used to describe tourists and day-trippers, of all shapes and sizes. Every year they flock in, but instead of dispersing into the countryside, some strange form of herd instinct seems to drive them closer together. Along the roadside verges outside Sandringham House, cars park in two straight lines making grockle-watching easy and entertaining. Many of them sit on picnic chairs within touching distance of their cars, reading papers, sleeping and eating; there are thermos flasks, sun shades, sandwich tins and dark glasses; it almost has the air of Brighton beach. There are no litter bins however; incredibly it was found that when bins were provided, more litter went outside than in, and so they were removed.

As we drove past, one small group sat almost totally enclosed by a gaudy windbreak, on a windless day, while an even rarer sub-species sat sleeping, her hair in curlers, her eyes shut, her mouth open and her feet resting in the open boot of her car.

Despite the throng of grockles along the road, the Country Park itself was almost deserted. From a hide overlooking a glade, a song thrush could be seen washing in a small pool, and bird song flooded the scene, this time with the sound of woodland birds. Warblers, the laughing cry of a green woodpecker, tits, chiff-chaffs, blackcaps, and the harsh warning call of a jay. A spotted flycatcher perched on a low branch of birch, occasionally flying out after flies, fluttering and twisting in pursuit, before returning to its perch. They are attractive little birds and to watch them flying for food gives much pleasure. Unfortunately, because of their drab colour, many people overlook them, and in so doing they miss an enjoyable part of summer.

Treecreepers and nuthatches searched and probed for bark-held grubs and a redstart flew. A starling joined the thrush at the water's edge, almost submerging in its enthusiasm to wash. The buzzing of insects reflected the warmth and a great spotted woodpecker began to hammer at dead oak, pausing only as a grey squirrel ran along a nearby branch. In just a few minutes of quiet watching I had seen a broad section of woodland life. It is from ordinary and simple encounters like this that a real interest and understanding of birds and animals can often grow.

Further into the Country Park, away from the paths, several damp flushes can be found, where marsh pennywort thrives; it gets its name from its almost round penny-like leaves. On slightly drier ground, near wood sage, were clumps of pincushion moss; when it becomes detached from its place of origin it rolls into a ball and keeps on growing. Another strange moss of the area still only has a Latin name – *Schistostega pennata*. It is a very small plant, found growing in the burrows of sand martins, and has the peculiar quality of seeming to glow in fading light.

With the ranger I walked on through the area of old pines, with its soft

Marsh pennywort.

Cotton grass on the bog.

floor and scented air. Goldcrests were again high up in the branches, where greenfinches were cracking cones. A blackcap sang vigorously, its beak opening still wider for each variation of song. Where the path descended towards the bog, harebells and centaury flowered, and bell heather was just beginning to burst into bloom. The floor of the bog was luxuriant and spongy with growing sphagnum mosses and cranberries. Cotton grass swayed gently in the breeze, but its name did not seem quite right; in sunlight the tufted heads bore little resemblance to cotton, for each white strand shone with the texture of fine silk. The golden yellow spears of bog asphodel added areas of even brighter colour to the transformed scene; it grows throughout Britain on the poor acidic soils of bogs, mountains and moors, and was once used for medicines as well as yellow dye.

Sundews were also coming out on to flower, small and white, rising above their sticky leaves, on long slender stems. From a clump of scrub the churring sound of a grasshopper warbler clearly showed the origin of its name; a redshank cried in alarm, perching at the top of a small pine, and a tree pipit climbed high into the air.

As we passed through bracken, by a group of birch trees, there was sudden movement caused by the fluttering and flapping of wings. It was a nightjar dragging an extended wing, as if injured. The patterns of its feathers were beautiful; a soft fusion of mottled browns, greys and tawny yellow, the colours of dead bracken, heather, fallen pine needles, and dried grasses over sand. It was a distraction display, for soon she flew, with a light, almost moth-like flight, to perch on a small branch. She was still difficult to see, for she seemed to lie along the branch. Unlike the bird, the two exposed eggs stood out clearly, white, marbled with brown. As we retreated she quickly returned to her nest where she immediately merged with the background. Even with binoculars I found it difficult to locate her, sitting tight, with her eyes narrowed into slits and no sign of breathing. We must have almost stepped on the nest to have flushed her, but her shock was not too great and she managed to rear one chick successfully.

Several pairs of nightjars return to the area each summer, but their numbers are slowly dropping. In the rest of the country the decline has been rapid over recent years, mainly through the destruction of heath-land, their traditional nesting sites, and disturbance. In many areas the country name for the nightjar is "goatsucker", for although its beak is small, it opens wide, and the bird was once believed to suck milk from goats during the night. The real reason for its unusually large gape is to take in insects, particularly moths, while on the wing. At Sandringham the choice of moth is wide, including the mottled beauty, rosy footman, common wainscott, straw underwing and true lover's knot. If their taste is as attractive as their names, then the nightjars must live very well.

By coincidence, a few yards further along, on more open, sandy soil, a

A nightjar.

Willow warbler.

willow warbler emerged from a small hole among grass. It was a beautiful olive-green, so dainty and fragile. She too feigned injury by spreading out a wing, to lure us away. Her tiny oval nest was on the ground, woven from grasses and feathers, with an entrance hole at the side. Inside were three new young and four still unhatched eggs. I was taken completely by surprise. Previously I had always imagined that willow warblers nested high up in the treetops, close to where they sang their tumbling, melodic song. Although a straightforward discovery, it made me feel quite elated, emphasising how much I still take for granted and how even in simple experiences there is always something new to learn.

Willow warblers and chiff-chaffs look very similar and can only be distinguished by an expert eye. Fortunately the birds themselves can tell the difference and they can best be identified by their songs; the willow warbler's is long and musical, while the chiff-chaff repeats its name with a pleasant onomatopoeic "chiff-chaff". Later it came as no surprise to learn that the chiff-chaff also nests low down and sometimes on the ground. I wonder if a pheasant has ever nested up a tree?

As we passed through a small village on our way to the sea wall, an old man waved us down. He was cutting the grass in front of his enormous weedless garden. It was full of vegetables, all large and pampered; potatoes, runner beans, marrows, lettuces, tomatoes and huge clumps of rhubarb. He claimed not to like rhubarb and gave it all away, as he did most of his surplus produce.

Before retirement he worked on the estate for forty-five years, and in that time he said that he had seen a decline in local wildlife. In the early days he could remember hearing, and occasionally seeing corncrakes, that have now been absent from East Anglia for many years, and otters were common in the fen. But other creatures continue to give him pleasure. He called them by their Norfolk names, not out of affectation, but as normal speech – "blue wagtail" – the pied wagtail; "cat owls" – long-eared owls; "snowy or white owls" – barn owls and "King Harry" – the goldfinch. I asked him what he called pheasants, expecting him to say "ol' long tails". Instead he replied: "I call them all sorts of names, especially first thing in the morning when they're on my garden." But the old names are both accurate and apt, and similar descriptive tags are still sometimes given to people. The present Agent, a very tall man, is known as "Long Braces". Sadly, country people, their dialects and their way of life are under just as much threat as the wildlife around them.

By a large barn many collared doves were feeding and flying. They are now common, having recently "invaded" Britain from the Continent. Moorhens and redshank were along several dykes, where occasionally garganey breed. They are small secretive little migratory ducks that spend their winters far down in Africa and even Australia.

The sea wall was covered with thistles, ragwort and countless butterflies made active by the sun; peacocks, small tortoiseshells, gatekeepers, small heaths, small coppers and meadow browns. It was hot, the salt-marsh shimmered in the heat, with the horizon losing all its definition in the movement of scorched air. Redshank displayed on quivering wings and seven kestrels were all hovering simultaneously as they hunted. We too were rewarded with food, finding many clumps of marsh samphire. When picked young it should be boiled until tender and then eaten with melted butter and new bread. The fleshy stems pull easily from the stalks, and with cockles and home-made wine it makes a memorable meal. It can also be chopped up fresh and added to salads, or the boiled stems can be pulled from the stalks with a fork and put into jars of malt vinegar. Pickled samphire is a tasty additive to salads, cold meat and meat pies; according to Mont another attraction is its reputation as an aphrodisiac.

To wile away an hour before darkness I walked by the Babingley. There were many sticklebacks in the shallows, ideal for the kingfishers that breed along the river, and swallows were flying low over the water, feeding on clouds of insects. On the bank I noted red and white campion, purple loosestrife, borage and yellow rattle, so named because the seeds rattle when ripe. Once, farmers did not consider hay to be ready for cutting until the seed pods of yellow rattle actually rattled. Brooklime was at the water's edge as well as water speedwell. As dusk fell bats began to fly and a tawny owl hooted.

Once in darkness a remnant of old heathland seemed to take on new life. Nightjars churred, a warming, soothing sound, reminding me of Africa. They flew in misty moonlight, flickering and fluttering like the fleeting shadows of giant moths. I threw a large stone wrapped in a white handkerchief into the air and a bird swooped down for a closer look, mistaking the white for the wing markings of an intruding male.

Long-eared owl.

The hunger cries of young long-eared owls came from a nearby conifer plantation, reminding their hunting parents of their where-abouts. The "ears" of the "cat owls" have nothing to do with hearing but are tufts of feathers, which, when raised, give the owl its characteristic and attractive appearance. They breed in the old nests of crows and magpies and feed on a variety of small mammals, birds and insects. Even in darkness it was good to know of their presence, for it meant that Sandringham had all five resident British owls.

But of all the areas of Sandringham in summer, the one that gave me the most gratification was the water-meadow, with its hedges and pond. On warm days it held in the heat creating a confection of scents, wings, colours and waving grasses. It is said that nostalgia distorts the accuracy of memory, and reluctantly I had come to believe that the grass meadows of my childhood, with flowers, butterflies and drifting pollen had become richer through romantic imagination. But the water-meadow confirmed that memory was not false, for it gave a full succession of flowers, butterflies and bird song, leading into high summer.

After cowslips and orchids came ragged robin, rosebay willow-herb, hogweed, bedstraw and banks of yellow fleabane. Moorhens called to their young on the pond; warblers caught insects with delicate deadly skill, and one morning in a corner of long, dew soaked grass, a spotted fallow doe was looking for a quiet, sheltered place to give birth to her fawn. Butterflies flew, insects hummed, and a pair of turtle doves dropped down to drink. Over the pond damselflies with bodies of brilliant turquoise-blue and lace-like wings seemed to float on air and larger dragonflies droned by, the four-spotted chaser and the larger brown hawker.

The meadow reached a climax in early August, with flowers, a profusion of colours, trailing grasses and tangled stems. There was hemp agrimony, silverweed, mayweed, knapweed, yarrow, meadow vetchling, selfheal, water mint, amphibious bistort, water plantain, goosegrass, forget-me-not, horse mint, dock, sorrel, marsh woundwort, fleabane, greater burdock, stitchwort, clover, bird's foot trefoil, marsh bedstraw, cocksfoot, Yorkshire fog, sweet vernal grass, common foxtail, smaller cat's tail and many more. If their taste matched their blend of scents then grazing in such a meadow must be sheer joy for a cow.

Butterflies were everywhere, common blues, meadow browns, small skippers, gatekeepers, peacocks, small tortoiseshells, red admirals, small coppers, large whites, small whites, green veined whites, wall browns, painted ladies and ringlets. Fourteen species in twenty minutes without actually looking for them. On such a day the meadow was a sanctuary, a place to stay, watch, lie in the grass, listen, smell and feel the sun. Other butterflies have also been seen in and around the meadow; brimstones, Essex skippers, orange tips, purple hairstreaks, small heaths and commas. It was like a living museum, maintaining a forgotten wealth and showing what has been lost in most other areas of rural England.

Of all the butterflies the most attractive was the small copper with wings of bright coppery-orange, on black. Sorrel is the food plant of the caterpillar; it is a wise choice, for in days gone by sorrel was much prized and even grown in gardens. The leaves have the pleasant tang of lemon which refreshes the mouth and helps to stave off thirst. In season, Mont often has a few leaves on the dinner table to restore the taste buds after each course.

At this time, although still only summer, birds are already on the move. Over the Wash oyster-catchers have flocked and groups of lapwings fly inland. Early migrants such as curlew sandpipers move through and often black-tailed godwits stop at the Duke's pools. In the farm fields the large combine harvesters devour the standing corn as harvest is in full swing. A year has almost died, with its death signalled by the rows of shattered straw. The ploughman adjusts his plough, ready to begin his urgent work and with the first furrows of freshly turned soil, the old year becomes the new.

Comma.

Buckingham Palace garden

BUCKINGHAM PALACE GARDEN cannot seriously be compared with the other Royal Estates, yet for London it does represent a large open area, relatively free from disturbance, and as a result it attracts some surprising wildlife. To birds passing over the great mass of concrete, noise and moving lights it must seem like a haven, a place where they can find food and shelter, with few people to disturb them. For plants and insects it can also provide odd corners where they can colonise and create the impression of "country" in the heart of Britain's greatest city. In various surveys over 250 wild and naturalised plants have been identified as well as more than 340 butterflies and moths.

The Palace and grounds cover just over forty-eight and a half acres, with the gardens taking up about thirty-nine, of which three and a half acres make up an attractive winding lake. The area was first mentioned in the Domesday Book as part of the Manor of Eia; a stretch of low-lying marshy ground that came into royal ownership in 1531. In 1609 James I turned part of it into a Mulberry Garden, hoping to produce silk, as the mulberry leaf is the food plant of the silkworm. Unfortunately his scheme was not a success, for silkworms flourish on the white mulberry – he planted the black. Parts were then variously let or sold until it was purchased by John Sheffield, Duke of Buckingham, a favourite of Queen Anne, who built "Buckingham House".

It returned to the Royal Family in 1761 when George III bought it for Queen Charlotte, and it became known as "The Queen's House". The King also liked it, as it gave him a place of peace and quiet away from the formality of the Court. It has remained in the possession of the Royal Family ever since, with various alterations and additions creating the Palace as it is known today.

In the early days there were still large areas of "rural" land in London and in 1709 the Duke of Buckingham wrote of his: "Little wilderness of blackbirds and nightingales". Even as late as 1834 a fence had to be erected around the flower garden: "In consequence of there being hares and rabbits and other game in the grounds."

Sadly, nightingales have now disappeared, as they have from all the Royal Estates, apart from the occasional passing vagrant, and house mice, brown rats and grey squirrels are the only mammals to have visited the grounds during recent years, although pipistrelle bats have been seen flying overhead in the summer. However, despite the gardens being largely formal and ornamental, other forms of wildlife still flourish and are encouraged. At the Queen's insistence wild areas of grass are left uncut and the fringes of the lake are not touched until the birds have finished rearing their young and the flowers, reeds and rushes have seeded. Because kingfishers sometimes visit the lake, which in itself is astonishing for central London, a special bank with suitable nesting holes has been created at the water's edge, in the hope that one day a pair will stay and breed.

But although the whole area is attractive, the roar of traffic and a permanent haze in the air always betray its urban setting. High office blocks also intrude and overlook, confirming that as planners have become more adorned with qualifications and grandiose titles, so their decisions have become increasingly insensitive, unimaginative, irrational and absurd.

The wildlife year in Buckingham Palace Garden starts very early, at the beginning of January, or even late December, when the winter heliotrope blooms, showing that the shortest day has already passed. The trees are bare and winter appears to be in full control, yet the strange white flower still appears. It is like a small white butterbur, but its scent is sweet, hinting of almonds and cherry blossom, and on a warm day it can even attract a few early bees. The flowers can be found on a mound above the old "ice house", at the end of a long tree-covered ridge. Before the days of electricity great chunks of ice were cut from the lake when it froze, to store underground in the ice house, as an early form of refrigeration.

Crocuses, daffodils and drifts of snowdrops signify the arrival of true spring, together with the swelling buds of alder and weeping willow. Activity on the lake increases and in the surrounding vegetation, mallards, pochard and tufted ducks all begin to incubate their eggs. Other water birds breed including moorhens, coots and sometimes even great crested grebes.

The garden has many fine holly trees and when the April sun feels warm, the holly blue butterfly appears. It is a small, fast flying butterfly, with wings of finely touched lilac-blue. Bird song can be heard clearly and reassuringly above the noise of traffic: thrushes, blackbirds, hedge sparrows, robins, wrens and chaffinches. Most breed in the garden, for

Tawny owl.

later, young birds appear, with food still being brought by their parents. But although they are town birds, they have to retain the sharpness and awareness of the country, for magpies, jays and carrion crows all nest in the garden and young fledglings feature prominently on their diets. Marauding herring and lesser black-backed gulls form another threat, particularly to young water birds, and kestrels can also take small chicks; they regularly fly over the garden, occasionally hovering to hunt.

Strangely, tawny owls appear to be present during the whole year and they are thought to breed, although so far no nest has been found. On my first visit a tawny sat in a tall bay tree, well concealed by the evergreen leaves, and on each subsequent visit there were signs of "kills"; a pool of pigeon feathers, usually with a half eaten carcass. Woodpigeons and feral pigeons thrive in the middle of London, and numbers are high; the dead birds were mostly headless with the breasts eaten, in the way that a few rogue tawny owls deal with young pheasant poults. It seemed that without a wide selection of small mammals, the owls had developed an efficient way of taking pigeons, probably at dusk when they went up to roost.

Not only does the Palace garden have one of the earliest signs of spring, but it also has one of the latest, in the form of two black mulberry trees. Although they both look ancient, it is doubtful whether they date back to James I, for even quite young mulberries look old, with twisted limbs and bark that suggests great age. The mulberry is one of the last trees to get its leaves, which usually show towards the end of May; hence it is a useful guide to gardeners:

> When the mulberry tree grows green,
> The last of winter's frosts you've seen.

An old writer describes it in even more detail: "The Mulberry is accounted of all other trees the wisest, because it never blossometh till all cold weather be quite past; so that whensoever you see the Mulberry begin to spring you may be sure that Winter is at an end." Later the mulberry gives juicy berries of a dark raspberry-red colour, with a slightly sharp taste. They can be eaten raw, used to flavour fruit pies, or made into a delicious jam. Apart from palace gardens, mulberry trees were once to be found in prison exercise yards, giving rise to the old rhyme, "Here we go round the mulberry bush".

In high summer, the garden can almost be confused with true country. On the lake there are families of ducks pattering among the lilypads and a small arched bridge shows through trees and luxuriant waterside vegetation. I was amazed to see a great crested grebe with two half grown young. One swam behind its mother while the other had "hitched" a ride on her back. On a nearby pine a pair of goldcrests fed their almost independent young, as if they too had bred, as urban birds. A heron flew

A bridge to one of the lake's islands.

Red-breasted geese on the lake.

Yellow iris.

in, wanting to fish, but was harassed in flight by a carrion crow. Eventually it managed to land and began to stalk slowly through the shallow water. From the many swirls and rises, fish do very well in the lake, and roach, dace, perch and gudgeon have all been caught. Only occasional frogs and toads appear and if they ever breed, few tadpoles would survive because of all the wildfowl. The lake also has a colony of Caribbean flamingoes and they too would make short work of any tadpoles. It was hoped to induce the flamingoes to breed, but so far all efforts have failed. On an island, red-breasted geese have been more successful; they are one of Europe's rarest geese and with help and advice from the Wildfowl Trust several young are reared every year. The old gardener who looks after them takes a great pride in his charges; he is a rare breed as well; he still retains his country accent and appearance; he sometimes rides from job to job on an old bike and he always carries a clip-on tie, then, when circumstances demand, he snaps it quickly into place.

A small flock of Canada geese flew in and splashed down in the water. Unfortunately they like to swim ashore and carry out their ablutions on the lawn, leaving discarded feathers as well as ample evidence of their active and efficient digestive systems. These wildlife signs are not appreciated by the wearers of over-shined shoes who attend Palace garden parties. However, some dogs consider goose droppings to be a great delicacy and the royal corgis are no exception; consequently the Canada geese are not encouraged.

While I was watching the geese a group of corgis were actually being taken for a walk by a footman. Among them was an attractive breed, unknown to me, being long, lower and hairier than a corgi. Apparently one of the Queen's corgis became too familiar with a dachshund belonging to Princess Margaret; the resultant offspring are known as "dorgis".

Damsel and dragonflies patrolled over both the lake and the land; the blue-tailed, the brown hawker and, most appropriately, the large, blue, emperor. Some of the moths found in the garden have equally well suited names; the marbled coronet, buff ermine, burnished brass and the common footman. There are many more humble intruders, however, including the turnip, the flounced rustic, the tawny speckled pug and the clouded drab. Among the most attractive moths are the buff-tip, the ruby tiger and the privet and elephant hawk-moths. Some extremely rare moths have been found, the very first *Monochroa hornigi* identified in Britain was caught in a light trap set up in the garden. Exotic species from abroad have also appeared, possibly arriving in the clothing or baggage of dignitaries from abroad.

Butterflies find it harder to survive in the city and over recent years only nine species have been seen in the garden, with two of those, the red admiral and painted lady, being immigrants from abroad; the holly blue

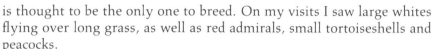

Peacock butterfly.

is thought to be the only one to breed. On my visits I saw large whites flying over long grass, as well as red admirals, small tortoiseshells and peacocks.

Around the edge of the lake were many wild plants typical of the land's swampy past; great hairy willow-herb, various rushes and reeds, water mint, marsh pennywort, gypsywort, and the attractive yellow iris. There was purple loosestrife too, whose old English name of ''long purples'', describes the flowering heads perfectly. Some of the plants have been deliberately introduced, while others have been blown in by the wind, or carried, stuck to the feet or feathers of birds. Although wild geese are not encouraged around the lake, several goose-foots can be found; plants with leaves the same shape as the feet of geese – the many-seeded goose-foot, the fig-leaved goose-foot and the red goose-foot.

The lakeside is undoubtedly the richest area, with a fine clump of royal fern, together with a spreading patch of adder's tongue. Adder's tongue is quite a rare plant, normally associated with old native grasslands, and its appearance has been unexpected but welcome; again its spores could have been airlifted in by wildfowl, blown in by the wind, or brought in accidentally with bedding plants or shrubs. It is a peculiar plant, having large, shiny, dark green leaves, like those of a plastic-coated cuckoo-pint, with the spore bearing stems resembling an adder's tongue. One was actually forked and looked almost venomous. It is hardly surprising that they were once crushed in medical concoctions to counteract the effects of snake bites.

Adder's tongue fern.

Nipplewort.

Scarlet pimpernel.

There are other more ordinary wild flowers, including yarrow, chervil, bird's-foot trefoil, bugle, daisies, chamomile and nipplewort. In places the chamomile spreads into the lawn, giving a beautiful green and springy sward. It is a useful plant to have in the garden and Gerard the herbalist wrote: ''It is a speciall help against wearisomnesse, it easeth and mitigateth paine, it mollifieth and suppleth.'' According to old medics nipplewort is another beneficial plant. Because of the shape of its buds, it was once said to relieve sore nipples, but a more simple use is to include the young leaves in salads.

Many of the wild flowers in the garden are normally classified as weeds, and among them I was particularly pleased to find the scarlet pimpernel. It is one of my favourite summer flowers, normally to be found in waste places, arable fields, roadside verges, as well as in cultivated gardens. The small scarlet flowers can be seen from the end of May until late September, although I have found them as late as November. On fine sunny days the flowers stay open, but when rain is on the way and the humidity rises, they close, giving the flower its common country name of ''the poor-man's weather glass''. It is certainly reliable, and more accurate than many of the orthodox forecasts. At one time the leaves were used to combat toothache and it was also claimed that a mixture of leaves and lard cured baldness. It is not said whether the restored hair also responded to changes in humidity.

The gallant soldier and the shaggy soldier are two other interesting weeds; the most obvious difference between them being that the shaggy soldier has hair and the gallant soldier is hairless. They are very numerous throughout central London, with small inconspicuous white and yellow flowers. They are South American in origin, but were taken to Kew Gardens, from where they escaped. They are also known as "Kew weeds" and "soldiers of the Queen". The flowers look nothing like soldiers, but for once the English name came from the Latin, as Galinsoga was turned into "Gallant Soldier".

Autumn seems to arrive late in the garden, with the leaves of the trees hanging on longer and the lingering buddleias and roses attracting the last of the butterflies. It is not just imagination, for due to the shelter of walls, together with the warmth from engines, lights, heating systems and ventilation outlets, the autumn and winter temperatures of London can be between 5 and 10°F higher than in open country.

Migrating birds pass through and boost the numbers of pochard and tufted duck and wild wigeon and shovelers become more frequent visitors. Even a common sandpiper has been seen at the lakeside on its journey south.

The leaves of falling willow form changing patterns on the water, and as the cover drops away, so the garden birds seem more conspicuous, with blue tits, wrens and robins appearing to have little fear. Small charms of goldfinches pick at willow-herb seeds and greenfinches are numerous. I was glad to see a coal tit searching for insects, grubs and eggs among the needles and cones of a conifer tree. It is the smallest member of the British tit family and the broad white patch on its black head makes it both attractive and distinctive.

Winter finally comes when fingers of ice reach out from the edges of the lake. Gradually they spread and thicken, allowing the black-headed gulls to roost in safety, and the wildfowl become confined to an ever shrinking area of open water. More occasional winter visitors have been seen to drop in; smews, an immature buzzard, curlews and woodcock. After snow, small holes appear at the edge of the lake where snipe have probed with their long, sensitive bills.

As I was walking slowly round on a cold winter's morning, I was given yet another surprise, by a treecreeper working its way busily up the trunk of a tree. I just had not expected to see this small bird of woodlands, parkland and large country gardens in the middle of an enormous city sprawl. They are delightful little birds, with slightly curved beaks and extra long claws on their toes to aid grip and balance. When seen at close quarters they seem almost too fragile and delicate to be real; in fact, like the treecreeper, many of our native birds and flowers are just as beautiful as those in more exotic climes, but we simply do not stop to notice or appreciate them.

From my visits, it became obvious that the Buckingham Palace Garden is an important area for urban wildlife. It is far richer than most of the London parks, as few people disturb it for most of the year. Now, whenever I pass the Palace, I shall not only look up to see if the Royal Standard is flying, but I shall be searching above the garden wall, hoping for a sight or sound of some of the other residents.

Windsor

OF ALL THE Royal Estates, Windsor came as the greatest surprise; previously I had only been through the Great Park, at speed, along the A332, while heading for the M3 and Dorset. With its parked cars, collapsible picnic chairs and wandering poodles, I had written it off as being largely a relief area for suburban dogs. In any case I had considered it to be too near London and commuter-land to hold much wildlife.

I was wrong, for although some people do misuse the Park, and despite the spread of roads and urban development, the Windsor Estate was a revelation. Just as Balmoral has areas of ancient and irreplaceable Caledonian pine forest, so Windsor has some of the oldest relics of broad-leaved woodland in Europe. As such it can give tantalising glimpses of part of southern England's distant past, for after the Ice Age retreated and the temperature warmed, so much of lowland Britain became covered with forest. Windsor was in the heart of this woodland, which was broken only by marshes and sandy heaths where heather, Scots pine and birches still dominated.

Evidence of Windsor's antiquity can be seen from the roadside in the aged hulks of once pollarded oaks. Some of them date back over 800 years and pockets of the old flora and fauna have survived with them.

The monarchy's association with Windsor goes back to beyond the time of even the oldest oak, to the Anglo-Saxon kings, for it was the place where some of them hunted and held Court; William the Conqueror continued the tradition and because of the area's strategic position, commanding both London and the Thames Valley, he built the first castle. Hunting was his great passion, however, and it was said of him: "He loved the tall stags as if he were their father."

Windsor continued to be popular with a succession of monarchs, for hunting was the accepted sport of the nobility, and the whole area was subject to the Forest Laws, which protected and preserved game for the king. Henry VIII and James I were particularly fond of "the chase", and falconry was another favourite royal sport; but to Elizabeth I Windsor was important for another reason. In the fine trees she saw oak to maintain the ships of her navy, and in 1580 she commanded her Chancellor, Lord Burghley, to plant acorns in the Great Park, to ensure future supplies of high quality timber.

During the Civil War Windsor became the headquarters of Cromwell's army and the Castle was converted into a prison. The Stuart connection was not totally severed, however, for Charles I became one of its prisoners. After the Restoration, Charles II spent much time and money at Windsor, and he began the impressive tree-lined avenue that became known as the Long Walk. The Long Walk was extended to the present length of three and a half miles by George IV, and under his direction the castle was altered to its appearance of today; he also erected the great statue of George III, dressed as a Roman emperor on a copper horse.

George III's association with the estate is probably the most important. He was a much under-rated king, with a keen interest in the agricultural advances and experiments of the time; he introduced some of them to Windsor, giving him the nickname of "Farmer George". It was also during this period that the finances of the monarchy were put on a more stable footing. The king gave up most of his land, including Windsor and Richmond, in return for the Civil List, an annual cash payment to cover the running expenses of the monarchy. Two estates were excluded from the agreement and remained in the ownership of the Royal Family – the Duchies of Cornwall and Lancaster. The old royal land is now managed by the Crown Estate Commissioners, and ironically, the income received for the State far exceeds the value of the Civil List.

The other matter to be resolved during the reign of George III was the title of Ranger to the Great Park. The Ranger was in charge of the day to day running of the Park and the appointment was usually made by the king. When George III succeeded to the throne, the Ranger was his uncle William, Duke of Cumberland – "Butcher Cumberland", who defeated the Scots at Culloden during the Jacobite rebellion, and continued to harass them without mercy. On his death in 1765, the king's brother Henry became both the new Duke of Cumberland and the new Ranger; but the two brothers did not get on. The Deputy Ranger during the reign of Queen Victoria was William Menzies and in his book *The History of Windsor Great Park and Windsor Forest*, published in 1864, he wrote:

A question having arisen between George III, who wished to hunt in the Park, and Henry Duke of Cumberland, who, as Ranger, closed or threatened to close the gates, His Majesty himself took the Ranger-

Prince Philip driving along the Long Walk in Windsor Great Park.

ship, on the death of the Duke, and the office has since been held by the reigning Monarch, or in commission for him, except during its tenure by His Royal Highness the Prince Consort.

As the land is no longer owned by the Royal Family, the title of Ranger is only honorary and advisory and the actual management of the estate is undertaken by the Deputy Ranger, an employee of the Crown Commissioners. However, as the present Deputy Ranger, Mr Roland Wiseman, explains: "Prince Philip is now Ranger and takes a very great and active interest in all the affairs of the Great Park. He makes various suggestions and is consulted about changes. The system works well and the relationship is very good."

The Royal Family still enjoys Windsor and visits it regularly. It is an "official residence", unlike Balmoral and Sandringham, which are private, but nevertheless it is a place where they can find respite from their formal duties, and where they can pursue their various equestrian interests, as well as experience a semblance of country living.

Today Windsor Estate totals 15,000 acres, with woodland covering 7,000 acres and the Great Park a further 5,000. The remainder is taken up by farmland, heath and open water, of which the Queen farms about 1,400 acres as tenant. In parts it is a pleasantly soft and undulating landscape, but unfortunately it has been scarred, divided and obscured by roads, housing development, Ascot Racecourse, dual carriageways and even a golf course. Yet astonishingly, despite all these intrusions, and with suburbia pressing in on every side, there continues to be a variety of birds, animals and wild flowers, despite some of them being under pressure. The old features of parkland, natural forest, heath and swamp are still there, but they have shrunk in size, although the estate has gained new elements too. Under the Duke of Cumberland in the 1750s the fashion for extravagant landscape gardening led to the creation of a number of large lakes, pools and ponds. Virginia Water, with its 120 acres, is one of them and they have become important places for many forms of wildlife. More recently, commercial forestry has covered much of the land with quick growing firs and pines, but the planting has been undertaken sympathetically, with wide grassy rides and trees such as copper beech and wild cherry concealing the serried ranks behind them. Many mature oaks and beeches have also been left within the forest and by following a deer path or a badger run, it is possible to come across an open glade, with the spreading branches of an old tree to one side, creating its own small world within a world. Some forms of wildlife live well in the much maligned pines; badgers and roe deer thrive, and the whole area is a long established stronghold of the sparrow-hawk.

Within historical times Windsor contained some of Europe's most spectacular animals and birds; wild cattle, beavers, wild boar, wolves, bitterns, black grouse and kites. Sadly they all passed quietly into extinction, through hunting, harassment, disturbance and changing conditions. The last ravens were seen towards the end of the nineteenth century, and at one time cranes were also common, with the name Cranbourne, of Cranbourne Chase, meaning "crane brook". Very recently a pair of cranes resumed breeding in Norfolk, but the chances of them ever returning to Windsor are remote.

Red deer have been part of the park for many centuries, but even they disappeared during the Second World War. They were removed when George VI was Ranger, as he wanted to bring the Great Park into maximum production to help the war effort. It was a sad but justifiable loss, for over the years the presence of deer had actually helped to fashion the appearance of the forest. At one time the oak trees were pollarded or "doddled", to provide food for the deer in cold weather. William Menzies wrote: "For the support of the deer during the winter; it was necessary to lop off the boughs of the oak and beech and throw them down for the deer to eat the bark. The law required that no bough larger than a deer could turn over with his horns should be cut."

Once the deer had eaten the bark the wood was not wasted: "The boughs stripped were the privilege of the Keepers as 'fireboote' or 'houseboote'." The regular trimming of the oaks led to the short trunks and huge girths of today and finished about 100 years before William Menzies wrote his book. In many country areas willow and ash were also pollarded, for building materials, implement handles, fence posts and firewood.

Reintroducing deer to the Great Park was Prince Philip's idea:

Windsor always used to be a deer park, but the hinds were taken up to Balmoral in the 1940s when much of the Great Park was ploughed up. They did not like their freedom all that much and used to hang about by a fence as close to the house as possible.

After the Park had been ploughed, productivity started dropping, access was difficult and the Long Walk was made into a complete mess. So we returned it back to grass, and deer from Balmoral were let loose in it in 1979.

The deer enclosure is 1,000 acres in size and it is good that the old continuity has been restored. The hinds and stags thrive in their historical lowland home and during the course of my visits they gave me some unforgettable encounters; a glowing sky in the early morning and their dark silhouettes among trees; dew, and the damp, liquid smell of a forest at dawn, with shafts of light picking out deer from the shadows; then, warm sun, a woodpecker drumming, and as a large stag stared at me, half hidden by bracken and branches, Concorde flew noisily overhead from Heathrow; it was a peculiar feeling to be looking simultaneously at both the ancient and the modern worlds – the natural and the supersonic, the permanent and the passing.

Although the roar of stags can be heard in the autumn, the wild and distant sounds come only from the deer enclosure, for the wildlife year on the estate as a whole begins with the gradual turn of winter into spring. It is sometimes signalled before the end of January by the first strains of the dawn chorus, melodic, but soft, as a few birds feel the far off changes in the air, long before they become apparent to man. As daylight begins to lengthen and dusk and dawn bite into the night, so early morning flows with bird song. Wrens, robins and hedge sparrows are among the first to sing, and they are soon joined by blackbirds, thrushes,

chaffinches and tits. The great tit's metallic double-edged song gives it
the perfect nickname of "saw sharpener" – a description I knew before
its correct name. Then, by mid-February, half an hour before sunrise,
the skylarks over the Great Park and the fields of the farms begin their
spring. Their songs fall from high up in the half-light, a tinkling vortex
of cascading, silvery sound. In the days when farm workers were "up
with the lark", it was said that:

> Merry larks are ploughmens' clocks.

On my numerous pre-dawn journeys to Windsor, they made getting up
early almost a pleasure.

The January or February start of the dawn chorus surprises many
people, and most miss it because of closed windows, or the hum of
internal combustion engines drowning the more pleasant sounds of bird
song. It is a sign that the birds are already concerning themselves with
territories and nesting sites, a fact noted by the early-risers of previous
generations who expected domestic geese to be laying, and wild birds to
be pairing, by February 14th, St Valentine's Day: "On St Valentine, all
the birds of the air in couples do join."

Deep in the forest other signs tell of the weakening power of winter.
The hazel catkins loosen into their attractive "lambs' tails"; the leaf buds
of honeysuckle begin to burst; the dull flowers of dog's mercury show;
and the distinctive arrow-shaped leaves of cuckoo-pint are clearly
visible. Gradually the tempo increases and the "sap begins to rise". It is
not an idle phrase, and the truth of it was shown to me by a retired
gamekeeper, who knows almost every path and woodland ride in the
Great Park and forest. Bert is a knowledgeable, gentle man, with a ready
smile, and before working as a gamekeeper he worked on a large private
reservoir, ringing and monitoring wildfowl. He was the sort of
gamekeeper that enriched his beat; he saw the place in nature of birds of
prey and understood that even some predators had their niche. Jays he
regarded almost as friends, for their harsh and persistent warning cries
can accurately inform of intruders – people on harmless country walks,
or poachers. With retirement he put down his gun, but still follows the
animal and bird movements around him through binoculars. His only
regret is that increasing age has brought a degree of deafness, denying
him the pleasure of hearing the birds sing. He is an excellent naturalist,
and one of those whose ability to identify birds was aided by his
knowledge of their songs; now he has to rely almost entirely on sight. As
a keeper, one of his greatest dislikes was grey squirrels, because of the
damage they do to trees and the nests they rob, and his view of them has
not changed. Unlike Mont, at Sandringham, he has never eaten grey
squirrels, although made into a stew with plenty of onions, they are said
to be extremely tasty.

Bert's speciality is birch sap wine, and on a warm day in late March he took me to a group of birch trees. Each tree had a small hole bored into it, about half an inch deep and of a similar diameter, and from every one a rubber tube led into a bottle. On a good day, when the sap is rising, he will get about a quart of sap per tree in four hours. But if the cold returns, the flow will almost cease. The sap tastes like muddy water, but the wine is beautiful; smooth, clear and clean, with the colour of apple juice.

According to Bert the recipe is simple:

1 gallon of birch sap	3 lbs sugar
2 lemons	1 lb raisins
1 sweet orange	Yeast and nutrient
1 Seville orange (optional)	

Peel the oranges and lemons, with no pith, and boil the peel and sap for twenty minutes. Add water if necessary to maintain one gallon. Pour the liquor into a container with chopped raisins and sugar. Stir until the sugar is dissolved. When cool – 70°F – add fruit juice, then the yeast and nutrient, one heaped teaspoonful of each. Cover with a cloth and keep in a warm place until fermentation has subsided a little. Stream into a demijohn and fit air-lock. Leave for about six months before bottling. The longer you keep the wine the better the flavour.

Not far from his home is a large lake, surrounded by willows, alders and dense rhododendrons, and that held many more obvious signs of spring. The catkins of "pussy willow" were silky soft, catching the light, while those of the alder were long and loose and full of pollen. Alder is one of the oldest parts of the landscape, and pollen grains found in ancient peat show that it has been growing in damp, marshy places for many thousands of years. The male catkins become long and pendulous from early March to the beginning of April. At the same time the new female catkins are small, round and green, although the catkins from the previous year can still be seen. They resemble small dark brown cones, and they release their ripe seeds in the spring. The seeds themselves are remarkable, for they are surrounded by air-filled webbing that enables them to float for up to a month; during that time they can be carried considerable distances and it helps to explain why alder was so numerous before the age of drainage turned it into a "weed". The seeds are loved by many birds and form an important source of food during the winter.

But not only is the alder an attractive tree, it is also unusual. Like the pea its roots can "fix" nitrogen from the air, and so the presence of alders can actually improve the soil where they grow. At one time, because the wood is a bad conductor of heat, alder was used for clogs, as it would help to keep feet warm and dry. It was also used to make window frames, toys and pencils, and its charcoal is ideal for the manufacture of gunpowder.

As we walked, two nuthatches were searching the trunk of a solitary pine, and a treecreeper flew to an alder. They made an interesting contrast, for the treecreeper busily worked its way upwards, before flying to the bottom of the next trunk, while the nuthatches were travelling both up and down the trunk, head first. They are the only British birds to travel downwards in this way. Another unusual feeding method of the nuthatch is to wedge a nut into grooved bark and split it by blows with its large pointed bill, a technique also used by woodpeckers.

Further along, a small flock of birds with a musical flight song flew into the topmost branches of alder and began searching for seeds in the old female catkins. They were siskins. At first glance, with their yellow and green plumage they looked like small, slender greenfinches; they are particularly fond of alder and birch seeds.

On a grassy bank several starlings were probing the soil for leather-jackets. Their beaks showed another sure sign of spring, for they had changed from the dark brown of winter to a brilliant golden yellow. In sunlight they are beautiful birds with a dark iridescent plumage that flashes with blue, violet and turquoise. One flew into a tree and began to sing, a throaty song; with its wings held open and its feathers ruffled, it looked distinctly reptilian.

Away from the trees and on open water were a few ducks; a pair of distant mandarins, mallards and tufted. Two more birds swam slowly towards each other; they were great crested grebes. The great crested grebe in spring plumage, with its rusty-red ruff and two prominent feathery tufts is one of the world's most handsome birds. In the last century, ladies of fashion agreed, and it was almost shot to extinction to decorate hats. Now, with protection and more gravel pits and lakes on which to breed, the great crested grebe has made a successful comeback.

One of the grebes dived, but soon surfaced with a large roach. Several times it tried to swallow the fish, but failed because of the size, eventually giving up. The injured fish swam close to the surface before diving, but the grebe dived too and recaptured it, again finding it too large to eat. Several times the fish was caught and dropped, almost like a cat playing with a mouse. Then, with a great extra effort, the roach was suddenly swallowed.

Hunger satisfied, the bird turned its attention towards its mate and the two swam together to begin their extravagant courtship display. With their necks stretched up, their ruffs fanned out and their tufts erect, they started shaking their heads vigorously, before preening in unison; the last act had almost the beauty of ballet. After a short pause the ritual resumed and during the head-shaking it was easy to see why one of the great crested grebe's alternative names is the "greater loon".

They drifted apart, before one swam in fast towards the other, until it stood upright on the water. Sometimes in a cloud of spray both birds attempt this "penguin dance". It is made possible because the grebe's feet are far back on its body; a physical feature shared with several other expert divers. It also gives it the coarse country name of "arsefoot".

A siskin and alder catkins.

Dabchick or little grebe on nest.

They dived, to surface with weeds hanging from their beaks, for among the half-submerged branches of overhanging alder they were building a nest. They drifted into open water once more, to continue their head-shaking and one swam so low that the water lapped over the base of its neck; they showed incredible variations of buoyancy. Returning to their nest they swam in fast, creating impressive bow-waves as they went, their necks held straight and low, only just clear of the water, like two homing torpedoes. They carefully inspected their work and began to preen normally. It had been an absorbing performance and one and a half hours had passed unnoticed. The display of the grebe occurs from late winter until well into spring, and egg laying usually begins in April.

As the grebes were preoccupied with courtship, elsewhere incubation was already well under way, and some young could even have hatched. Herons are among the earliest birds to breed, often starting in February, and there has been a heronry on the estate since at least 1607. Despite the cold, the early start is not as foolish as it first seems, for the hatching of the young coincides with the emergence of frogs to spawn. This, in the past, made fishing and feeding easy; frogs and toads still breed locally, but their numbers have fallen in recent years.

The heronry is among huge old Scots pines and cedars of Lebanon, planted well over two hundred years ago. They are the tallest and most magnificent pines I have seen, with the dishevelled stick nests at the very tops of the trees. The heron population has also decline recently,

Courting great crested grebes.

possibly because of drainage schemes, pollution and disturbance in the area as a whole, which have made feeding more difficult. There are still usually over twenty pairs, however, and they make a fine sight. To see herons perching high up in the trees, tall, still and patient, is to understand why a group of herons is called a "siege".

They are large, grey, melancholy birds, and for most of the year they are solitary. Their mood of desolation is accentuated in winter, when it is a common sight to see a lone bird standing hunched up by ice or wading slowly through mud and drifting fog. At one time herons were royal game, and hawks were flown at them. According to the Book of St Albans: "If the hawk getteth the upper place, he over throweth the heron. If the heron get above the hawk, then with his dung he defileth the hawk, and so destroyeth him, for his dung is a poison to the hawk, rotting and putrefying his feathers."

There are several unusual old beliefs about herons. They were said to fly and nest high, to avoid the wind and rain, and it was even suggested that they made two holes in their nests to allow their long legs to hang through during incubation. If a heron caught an eel, then it was supposed to stand with its tail against a rock or tree, to stop the creature wriggling straight through.

Because of the heron's success as a fisherman, it was believed that its legs gave off a strange substance to attract fish. As a result the legs of herons were boiled up by early anglers, and their hooks, lines and lures were soaked in the soup, in the hope that the bird's strange attraction would be transferred to their tackle.

Away from the water March had brought other signs of spring. Within the woodland there were flowers, swelling buds and many signs of birds. "Pussy willow" shone, with the willows and sallows not yet drawn into the anonymity of summer foliage. Carpets of flowering primroses covered patches of damp ground, showing the warmth and hope of the new season. John Clare caught their charm and mood with beauty and simplicity:

> Welcome pale Primrose starting up between
> Dead matted leaves of ash and oak that strew
> The sunny lawn the wood and coppice through
> Mid creeping moss and ivy's darker green
> How much thy presence beautifies the ground.

By a stream, luxuriant beds of lesser celandine spread, bright and golden, known in many places as "kingcups", in preference to the larger marsh marigold. High up in the old oaks there was much activity, for there is great competition for nesting holes. Windsor is a haven for birds and many of them nest in holes, including the tawny owl, kestrel, great spotted woodpecker, lesser spotted woodpecker, green woodpecker,

Tree creeper.

Long-tailed tit.

treecreeper, nuthatch, jackdaw, starling and even the mandarin duck. Mallards too will sometimes nest in trees, and on its arrival in April the redstart is another that requires a suitable hole in which to build its nest. The woodpeckers are fortunate as they can excavate their own, and old abandoned woodpecker nests are quickly claimed by other birds. The nuthatch has an interesting method of reducing the attraction of its hole, for if it is too big, it will plaster the entrance with mud to make it smaller.

Six of the seven British tits nest at Windsor, and five of them, the great tit, blue tit, coal tit, marsh tit and willow tit, all choose holes. The marsh and willow tits are very difficult to separate and identify, and whoever named them got it slightly wrong. A helpful, but not completely accurate guide is: "If it's in a willow it's a marsh tit, and if it's in a marsh it's a willow tit." It is rather similar to the old country method of identifying a rook from a crow: "If you see a single rook, it's a crow, and if you see three crows, they are rooks." This is based on the fact that crows are normally solitary birds, and rooks are gregarious. Both rooks and crows flourish at Windsor and there are several rookeries in the area. After rain, rooks are particularly fond of the polo pitches at Smith's Lawn, where they arrive in large numbers to probe for leather-jackets, the larvae of crane-flies, and "wireworms", the larvae of click beetles.

The only tit breeding at Windsor that does not nest in a hole is the long-tailed tit. It is the most beautiful member of the tit family, being black and white and tinged with rose-pink. Its name comes from its long tail that takes up three inches of its five and a half inch body. Once the young have fledged, up to twelve of them, they brighten up many hedgerows by remaining in family parties throughout the winter. They even have more character than the crested tits of the Spey Valley, another tit that nests in holes.

The nest of the long-tailed tit is a work of art, a delicate dome of wool and moss, lined with feathers, often over 2,000 of them, and covered with lichens and spiders' webs. Because of her length, the female incubates with the end of her tail protruding from the entrance hole, which is at the side. The nest can be among brambles or wedged into a natural fork between branches. In Norfolk, the shape of the nest has led to the long-tailed tit being called the "pudding bag"; a rare case of a country name not doing justice to the bird. Other more suitable names include "oven builder", and because of its ruffled feathers, the "long-tailed mufflin". The covering of lichens adds to the delicacy of the nest; the birds have a wide choice as there are over seventy types of lichen found in the Great Park and forest. Sadly a decline is slowly under way as lichens cannot tolerate pollution, and exhaust fumes from Heathrow and the nearby roads are gradually taking their toll.

In woodland, May is the month when hesitant spring grows into lush full summer. Early on the bursting buds of hawthorn, birch and larch, hang a green haze in the air, and even the late leaves of oak swell quickly.

Below, on the forest floor, other flowers have joined the primrose to shine with colour and early morning dew; violets, ground ivy, patches of bugle, stitchwort, and wood sorrel. Bugle is the food plant of the chequered skipper butterfly, but its caterpillars no longer feed on the leaves as it is now extinct in England, although conditions look ideal in several places. It hangs on in Scotland, and will only return south if reintroduced by man. Wood sorrel is a most attractive flower, having lined, white petals with a hint of pink or lilac; the leaves are clover-like, folding down the stems at night, giving it the name of "sleeping beauty". It is one of the plants thought to be the "shamrock", chosen by St Patrick to illustrate the Trinity. He also used it to drive the snakes out of Ireland. It has not been successful at Windsor for grass snakes live well in the woods, and one slid over old leaves and new grass, to coil up for protection against the trunk of an oak; it held its head back and hissed defiantly, despite being non-poisonous and quite harmless. On the heath land, too, there are many adders, as well as slow worms and common lizards. Perhaps the supposed link between snakes and "shamrock" was the first Irish joke.

Among the buds, flowers and greening grasses of the deer enclosure, the stags, hinds and growing calves looked well, being sleek and fat, with plenty of food. They made an interesting comparison with those at Balmoral, still struggling on, thin, weathered and waiting for the spring to reach them.

It is at this time, before the trees are in full foliage, and the vegetation is low that badgers can be seen at their best, and there are many setts throughout the whole estate. I checked one at midday, with the sun warm, approaching over a grass field, to a wood of pine and beech. A fine roe buck with excellent antlers rested in the shade of a tree, quietly chewing the cud.

Moving into the wood was like drifting into a rich blue mist. Bluebells were everywhere, confusing distance and depth, like a mixture of sky and sea from which the trees floated, in pools of dancing, rippling light. Close to a bluebell wood seemed a superb place for badgers to have their sett, and there were many signs that they had been rootling for roots, insects and worms. Where the bluebells thinned, wood sorrel and wood anemones took their place and then dark shadow came as dense pines replaced mixed woodland. There were many entrance holes to the sett, all well used, and a fox ran off as if it had been checking up on its neighbours.

I returned along a ride between pines, in almost total silence, apart from the occasional tit, and the running hooves of an unseen roe deer. The silence found in tracks of coniferous forest is not unnatural, as often suggested. William Menzies noticed it many years ago: "A fir forest is always a silent one. Birds almost invariably choose deciduous trees to sing in. An engineer officer attached to the Baltic expedition in 1856

Opposite page: The bluebell wood, close to the badgers' sett.

mentioned to me the silence of the great pine forests in Sweden, Norway and Russia as very remarkable."

Conifers have birds, but they are quieter and more secretive than those that sing in the great stands of ancient oak and beech. Among Windsor's firs and pines, goldcrests and the scarcer firecrest breed successfully; Britain's two smallest birds.

At the edge of the ride, bathed in sunlight, the large mound of a wood ants' nest had erupted into summer life and activity. It was made of pine needles, soil and fragments of twigs, leaves and grass stems; the ants are closely related to those that occupy similar ant hills at Balmoral. Each nest houses a number of queens and up to 100,000 workers, and they are constructed in a clearing, or gap in the trees, to collect the maximum amount of sun. Every worker scavenges far and wide, often climbing to the top of the tallest trees, and they set off and return along well worn paths. They do not sting but can squirt formic acid at an enemy, and their powerful jaws bite hard.

The silhouette of a bird appeared above the pines; it was a sparrow-hawk spiralling upwards on a bank of rising air. The edges of its wings were aflame with incandescent white light as it climbed towards the sun. Its mate appeared flying hard to join it, mewing loudly the closer it flew. They seemed to touch, then both plummeted downwards like falling stones into the treetops. It meant that the sparrow-hawks too had been aroused by the spring.

Near a lake, cuckoo flower grew, and coots were creating clouds of anger and spray as they threatened and displayed. Moorhens were feeding at the water's edge; a mallard swam with her seven newly hatched young under an over-hanging arch of dark rhododendrons and a dabchick or "little grebe" was collecting old vegetation. It was probably repairing its nest, a floating tangle of weeds, anchored on to reeds or submerged aquatic plants, while its mate incubated the eggs. They nest on several of the pools and ponds and the young can swim almost immediately after hatching; they also ride on the backs of their parents, sometimes completely hidden by feathers, or with just a head protruding from the warmth. Often in the spring it is worth focusing binoculars on a swimming dabchick, or a great crested grebe, to see if chicks are on board.

Bert wanted me to visit another badger sett, to determine whether it was being used, for after several years of occupancy it had suddenly been deserted. The heronry was very active with herons flying over and "cronking" to their incubating mates. From several nests came a strange wheezing-whirring noise; it was made by young herons, inducing their parents to regurgitate food. One young body was hanging dead in the topmost branches, close to its nest. It could have been knocked over the edge as a parent had taken to the air, or blown out during high winds. The fate of the small, sorry figure showed that even building high did not give complete safety.

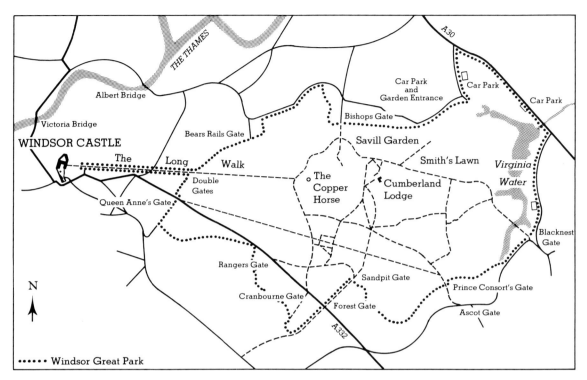

····· Windsor Great Park

Young grey squirrels, already out of their dreys, scampered up large tree trunks and a magpie flew, holding a stolen egg in its beak. The sett entrance was on a bank at the base of a large yew, half concealed by the leaves of a sprawling rhododendron bush. No cobwebs were strung over the hole and the soil was freshly disturbed: "They're back," Bert said with pleasure, "and from the tracks they've got cubs."

I can never resist the opportunity to try to see badgers and an hour before sunset I returned quietly to the wood. Birds were still singing including willow warblers and chiff-chaffs, fresh voices of summer, and high above the trees the first swallows flew, promising a fine evening; a rabbit scuttled from a clump of brambles. I moved into the gentlest and narrowest of small valleys, covered with once coppiced sweet chestnuts. The long fallen leaves of autumn deadened my footsteps and they showed too where badgers had been looking for food.

I stood behind a tree, thirty yards from the sett, to wait. The long, slow wingbeats of a passing heron exaggerated the hurried flight of an early bat as it hawked after insects. When the light began to fade a tawny owl flew silently from a yew and perched near to me. It had just roused to begin its night's work – it stretched, scratched and swivelled its head around before flying off to hunt.

It is pleasant simply standing or sitting, deep in a wood, listening and watching as the sounds and light change. The mind rests and time slips away unnoticed. Suddenly there was a distinctive black and white striped

Halfgrown badger cub sniffing a fading rhododendron flower.

head, followed by two more. Three badger cubs had emerged, not from the hole I had been watching, but from another, hidden deeper within the rhododendron bush. They were about two months old, smaller than poodles, and were bouncing and rolling in play. As two skirmished, the other dug its nose into leaves, before scratching with obvious delight. The itch was soon forgotten as hide and seek began, inside and outside the confines of the bush. A sudden breeze carried eddies of air through the trees, taking my scent with it. From within the sett a warning snort sounded and the cubs scampered underground. The full moon had risen, casting long shadows among the trees, and a tawny hooted. I crept silently away, wishing to intrude no further; it seemed impossible that the very centre of London was only twenty-seven miles away.

By the end of May foliage had transformed the forest, creating gently moving canopies of fresh melting greens – birch, horse chestnut, hawthorn, blackthorn, willow and spreading oak, beech and sweet chestnut. The leaves brought with them shafts of light streaming through their new translucent shades and shapes; but most of all the full leafed forest brought bird song. The dawn chorus had moved to a full hour before sunrise, reaching a peak as the sun began to strengthen. The birds continued singing all day, and those that sang in February had been joined by summer visitors – garden warblers, wood warblers, willow warblers, chiff-chaffs, redstarts, whitethroats, blackcaps, spotted flycatchers and cuckoos. Some had added music to the woodland symphony, while others gave brief snatches of adulation or anger. With the leaves confining and magnifying each note the chorus ebbed and flowed through the branches and across the rides in vibrant harmony. Other calls punctuated the interwoven threads of sound – cock pheasants crowing and the drumming of the great spotted woodpecker.

Great spotted woodpecker.

Drumming is territorial, made by striking hard, dead wood, in short bursts of eight drums to the second. They also use their beaks to chip out grubs, eggs and insects, but then the drumming is more regular and workmanlike. Great spotted woodpeckers are found all over the estate, since they are equally at home among conifers or deciduous woods. The green and the lesser spotted woodpeckers prefer broad-leaved trees.

The old oak forest is ideal for all three woodpeckers, as Windsor is one of the richest areas of insect life in Europe. Insects that bore into wood, hide under bark and even roll themselves in leaves. They need dead and dying wood, as well as leaf litter, and in the Park and forest they have all three in large quantities. Because of its wealth and importance, the Crown Commissioners allow some trees to mature and grow old naturally, so that the full cycle of live, dead and dying wood can satisfy the highly specialised creatures that depend on them.

In 1956 a forty-five-acre area of ancient woodland was declared a Forest Nature Reserve, and it is left totally untouched, without management or disturbance, and is regularly monitored by the Nature Conservancy Council. The importance of each type of tree is shown by the number of insect species associated with it; the oak has 284, sallow and willow 266, birch 229, hawthorn 149 and sloe 109. The least important for insects is the lime with only 31, and surprisingly, ash with 41.

One of the ancient oaks of the forest, complete with props.

Some of those insects dependent on ancient oak and beech occur nowhere else in Britain. As proof of their rarity, most are still only identified by their long Latin names – *Elater nigerrimus, Lacon quercus* and *Chrysopilus laetus*. There are others too that require very special conditions, from the nests of hornets, to hawthorn blossom.

Of the 4,000 British beetles, over 2,000 are found at Windsor. One of the more common ones is the stag beetle, easily identified because of the male's large antler-like jaws. It grows to over two inches in length and is Britain's largest beetle. The grubs live for several years in rotting tree stumps and are loved by badgers who try to dig them out.

The stag beetle larva is very fond of oak, and as oak trees often get hit by lightning, the beetle was once associated with thunderstorms and it was even thought to attract lightning indoors. A similar link gave the green woodpecker the name of "thunder bird", because its tapping imitated and attracted rain, and its red crown signified lightning. As a result of the "thunderbird's" liking for the insect-rich wood of mature oak, the tree became known as the "thunder tree", and old observers believed that the chances of a lightning strike on oak was ten to twenty times greater than for beech.

Despite the old adage, "Avoid an ash, it courts a flash", William Menzies also believed that oak was struck more than any other tree, and he wrote:

> Shakspere had observed another peculiarity of old oaks – their liability to be struck by lightning. In *King Lear* he speaks of
> > You sulphurous and thought-executing fires,
> > Vaunt-couriers to oak-cleaving thunderbolts.
> Of all the forest trees, oak are, in my experience, the most dangerous. If they have a large spreading head, they are shivered into shreds when struck; if they have long tapering stems, and thus can act almost as conductors, they are not so dangerous, and the lightning will run down the side, ploughing out a deep furrow. I have once seen a beech struck, an ash once, an elm once and a cedar of Lebanon once, but never any other trees except the oak. And while the others stood comparatively singly on an open space, the oaks have been selected and struck in the midst of a thick wood.

As if to confirm this, there was a violent thunderstorm during one of my visits and sure enough two oaks were struck. One in thick woodland was shattered. The other, standing in the more open land of the Great Park was singed and split. The leaves at the top were brown and scorched, while a broad white scar was gouged from the top of the trunk to the bottom; tattered and burnt bark lay strewn on the ground. It was an impressive display of natural power beyond the control of man. The tree survived, and within days, jackdaws had claimed a new nesting site where a small branch had been ripped away; soon insects would also invade the areas of scorched and dead wood.

Scientists have attempted to explain why oaks are hit so often. With smooth barked trees, such as beech, rain water streams down the trunk evenly, making it a good conductor. If the tree gets struck, little damage is done. The oak with its grooved bark, however, holds water, causing it to be a bad conductor; consequently, when it is hit the tree sometimes explodes. Elder, on the other hand, is rarely struck, the non-scientific explanation is simple; Judas hanged himself in an elder tree, and so all elder has the Devil in it. Judas also left his mark on the tree, for the brown Jew's ear fungus usually only grows on the dead wood of elder. It looks like a human ear and its name is thought to have come from ''Judas's ear''. Like many ugly fungi, it is edible and can be made into a tasty soup.

Towards the end of May, change also comes beneath the trees, with the bracken unfurled, the brambles in full leaf and the grasses growing high in the glades. It is a welcome transition, for between the middle of May and the middle of June the female roe deer seek out quiet, secluded places, with plenty of cover, in which to have their young. The roe is the smallest of our native deer, as well as the most graceful and beautiful. Newly born red deer are called calves, fallow are known as fawns, but with roe it can be either fawns or kids, with kids being the most usual. Seventy-five per cent of the does have twins, twenty per cent have single kids, while the remaining five per cent have triplets. The young have bright white spots on their sides, to match the dappled light, but after six weeks they begin to fade, and by the time they get their first winter coats in October, they have disappeared. During daylight the kids are left alone, and remain hidden, the doe returning only to feed them; it is during these first few days that they are vulnerable to foxes and dogs. The presence of young is first revealed by their tiny slot marks, appearing in sand or soft mud, although there are also many muntjac in the area and they too have very small hooves.

It must be a pleasant start to life looking up at the light through new oak leaves, for they are normally fully formed towards the end of May, when the softness of their colour matches their touch. In a normal year the leaves of oak and ash appear at almost the same time, but in the spring of 1983 the oak was well ahead of the ash:

> If the oak is out before the ash,
> Then you'll only get a splash.
> But if the ash beats the oak,
> Then you can expect a soak.

After a cold wet spring it turned into a long hot summer, the best since the drought year of 1976, and so the old weather lore was proved correct.

Young oak leaves attract the caterpillars of several moths including the maiden's blush, the oak beauty, and the green oak-roller; the green oak-rollers lower themselves from branch to branch by long silken threads. On a warm day, thousands were just hanging, with some falling to the ground, and starlings and jackdaws were having an unexpected feast. Having so many old trees with lost limbs and holes enables jackdaws to thrive in the Great Park; inevitably a rare insect thrives with them, for the *Atomaria moria* lives in birds' nests, particularly those of jackdaws. Jackdaws were once very common in my own parish, nesting in holes in pollarded elms, but with the coming of Dutch elm disease and the removal of trees for arable agriculture, their numbers have dwindled. It is only after memory has been jogged by seeing once common sights, that the true scale of the wildlife losses in the ordinary countryside is fully realised.

In one oak a little owl was quite uninterested in caterpillars, watching me pass before flying off quickly with its undulating flight. Little owls and barn owls are two more birds that nest in the holes of the old oaks. They have an abundant food supply for the whole area is rich in small mammals, including the water vole, short-tailed vole, bank vole, common shrew, pygmy shrew and water shrew. In addition there are many wood mice, sleek little animals with large dark eyes; most country people know them as "field mice".

Britain's smallest rodent, the harvest mouse, is also found at Windsor. At one time, as its name suggests, the harvest mouse was common in the cornfields at harvest time. It is even more attractive than the "field" mouse; with a gingery brown coat, and small, flat hairy ears, it is immediately recognisable. In earlier times its nest was the most obvious indicator of its presence; a woven ball of grasses, sometimes over eighteen inches above the ground, joined to stems of corn. Unfortunately sprays and combine harvesters have caused numbers to fall drastically, and at Windsor it is not found in the fields, but in the dense vegetation of grasses, rushes, reeds and great reed mace, around one of the large lakes. Conditions are perfect; it suffers from little disturbance and a pair can have several litters during the course of a summer.

In the dense vegetation of the same lake, garganey breed, as well as the equally furtive water rail, a small dark bird with gangling legs and a distinctive long red beak. I stopped at a grassy bank on the water's edge after encountering the caterpillars in the oaks; there were several broods of young mallards, tufted, coots and moorhens, as well as single broods of Canada geese, feral greylags, and mute swans. A female mandarin swam off fast, with her four ducklings. Kingfishers also breed on the estate in small numbers, with one of the nests sometimes excavated in a bank of sand, well away from water.

Not only did the fringe of reeds conceal garganey, water rails and harvest mice, but they had become alive with reed and sedge warblers.

Harvest mouse.

Heron.

Kingfisher.

Swallows and house martins were skimming low over the surface for flies and a heron perched on a branch of hawthorn overhanging the water. It was not resting, but staring downwards with great intensity. Without warning it jumped clumsily down, striking with its beak as it landed and catching a fish. I have seen herons fish like this on other occasions, once in deep water; after catching a small eel, it flapped its waterlogged way back to the bank. More movement came from the reeds, to reveal a pair of ruddy ducks, without young, but living quite wild. They are North American in origin and numbers are small, but slowly increasing; the British population started from birds that escaped, or were released, from wildfowl collections.

Above Bert's lake more swallows and house martins were feeding and a great crested grebe, with a chick swimming close behind, drifted towards me. Something was not quite right; it had two heads, both looking directly at me. As it swung round the mystery was solved, for there was quite a large second chick, riding on its mother's back. Soon the parent bird, tired of carrying her cargo, tipped her offspring into the water and began to preen.

As dusk approached the swallows and house martins over the water were replaced by bats. With old trees in which to live and a high insect population, the area is ideal for bats, but due to the problems of finding and watching these attractive little night-flying mammals, it is not known exactly what species are present. Four types have been identified, however, with a "bat detector", a receiver that picks up the ultrasonic sounds emitted by bats to direct their flight. Most of the sounds are well above the range of the human ear, but with the help of a "detector" it is possible to pick up the distinctive sound patterns of individual species. Unfortunately it is only effective with nine of the fifteen British bats, and it is not possible to use it successfully in dense woodland, which rules out much of Windsor. Those positively identified so far are pipistrelle, Daubenton's, a solitary serotine and either noctule or Leiler's, which is also known as the lesser noctule. The serotine is a large bat with a wingspan of up to fifteen inches and it is fond of old woodland; as one was "detected" it would be strange if there were not several more in the area.

After the early flush of spring flora, Windsor does not have any great quantity or variety of flowers. It has a few orchids, the spotted and the spotted heath, as well as the common twayblade, which for an orchid is very dull and ordinary. Similarly the name of the broad helleborine, which is quite common, is more attractive than the plant. There are two rare helleborines, the green-flowered, which is also known as the Isle of Wight, and the violet. One flower I was pleased to find was the yellow pimpernel, a plant of damp places, previously I had only seen the abundant scarlet; they are both members of the primrose family. The area of natural grassland around the Copper Horse on Snow Hill is quite rich in flowers, despite being trampled by many visitors. It has bitter vetch, lousewort, and harebells, together with adder's tongue, growing in more normal surroundings than those of Buckingham Palace Garden.

On a day of rain I saw several common flowers in a mixed wood of oak, ash, beech, birch, larch and pine. It was almost possible to feel the age of the area through the softness of its floor; it had a pleasant springiness, with leaf mould and dead bracken fronds – a covering that has been laid down each year for centuries. The rain dripping through leaves gave a soft, soothing sound and the aroma was moist, rich and earthy. Dewberries had just come out on flower, with raindrops bending their soft-white petals. Their name comes from their fruit, like large blackberries, which because of their bloom, look as if they have a covering of fine dew. There were patches of stitchwort, enchanter's nightshade, lesser skullcap, and in a marshy clearing, corn mint. There were many families of tits busy feeding in the foliage, blue, great and long-tailed; some of the young looked very damp and bedraggled. Two magpies fed at the base of a tree; a jay flew across a ride, and the laughing cry of a green woodpecker sounded from among the branches of an old tree. A winding stream, with a firm, sandy bed, flowed at the bottom of a valley and from a bend, a pair of mandarins rose up in flight. They often nest deep in the woods, using holes in trees as high as forty feet above the ground. Soon after hatching, the ducklings tumble down and the mother can trail them quite long distances to a lake or pond. Mandarins are not good parents, often foraging for food away from water, where the young become easy prey for crows, magpies and jays; in rainy conditions the dripping vegetation through which they trundle can make them wet and cold. The mortality rate is high — by the time they have their feathers, only three or four will have survived out of a large brood.

The growth along the banks of the stream was lush and green, with grasses, sedges and rushes, as well as great hairy willow-herb, lady's bedstraw, hedge woundwort, herb robert and herb bennet. Herb bennet is also known as wood avens and is a close relative of water avens. Where the two grow close together they often cross to produce a variety of peculiar but not unattractive offspring. Even sprawling goosegrass had small white flowers and there were ferns too, in addition to bracken, including the broad buckler and the pleasant lemon-scented.

It is always relaxing to walk in the rain, and at a great fallen copper beech I met a fox who seemed to agree. We were within a few feet of each other and both of us stopped to assess the situation. It had beautiful deep brown eyes and a white tip to its brush. Without panic it calmly turned round and trotted back along a small pathway through a tunnel of bracken and brambles. From the amount of flattened vegetation it looked as if cubs had been playing around the trunk and twisted branches. White honeysuckle climbed and trailed over young saplings, with the petals closed because of the rain. Where I crossed the stream, slot marks showed that a solitary roe had recently passed under a natural arch of flowers. Climbing up through tearing scrub I reached a wide open ride, with long grasses, clumps of stitchwort and grass vetchling, an uncommon plant with single or paired flowers like small, elongated sweet peas. Appropriately too, there was a large patch of orange hawkweed; a bright conspicuous wild flower with the alternative name of "fox and cubs". It is quite uncommon and was originally found only in cottage gardens.

The forest has a whole network of grassy rides, which when the rain stopped, began to steam under a watery sun. Meadow brown butterflies flopped in low flight, and unusually for them, fed on a brilliant patch of buttercups with their wings open. Blackberry buds were beginning to burst, showing patches of tight pink petals; soon the change from bud to flower would be matched by the metamorphosis of caterpillars into beautiful woodland butterflies. As if to emphasise the fact, a speckled wood flew down to settle on a bramble leaf; it was exactly the right colour for both its name and its home – dark brown, speckled with light primrose yellow. The wings were clear and fresh as if they had just emerged from a chrysalis. Speckled woods are fast flying butterflies that seem to enjoy fluttering in and out of dappled light; for creatures so light and delicate the males are very territorial and, surprisingly, aggressive.

Already, as the sun faded, the air was warm and dry and with dusk came the open flowers and sweet scent of honeysuckle hanging thickly in the air. The clockwise climb of its trailing arms gives it the name of "woodbine"; sometimes they can become so tight on a growing stem that the shape is affected. With blackthorn this constriction creates an attractive spiral, ideal for a country walking stick. In the same way that I prefer the wild rose to cultivated varieties, so I love to see honeysuckle wild in woods and hedgerows. The seventeenth-century herbalist John Parkinson felt the same way, for he wrote:

> The Honisuckle that groweth wilde in every hedge,
> although it be very sweete, yet doe I not bring into
> my garden, but let it rest in his owne place, to serve
> their senses that travell by it, or have no garden.

I enjoyed seeing the foxes at Windsor and later, on a hot day, I saw another, in the grass field where the roe buck had been lying in shade. At midday the fox was sniffing around troughs put out for cattle, either seeking insects or spilt cattle food. When I approached, it nonchalantly trotted off through rough grass, briefly stopping to look back.

They are one of my favourite animals and I have had several as pets. But although I love to see them, and each year try to watch cubs, they sometimes make appreciation difficult, because foxes can cause much damage to wildlife and domestic fowl. As they are intelligent and adaptable, they are one of the few creatures to have increased in number over recent years. Their increase dates back to myxomatosis, for despite the hideous disease taking an item of food off the fox's menu, it also made rabbit trapping uneconomical, and with traps and snares rabbit-trappers killed thousands of foxes each year. As a result, when trapping ceased, the single greatest pressure was removed from the fox and the population has increased ever since. Even in winter they avoid hardship by scavenging in gardens and dustbins, and some have moved into towns and cities.

The greatest problem caused by the fox is not the fact that it will kill the odd hen or pheasant, but that it occasionally indulges in "surplus killing". This means that a fox in a hen-house may kill many hens, or a vixen along a hedgerow can take all the sitting pheasants in a single night. In addition, on a nature reserve, colonies of ground nesting birds, such as terns, are all at risk and can be wiped out in a few hours. Scientists make various claims to explain this behaviour; some suggest that the fox intends to return, to store the surplus food for later use, and that the flapping and alarm in a hen-house makes it panic and lose control. From the behaviour of my foxes, and after seeing a wild vixen with large cubs killing hens I believe the explanation is far more straightforward. Foxes are very playful animals and are attracted by things that flutter and move, so they actually enjoy the act of killing. It can become a game in which the flapping bodies and feathers are chased and thrown in the air; when movement stops another victim is found to replace the old. Of course this is much too simple for some "experts", after all, few research grants or PhDs are given for stating the obvious.

Fox.

Some years on the farm, foxes cause great problems, ripping boards out of hen-houses to get at the hens, or trying, sometimes successfully, to climb in through the windows. Once break-ins occur they continue, as if the fox reponsible acquires an insatiable appetite for hens; unfortunately when this happens we have to try to kill the offending animal. At other times, although fox tracks go through the farmyard, we get no trouble, suggesting that those particular foxes prefer other food. As a result, some years we will kill one or two foxes, and the rest of the time we can leave them alone. Almost every year cubs are born on the farm, and we see foxes at most seasons; usually we enjoy having them.

The view that individual foxes develop likes and dislikes is supported by Bert. He once caught a fox that appeared to be pregnant at the wrong time of the year – in mid-summer; he carried out a post-mortem to find that it had gorged itself on 203 young mice and voles. It had found a field of rough grass with many tussocks of cock's foot, ideal for breeding "field" mice and short-tailed voles. He believes that a fox's diet depends on personal taste, the season and the availability of food. When food is short they will eat carrion; in the autumn they like wild strawberries, blackberries and rowan berries, and at other times they will take mice, moorhens, rats or pheasants, depending on mood and opportunity.

Consequently, if a gamekeeper complains that foxes live solely on his pheasants and other game, both his natural history and his competence are highly suspect. Similarly, if an apologist for the fox suggests that they eat nothing but creatures harmful to the farmer such as rats, mice and slugs, then he too has replaced fact with fiction and probably hears the cuckoo in October.

It seems that Oliver Goldsmith also heard the cuckoo in October, as he makes some unusual comments about the fox's hunting methods:

The hedge-hog in vain rolls itself up into a ball to oppose him: this determined glutton teases it until it is obliged to appear unconcerned, and then he devours it. The wasp and the wild bee are attacked with equal success. Although at first they fly out upon their invader, and actually oblige him to retire, this is but for a few minutes, until he has rolled himself upon the ground, and thus crushed as stick to his skin; he then returns to the charge, and at last by perseverance, obliges them to abandon their combs; which he greedily devours, both wax and honey.

Strangely, he also identifies three types of fox: ''The greyhound fox is the largest, tallest, and boldest; and will attack a grown sheep. The mastiff fox is less, but more strongly built. The cur fox is the least and most common; he lurks about hedges and out-houses, and is the most pernicious of the three to the peasant and the farmer.'' Samuel Johnson, a contemporary of Goldsmith was not very impressed, commenting: ''If he can tell a horse from a cow, that is the extent of his knowledge of zoology.''

Of all the predators at Windsor, two stand out for their mixture of grace and primeval anger – the sparrow-hawk and the hobby; they are magnificent birds, but both are ruthless and efficient killers. Once the sparrow-hawk was common, all over the country, but the hobby has been scarce for many years, arriving in late spring from Equatorial Africa and staying for the summer.

I went to check the nests of the hawks and hobbies with Ted, a self-taught naturalist who from his boyhood days has spent nearly all his spare time in the Great Park and forest. During the week he works as a laboratory technician, but then acts as a voluntary warden for the Nature Conservancy Council, monitoring the natural fluctuations of Windsor's wildlife. In the course of his walking and watching he has become an acknowledged expert in fungi and flowers, reciting the scientific names as if Latin was his mother tongue. Over many years he has carried out a survey of the breeding sparrow-hawks and he has also helped to ring and blood-test hundreds of chicks, to check the population trends and patterns.

He is an interesting and amusing man, a Royalist with political views

Hobby.

that sometimes appear to be slightly left of Lenin, but Lenin, from his writing, had no sense of humour. Ted had a hard start to life; when he was a young boy in the Second World War his father was killed by the Japanese in Hong Kong. He and his mother were then evicted from their London home; so he has some justification for his feelings, as political views are nearly always a mixture of experience and prejudice.

Ted took me along a ride cutting between mature trees, with patches of flowering self-heal at the sides, and almost immediately we saw birds of prey. They were circling, mewing to each other, and gradually climbing with fast, almost flickering wingbeats. One briefly tucked in its wings to fall fast, in a short stoop, probably at an insect, before pulling out and again beginning to climb. They were hobbies, about the same size as kestrels but darker and more streamlined, with sickle-like wings. In shape and appearance they almost resemble miniature peregrines, and like the peregrine they have complete mastery of flight, culminating in spectacular stoops to kill their prey.

The pair had chosen an old crow's nest in which to breed, and hobbies will also occupy deserted magpie nests or even squirrel dreys. A branch of a nearby tree was being used as a "plucking post" and several feathers were scattered on the ground. They were from young swifts, confirming the hobby's airborne ability. A swift is streamlined and fast, and to knock one out of the air a hobby would have to fall straight and true at great speed, often through turbulence and swirling air to make its strike. Around Windsor they also take swallows and house martins, as well as many insects.

Not only do the birds perform spectacular flights when hunting, but they also seem to fly for sheer pleasure. They climb high, tumble in air currents and loop the loop, as if loving the freedom of the open sky and the skill of their wings.

Not wanting to linger too near we moved deeper into pines, stopping beneath a mature tree. There was another nest three quarters of the way up, looking like that of a pigeon. A hen sparrow-hawk flew, showing in shafts of light and disappearing in shadow as she circled, flying expertly between branches and foliage. White down was caught in cobwebs close to the nest, revealing the presence of young, and later Ted would return with help to ring and weigh the chicks.

Sparrow-hawks are distinctive birds, with the female being larger than the male, which is not unusual in birds of prey. At a distance, whether perching or flying, they can be mistaken for cuckoos, but at close quarters their beaks show the sharp, piercing hook for holding and ripping. Before migration was understood, cuckoos were thought to change into sparrow-hawks for the winter.

To see a sparrow-hawk at close quarters is a slightly chilling experience, for the fierce yellow eyes are totally empty of feeling; they are wild and savage, and to look into them is to see the primitive world as it was

Sparrow-hawk with kill.

when the earth was young. They kill a wide range of birds from those as small as blue tits, to full grown carrion crows larger than themselves. At Windsor they seem to be particularly fond of birds about their own size, wood pigeons and jays. I had always imagined jays to be brash, fearless birds, but many get taken. Bert believes that hawks and falcons develop likes and dislikes, in the same way as foxes, and he has known a pair of sparrow-hawks to clear all the jays from even quite a large wood.

Sparrow-hawks suffered considerably in the late fifties and early sixties through the toxic chemicals used on the farm land. Small birds would eat contaminated corn or insects and then the hawks would prey on them. Infertility resulted, as well as eggs with very thin shells. They were easily damaged, and numbers quickly fell. They disappeared about then from my own parish and they have never returned. Those at Windsor were slightly more fortunate, although numbers did fall, a substantial area of the Great Park and forest remained almost free from the effects of pesticides, and an adequate breeding population survived. Occasionally unhatched eggs are still found, containing traces of poisons, and so a check continues to ensure that warnings are heeded and future wildlife catastrophes avoided.

A plucking post was situated close to another nest, littering the area with the feathers of many small birds, including those of young blue tits. Both the sparrow-hawks and hobbies feed their young each year at the time when inexperienced fledglings are just on the wing. Many get taken, and the survivors soon learn the importance of constant alertness. Large victims such as carrion crows would also be young birds just out of the nest, not yet aware of the dangers around them. Man's great admiration for birds and animals that kill is hard to explain, but the lion and the eagle always seem to hold more attraction than the antelope or sparrow. Perhaps it is some subconscious link with our past, when the reality of our killing was not hidden by the pre-packed presentation of supermarket meat; now, to most people, beef steak or lamb chop is a "product" not part of a "kill" and a once living animal. For some time I had wanted to reintroduce sparrow-hawks to our farm, but on seeing the blue tit feathers I decided against doing so.

Returning from the second nest we passed over sandy heathland with birch scrub and scattered Scotch pines. Two birds flew with a sharply undulating flight; they were woodlarks. A few pairs breed in the area, but numbers have declined in the last thirty years, as they have throughout the country; now they are found only in southern Britain. Why the population has fallen so drastically is not known, although the birds are particularly vulnerable to cold weather, and suffered badly in the 1950s, as well as in the long cold winter of 1962–3. Their fall could also indicate a slight change in the weather, with colder, wetter springs affecting breeding success.

Nightjars and tree pipits are also found on the heathland, but one rare

Silver-studded blues on bell heather.

bird that nests at Windsor spurns both the heathland and the seclusion of the forest, for the black redstart chooses the castle itself. It is a bird that did not nest in Britain regularly until 1923, but now a few pairs breed each year mainly in south-east England. They seem quite at home in urban conditions, nesting in old buildings and walls, although some prefer the more natural surroundings of rocky cliffs and boulders. The black redstart is a summer visitor, spending its winters around the Mediterranean.

Bog asphodel and cotton grass confirmed the advance of the season and then small, deep blue wings, the same colour as the sky, settled on flowering cross-leaved heath. It was a silver-studded blue, a beautiful butterfly of heathland, with wings edged in white. Soon a female flew by and the two fluttered dizzily before joining together to mate; their wings closed, showing the undersides dotted with spots of black and orange.

The appearance of the silver-studded blue suggested that it was a day when butterflies would be flying and so we returned to the old forest. Speckled woods and ringlets darted in and out of changing light and a silver-washed fritillary passed at speed; then, high above, at the top of old oaks came the flashing brilliant white of flying wings. White admirals were dancing in flight before gliding down to feed on the open blossom of brambles. It was my first sight of their soft, velvet wings, held open and crossed with white, as they fed on nectar. I could understand why the butterfly was once known as the "white admirable". The ride was perfect for them; oak trees in which to fly and rest; brambles giving flowers and plenty of sweet food, and honeysuckle on which to lay their eggs. Another woodland butterfly, the purple hairstreak also briefly flew, again in oak, and the leaves form the main food of its caterpillars.

White admiral on bramble.

In addition, the old mixed woods have one of Britain's most scarce but attractive butterflies, the purple emperor. Bert once saw a male resting open winged in a ride; he caught it and admired its fragile beauty before giving it back its freedom. They love the sun and can only be seen in their true splendour when the light catches their wings to make them shine, a dazzling iridescent purple. Because of the angles involved in flight, the wings are caught alternately, and so in bright light the colour constantly flashes and changes. The purple emperor is only bettered in size by the swallowtail, and is now confined to just a few oak woods in central southern England. It lays its eggs on the broad-leaved sallow, which can also be found among the trees of Windsor Forest. The eggs are laid singly and are very difficult to find. Unfortunately the beauty and romance of the purple emperor are spoilt by its feeding habits, for it is attracted to corpses, droppings and stagnant puddles. They are aggressive butterflies and have been seen to chase off other insects and even small birds from their territories.

In my efforts to see the purple emperor, not only did I make several special journeys to Windsor, but I also went to see ''BB'', Denys Watkins-Pitchford, the old country writer, who had just finished what he claimed would be his last book. He has successfully introduced purple emperors to a wood in Northamptonshire, but again I was unlucky, having to make do with a single large chrysalis, suspended from the underside of a sallow leaf.

To see the butterfly that Bert had described so enthusiastically I eventually had to visit Gordon Beningfield, to look at his cased specimen, bought from an old collection dating back to the days when butterfly collecting was popular with many country gentlemen and vicars. Despite its age it was still possible to appreciate its ever-changing beauty.

A clergyman who was formerly at Windsor, kept up one of the traditions of his calling and was very interested in ''lepidoptera''; he too failed to see a purple emperor, but he had reliable reports of sitings from several different areas of the forest. He also made use of the grassy rides, and in 1971 successfully introduced marbled whites, from an area of Dorset grassland that has since been turned into arable fields.

As we left the white admirals still flying and feeding, several butter-flies of grassland and hedgerow flew among the seeding grasses of the rides – skippers, meadow browns, gatekeepers and small heaths. Many flies and varieties of wasp also flew, some feeding on wild ripe cherries, and spiders had suspended their webs to trawl the breeze for insects. A red admiral in perfect condition basked with its wings open on the track, until a magpie landed and tried to peck it. The butterfly flew ten yards further on, before landing again, only for the magpie to hop in pursuit. This happened at short intervals for about sixty yards, until the magpie finally lost interest.

While the woodland butterflies are flying the rut of the roe deer takes place, deep in the forest. It has nothing in common with the ruts of the red and fallow deer, as it takes place during a different season and the bucks remain silent. The surest sign of the rut is to find a circle of trampled grass in a ride or around bushes, known as the "rutting ring". When it is being worn, the in-season doe leads the buck in circles, as if trying to excite him, and when she stops, he mounts. The procedure can last for many hours and it is seldom seen. I have been fortunate enough to see it once, not at Windsor, but in Thetford Forest. Although the egg or eggs of the female become fertilised, the roe is one of those animals in which delayed implantation takes place. Normal development does not begin until later, when the egg implants itself in the uterus wall, sixteen to eighteen weeks before the kids are born. Delayed implantation is also found in the badger, and scientists still do not understand all the mechanisms involved, or what triggers them off.

The roe buck is a handsome little deer, with large active ears, doleful eyes and a dark, damp nose. It also has small upright antlers with one or two simple tines. Unlike our other native deer, the antlers are cast from October to December and the new set are free of velvet by about the end of April. Each buck endeavours to set up its own territory, which it maintains the whole year. The deer are mostly solitary, although in winter they often stay in small family groups.

The other wild deer of Windsor, the muntjac, is also solitary and because of its small size, only eighteen inches at the shoulder, it is not often seen. The area is ideal for it, with dense brambles, gorse, bracken and rhododendrons. In summer both bucks and does are a beautiful chestnut brown, but at first glance, because of their size they can be mistaken for hares. Despite their lack of height they are very fast and can jump well; as a result, in Britain as a whole, both their numbers and their range are steadily increasing.

Originally two closely related species, from India and Southern China were introduced into Woburn Park by the Duke of Bedford at the turn of the century, and inevitably some escaped. They have young at any time of the year, and the two species interbreed freely. Because they give out a loud "bark" when frightened, they are also known as "barking deer". The buck has small antlers, and with age harmless tusks develop. Normally only fleeting glimpses are obtained, when they are surprised in open ground and rush for cover. One evening I saw a buck approaching along a narrow woodland path; I stood still and it continued on its way before stopping, just ten yards away. We studied each other for several minutes, before it trotted off into the undergrowth. Bert has seen them quite often at the edge of a small lake, browsing on new rushes.

In addition to butterflies, other translucent wings fly in late summer, for the great areas of water are rich in dragon and damselflies. In fact Windsor has at least seventeen species, well over a third of those that can

A roe buck.

be found in Britain. I sat by a lake on a still humid morning, in bright sun; there were thousands of damselflies, red and sky-blue, as well as turquoise and emerald with fine metallic sheens. Some had just emerged from the water, their lace-like wings drying and stretching, while others flew; shimmering concentrations of colour and scattering light, held up by wings of flickering silver.

Their movement created three surfaces; the clear blue water, the flying wings and their deep, gently rippling reflections. At one time they were known as "Devil's darning needles", but the name is more appropriate for dragonflies. They too were droning over the lake, with the menacing look of the hunter; blue and brown, long, and in the case of the four spotted chaser, squat. They take many insects as they fly, and a friend once saw a small copper butterfly seized in mid-flight. The English names of damsel and dragonflies describe them perfectly, a mixture of darters, hawkers, chasers and skimmers. The Windsor population includes the ruddy darter, the brilliant emerald, the common hawker, the broad bodied chaser, the black tailed skimmer, the red-eyed damselfly and the emperor dragonfly. Once it was believed that dragonflies only hovered above places where fish were plentiful.

Dragonflies do not get things all their own way, for when they are flying hobbies often visit the lakes; they are partial to large insects and eat them while still on the wing. As a line of defence a dragonfly will climb vertically when a hobby approaches, but Bert has seen a falcon simply flip over on to its back and snatch the rising insect with her talons.

In one corner a dabchick was diving after food for her two young. There was a marked variation in size suggesting that incubation began as soon as the first egg was laid, resulting in the chicks hatching at different times. As soon as she dived they both began calling and trying to anticipate where she would reappear. Sometimes one would get it right, and then the other. She was successful with almost every dive; dabchicks feed on small fish and various aquatic creatures, including dragonfly nymphs.

I called at the large pond where the ruddy ducks had been, but there was no sign of them, just tufted, pochard and two pairs of shovellers. A heron was hunting in orthodox fashion, slowly stalking in front of reeds. I was standing on a walkway of rotting wood, that once led to a duck hide, when a large eel slithered beneath me in the shallow water; it was by far the largest eel I had ever seen in fresh water.

Soon it would be making its way back to the sea, for the life cycle of the eel is just as remarkable as that of the salmon, but it lacks the romance; sliding through mud holds less appeal than leaping into clouds of falling spray. The eel's journey is the exact reverse of the salmon's; it begins life at sea and moves into fresh water, only returning to its ocean of origin to breed. It is thought that the eggs are laid in the Sargasso Sea, between the Caribbean and the bulge of the West African coast. They grow into leaf-like larvae that drift to the Continental shelf of Europe, there they change into elvers and swim into fresh water. They remain in lakes, rivers and streams for several years, until maturity, when again they head for the seas. On reaching salt water they begin their homeward journey and change from the colour of mud to a sea-going silvery-grey. It is an astonishing story, and as the eel is so common, many millions of larvae must drift to Britain every year.

Bert's lake had other fish, large carp, breaking the surface as they idled in the top layer of sun-warmed water. Some of the pools had flowers that confirmed the maturity of the season; pink amphibious bistort, meadowsweet, the "pokers" of great reed mace, water mint, yellow loosestrife and water-forget-me-not.

The old art of landscape gardening did not die with William Duke of Cumberland, for in the Great Park there are two large gardens, the Valley Gardens that cover 400 acres along the northern bank of Virginia Water, and the Savill Gardens, thirty-five acres of exotic flowers, plants and trees near the Obelisk Pond, and the wildlife of the area spills over into both of them. The Obelisk was erected to commemorate the military feats of "Butcher" Cumberland. In the Savill Gardens there is an area of rough grasses where common spotted orchids grow and under large beech trees, near the entrance, is a remarkable carpet of white fork moss, an entirely natural expanse of olive green. Ringlets and speckled woods fly among the trees and mandarin ducks land on the ponds. It was on one of the ponds that I watched a simple piece of bird behaviour; a pair of moorhens had several jet black, fluffy young, the second brood of the summer. The chicks of the first brood were fully grown, but they were still with their parents, and helping them to feed their new brothers and sisters. It was something I had never noticed before, and apparently, even during the second period of incubation, the chicks from the first, will help to repair the nest. The moorhen is not a bird of the "moors"; the name comes from "mere-hen", and so with its many acres of water and reed beds, Windsor is ideal.

The onset of autumn in the Park and Forest is a time to absorb and to remember; a brilliant morning in late September with the sun rising pink behind mist. It was cool and damp with the grasses and bracken heavy with dew, close to frost. Spiders' webs concentrated the sun into dripping diamond strings, and beads of fine moisture filled the grassland with sparkling light. Pheasants were feeding on stubble and perching on hedgerows that hung heavy with ripe hips and haws. The leaves were beginning to turn, gently and slowly into the soft colours of the new season.

As the sun strengthened it searched out the shadows, illuminating the heads of deer, their breath cooling as draughts of drifting steam, and their bodies lost in shade. A stag with antlers out of velvet snorted and

Beef steak fungus.

then two more appeared, antlers clashing, heads pushing and fallen leaves flying. By the time the dew had dried a stag rested under a large oak, with two jackdaws perched on its back; then came a familiar sound from deep within the trees, a challenging roar; the rut of the red deer had begun. Immature green and great spotted woodpeckers were flying and feeding, and disturbances in the leaves warned that acorns were falling.

It was the time for fungi, and again Windsor is very rich, with about 500 species. Ted took me to see one of the rarest along a wide sandy ride. A green woodpecker flew up from the ground, it had probably been eating ants. In the eighteenth century, the Reverend Samuel Ward had theories that went beyond eagles, as he also claimed to know how woodpeckers ate ants: "The wood-pecker pecks at their hills, in order to call them abroad; and, thrusting out its long red tongue, which resembles their usual prey, the ants come in crouds to settle upon it; the bird watching a favourable opportunity; withdraws its tongue at a jerk, and devours the devourers."

Ted found the rarity with ease – *Pisolithus arhizus*. It has been described as looking like a large brown fist or even a ball of horse dung; to me it looked like an old potato. It is normally found in southern Europe and the countries of the Mediterranean, but because it grows close to the old Roman road of the Devil's Highway, Ted believes that the spores could have come over with the Romans. It is a romantic idea and he could be right. There were numerous other fine specimens; on the stump of an old pine the great spongy mass of brain or cauliflower fungus. It looks almost identical to a rubberised brain, or a cauliflower that has been frosted. The small hedgehog fungus is so named because its gills resemble the spines of a hedgehog. It is edible and very popular in Europe. Real hedgehogs also thrive in the whole area, with plenty of food and old leaf litter in which to hibernate.

One of the strangest fungi is a parasite that grows on oak or chestnut. The beef steak fungus looks exactly like beef steak; it even contains a substance similar to watery blood. On oak it turns the wood dark, which makes it popular with furniture makers. Needless to say, the Windsor woods have many disgusting stinkhorns; most inappropriately, some grow close to an army theological college. Deep within the pines several jays began scolding; to Ted it sounded as if they had found a perching tawny owl. Long-eared owls are seen occasionally; they do not nest in holes like most of the other owls, but use the deserted nests of magpies and crows. In the old forest beneath tall beeches we found clusters of chanterelles. They are probably the tastiest of all fungi, particularly when fried in butter or put into omelettes.

Further along, the white admirals had gone and the bramble blossom had grown into ripe blackberries, but they still attracted late butterflies, red admirals and several commas. The comma is a most attractive and unusual butterfly, rather like a small tortoiseshell with tattered wings.

Its name comes from the small white comma that shows up clearly when its wings are closed. It is one of the year's last butterflies and is very fond of over-ripe fruit. The closed wings also look similar to old fallen leaves, ideal for camouflage during hibernation. Many survive the winter to emerge unharmed in the warmth of the following spring; the comma is one of the few butterflies to be increasing in number.

Hornets were also feeding on the fruit; they resemble large gingery wasps. Contrary to popular belief they are very docile creatures; they rarely get angry and their nests should never be destroyed. Late leather-jackets had hatched and many crane-flies or "Daddy-long-legs", were flying. Just as starlings take leather-jackets from the ground, so they were feeding on the crane-flies in flight. They were flying out from high perches, to take them in mid-air, like large dark flycatchers.

As an indication of its age the forest also has a few wild service trees, which are usually found in old deciduous forests. Locally it is called the "chequers tree" but the origin of the name is not known, although the bark of the mature tree peels off to produce a chequered effect. One story suggests that the "chequers berries" were made into a potent alcoholic drink, thus leading to many old public houses in the area being called "The Chequers". The main reason for its scarcity is thought to be the fact that the wild service tree makes excellent charcoal and was once very popular with charcoal burners.

Later, in October, early morning was full of mist and moving deer. Stags were roaring and autumn was at its peak. The leaves of the trees were a mixture of burnished golds, yellows, coppers and bronzes, and with the colours had come the rich harvest of forest food. Acorns had fallen, as well as beech mast and sweet chestnuts. Autumn is normally a time of plenty, when hunger is almost unknown. Jays, rooks, and jackdaws were flying with beak-held acorns and even mandarin ducks sometimes fly under the trees to feed. Tits are attracted to beech, and marsh, willow and coal are all thought to make stores of the small nuts for winter.

Grey squirrels also hurried and scurried with acorns and sweet chestnuts, hoarding food; they were introduced into Britain from North America between 1876 and 1929. There is little doubt that although attractive little animals their arrival has been a major wildlife disaster; they do considerable damage to our native trees, they destroy birds' nests, and the red squirrels have been unable to cope with their new competitors.

At one time, according to John Evelyn in the seventeenth century, acorns were collected by people as well as squirrels:

Water distilled from acorns is good against the phthysick, stitch in the side, and heals inward ulcers, and refrigerates inflammation. Nay I read in one Paulis, a physician of Denmark, that an handful or two of small oak buttons, mingled with oats, given to horses which are black of colour, will in a few days alter it to a fine dapple grey, which he attributes to the vitriol abounding in the tree.

The red deer in the enclosure, and the roe deer outside, are very fond of acorns, which put them in perfect condition for the winter. In the mixed woodland at dusk and dawn, one of the ways to see roe is to find the oak trees with their fallen acorns. Deer also like sweet chestnuts, and if a badger sett is close by, it is very much a case of "first come, first served". The original trees in Britain were probably introduced by the Romans. They can grow up to 100 feet high, and the description of the "spreading chestnut tree" could apply to the sweet chestnut, just as well as to Longfellow's horse chestnut. They have attractive grooved bark, which if the tree grows quickly begins to spiral and crack, spoiling the wood. Once it was coppiced for fence posts and hop poles. It is often said that in England the chestnuts do not ripen or germinate, yet at Windsor there are many natural seedlings. The reason for non-growth in some areas is possibly because grey squirrels eat the shoots. The ripe nuts are also very popular with people; it is traditional to roast them, and chestnut stuffing helps to bring out the flavour of the Christmas turkey.

There is still another tree that provides much autumn food, especially for birds, and hornbeams grow in small groves or as single trees throughout the Great Park and forest. It is a beautiful tree, indigenous to south-east England, with great fluted trunks producing wood so hard that it is still used for mallet heads and chopping blocks. The many small clusters of nuts have wings, rather like the seeds of ash, and they are a particular favourite of the hawfinch. Hawfinches are the largest and shyest of our finches, with large, very powerful beaks that open nuts with ease. They breed at Windsor, and during the winter small flocks of them can be seen foraging for food.

The one animal missing from the autumn forest is the wild boar. Although it still thrives in parts of Europe, even in quite densely populated regions, the last truly wild boar recorded in Britain was in 1676, although introduced animals were to be found in the New Forest until the end of the eighteenth century. So far there are no plans for any reintroduction and Prince Philip is not keen on the idea: "There are too many people in the area. I have seen wild boars in Europe and they can be very dangerous. With their tusks they unzip dogs easily and if released here I think there would be problems."

The pools and lakes also change as autumn becomes almost winter, with the rushes and reeds turning the colour of old straw. Odd bitterns, ideally camouflaged, usually drop into the reed beds and occasionally a purple heron is seen hunting in the shallows for food. Calling Canada geese flop down on to the water, and in one flock there is a solitary barnacle goose; it is almost certainly another escapee from a wildfowl collection. The Canada itself was first brought back to Britain from

Hawfinch at water.

Jay with an acorn.

North America as long ago as the seventeenth century, but it is now classified as a wild goose, Britain's largest. There are a few records of probable wild birds having been blown across the Atlantic, arriving at places as far apart as the Hebrides and the Isles of Scilly, but almost the entire British population comes from once captive stock.

With the first frosts and winds of winter, the leaves descend in great cascades of swirling gold. Bird song briefly revives from the silence of late summer, as if the birds are establishing their territories for the following spring. On a damp November day I even saw a blue tit drive off a larger great tit from a hole in a tree.

Bunches of mistletoe show up clearly once the leaves have gone from the trees, particularly in once pollarded limes and horse chestnuts. In early times it was given magical powers, simply because the people did not understand how or why the plants grew in trees. The reason is quite straightforward; the berries are liked by thrushes, particularly mistle thrushes, and the seeds are either wiped off the birds' beaks, or passed right through them, when they are in the treetops. The seed then germinates where it lands. It is partly a parasite, drawing much of its nourishment from the tree on which it grows. Thomas Bewick believed that it had to pass through a mistle thrush in order to grow, and that no other bird would do.

The name of the plant actually explains the way it grows, for it comes from the High German ''mist'' – dung – and so it was known as ''the dung twig'', spread by birds. The Druids used mistletoe in their rituals and according to folklore it is said to cure epilepsy and make women fertile. In many homes sprigs of mistletoe were hung on beams as a protection against lightning. It has always been considered to be a lucky plant and that is why the tradition of kissing under the mistletoe at Christmas time began.

On a cold bright morning I returned to the bluebell wood. Once among pines, the old fallen needles were quiet and soft underfoot. Almost immediately I saw a roe doe, standing in the shade watching and enquiring; her winter coat was as dark as the pine trunks behind her, and if there is a more beautiful animal, I have yet to see it. She trotted off to stand on a small bank bathed in a brilliant shaft of light; her coat seemed to absorb the sun, for she immediately matched the new trunks of winter bronze. Suddenly she bounded off, gracefully leaping a stream, her hooves sending up spurts of pine needles, and her white rump bouncing between the trees.

In place of bluebells were fallen leaves, where a woodcock flew silently between the trees. Just as Mont at Sandringham is adamant that woodcock do not carry their young, Bert is definite that he has seen it: ''The first time I could hardly believe it. The bird was carrying a well developed juvenile bird that later flew unaided. I have seen the same thing several times since. A colleague has seen much younger chicks being carried." Ted too sees it nearly every year. "They seem to call the young and then carry just one chick, with the adult's tail well tucked in. I've seen it with very small chicks and those nearly full grown. Sometimes it seems in response to danger, but I have also seen them carry young from dry ground to wet, in order to feed. One year several of us saw a mother carry one from the middle of a forest road." Perhaps this strange behaviour is local; in some areas the birds carry their young and in others they do not. The entrance of the badger sett showed signs of activity with dropped twigs of fresh pine, as if they were being used for bedding.

It is with the leaves down that better views can be obtained of muntjac, but as I returned all I saw were the tiny slot marks where a deer had been. Redpolls were up in birches feeding on seeds and a great spotted woodpecker as well as a nuthatch were busily searching for insects.

At one of the lakes three cormorants were perching on an old wooden frame, one with its wings open to dry. Numbers of tufted duck and pochard had increased and would remain high until the spring. There were several mandarins and from autumn onwards is the best time to see them. Most of the year they act as genuinely wild birds, not like some that can be seen in city and "country" parks; but when they congregate in the winter it is sometimes possible to see them at close quarters. They are beautiful birds; the drake is extravagantly coloured with "side whiskers" and feathers on its wings that can be erected, like miniature sails, when trying to impress a mate. The colouring of the female is more modest, but she is just as attractive with feathers of finely marbled grey.

Mandarins were originally found in China and Japan, but because of their beauty they were brought back to Europe by early travellers and were mentioned as far back as 1599. The ducks at Windsor are probably related to birds introduced into Surrey in 1928. Ironically the mandarin is now doing better in Britain than in China, where much of its woodland habitat has been destroyed. Goldeneye, goosanders and smew are some of the other regular winter visitors to the Windsor lakes; smew are distinctive black and white ducks that nest in the vast tundra regions of Scandinavia and northern Europe. Goosanders move southwards to avoid the harshness of the northern winters, and when they dive for fish, black-headed gulls often follow their underwater paths to fall on any small fish or nymphs that appear. A gannet was seen flying over a lake on one winter's day as if wanting to fish. It had probably been blown inland by strong winds.

I searched the standing reeds with my binoculars hoping for a sign of a kingfisher, but all I saw was a hunched up heron. A more orthodox fisherman was fishing with a rod and keep-net; he said the fishing was very good with large pike, perch, tench, bream, roach, carp and eels. Because the cormorants were immature birds he assumed that they had

A pair of mandarins.

Pine marten.

been reared in the area and called them "crails", a local name for freshwater cormorants. In fact ringed cormorants have been caught at Windsor and they have all been birds that were hatched on the coast of Pembrokeshire. Why or how they should arrive along the Thames Valley for the winter is not known. A few cormorants do breed by fresh water, but most of those are confined to Scotland and the Lake District.

In the evening I returned to the bluebell wood to try to see a badger in winter, but movement made me stop. I hoped it was an animal about which there is still much mystery, but I was disappointed, for it was only a stoat; yet since 1956 there have been persistent rumours of pine martens in the Windsor Forest. Reports have been infrequent and unconfirmed; but the pine marten is a very distinctive animal with a clear white throat and cannot be confused with any other animal. Then, in 1979 three woodmen saw a single marten playing in old timber, and from their description it could be nothing else. Someone could have tried to introduce pine martens to the area, or the animals could be part of a very old population, hanging on. Because of the nature of the Forest and the habits of the animal it is a mystery that could remain unsolved for many years.

The shadows lengthened, tawny owls called and the sound of a stream was as clear as its flow. Canada geese flew over, just visible, outlined against the grey sky. Sadly the day was too short and I quickly ran out of light, with no sight or sound coming from the sett. Normally the glow of the vanished sun aids direction immediately after dusk, but where was the sun? There were many pools of reflected light in the sky, most glowing from concentrations of street lamps. It was a reminder of just how urban the surrounding areas really are.

It is at dusk that starlings can also be seen for in the same way that they give an indication of the start of the year, so they show its end with a roost, that ranks as one of the most remarkable wildlife sights in the world. Hundreds of thousands of birds fly in, and some estimates even claim that it reaches well over a million. In wind they come in great straggling waves, flying low, but in still weather they arrive high, falling from the sky like clouds of fluttering leaves. The coverts and copses become black with birds and the noise, which continues all night, shows why a gathering of starlings is known as a "murmuration". On seeing such a roost it seems incredible that in the early nineteenth century they were so rare that one country name for them was the "solitary thrush". Just as quickly as numbers build up, so in December they often fall away, with the birds moving elsewhere.

December 21st is the shortest day of the year, and by 25th daylight is said to have increased by the length of a gnat's yawn. On Twelfth Night light increases by the size of a deer's leap, and by the time it has extended to the length of a lark's rise, then already the first notes of the dawn chorus can be heard; the year has run its course and spring is approaching.

The Duchy of Cornwall

In overall size the Duchy of Cornwall is the largest of the Royal Estates, totalling almost 130,000 acres spread over eight counties, or nine if the forty-five acres in Greater London, complete with the Oval cricket ground, are included. In addition it owns or has rights over 200 miles of foreshore in the South-West, as well as the fundus (the bed) of several rivers and estuaries. It also has mineral rights: copper, wolfram and arsenic have all been obtained in the past, and tin mining is still taking place today.

It is the oldest English duchy and was created in 1337 when Edward III made his eldest son Prince Edward, Duke of Cornwall. The land originated from the old Earldom of Cornwall which had lapsed to the crown. The title "Duke of Cornwall" is now held automatically by the monarch's surviving son, who is also heir to the throne – the title "Prince of Wales" is usually conferred on the first-born son. Prince Charles became Duke of Cornwall on the accession of the Queen in 1952. The previous Duke of Cornwall was Edward, Prince of Wales, whose title went into abeyance in 1936 when he became King Edward VIII.

As one purpose of the Duchy is to provide revenue for the heir, Prince Charles draws no money from the Civil List; indeed he gives up twenty-five per cent of his income as a voluntary contribution to the Government. But although Prince Charles receives income from what is a private estate, and he is Chairman of the Prince's Council, which manages the Duchy, the holdings are run in accordance with the Duchy of Cornwall Management Acts of 1863 to 1982. These permit Prince Charles to receive the income, but not the capital from the estate, which effectively makes him the tenant during his dukedom.

Over the years, the size and shape of the Duchy have changed considerably. At one time land was held in much of the Midlands, southern, and eastern England, as well as in the West Country. Henry V exchanged land in Somerset for land in Middlesex, and under Henry VIII more estates in Cornwall were obtained for holdings in Oxfordshire. In the late eighteenth century, the Duchy shrank when large areas of Lincolnshire, Berkshire, Leicestershire and Cornwall were sold to pay the Land Tax.

The present character of the Duchy was established between 1842 and 1861 when Prince Albert acted as Lord Warden, supervising the management of the estates. Since then, additional land has been purchased in Gloucestershire, Devon and Cornwall; in 1983 a significant addition was made with the purchase of a holding in Glamorgan – the first Welsh estate since the eighteenth century.

The single largest area of Duchy land is to be found on Dartmoor – a 70,000-acre block of the highest part of the moor which has been in the Duchy since 1337. The rest of the land is scattered throughout the South-West:

County	Acreage
Avon	8,501
Cornwall – Mainland	25,946
Isles of Scilly	4,085
Devon	72,599
Dorset	3,598
Gloucestershire	1,590
Greater London	45
Somerset	7,830
Wiltshire	3,795
Glamorgan	709

Inevitably with such a large, dispersed acreage, some of the holdings cover places rich in wildlife, from Maiden Castle in Dorset, near the eastern edge of the estate, to the Isles of Scilly at its seaward, south-western tip. But although the Duchy has a number of important sites, Prince Charles sees conservation extending beyond a few isolated areas, for he considers the general countryside to be just as important. He understands the need for efficient, well run farms, which allow the farmers to make decent livings, but he believes that conservation and farming can get on well together if encouraged and given support. Because of this a number of "demonstration" farms have been established throughout the Duchy, where conservation schemes and good farming can be seen working together. An Advisory Group on Wildlife and Landscape has also been set up to keep a watchful eye on both landscape and habitat, and a similar body has been formed to monitor and advise on the many important archaeological sites on Duchy land.

Prince Charles working on a Duchy
Farm in the winter of 1983.
(The Western Morning News Co. Ltd.)

Despite these developments, Prince Charles does not take a detached view; in the winter of 1983 he worked for a week on one of the Duchy farms, getting both his boots and his hands dirty. He visits the Duchy regularly, and attends some of the meetings of the Advisory Groups. His views on conservation are clear, considered and refreshing:

The Duchy covers some most interesting and beautiful country and we must try to preserve it. One of the justifications for the Duchy as it exists today, is that it gives a wonderful opportunity for enlightened land management – it is not run simply in the interests of the owner, but also in the interests of those who live and work on it. But at the same time we have a duty to take conservation into consideration for we must have a sympathy and a respect for our natural surroundings and for the flora and fauna which share our land. That is why we have created some demonstration farms, where good farming tenants will encourage conservation. We hope that as a result other tenants will see what there is still to be done, for people do notice what their neighbours are doing. I would like to see conservation become fashionable with farmers – once it has become a fashion then the problem is solved. If the Duchy can help to set that fashion, it would make it all very worthwhile

But conservation is important not just for us, but for the future. We must ensure that the countryside remains a beautiful as well as a productive place for our children and our grandchildren.

There is no doubt that at the moment the Duchy of Cornwall is both beautiful and productive; it is in good hands.

Maiden Castle itself forms part of the Dorset Manor of Fordington, to the south of Dorchester. Most of the land owned in Dorset is intensively farmed except for the castle itself and a few water-meadows by the River Frome.

Dorset is a strange county to visit, being largely off the beaten track and containing a jumble of ancient and modern. Those wanting to see the land described by Thomas Hardy will be disappointed, for the small fields with their hedgerows and shocks of corn have, in the main, been replaced by larger fields, which during harvest become dotted with new "big bales"; Hardy would find it difficult to recognise the transformed landscape. Areas of old downland, with their sheep, have also gone, lost to the plough; each year they vanish beneath a sea of wheat.

Small glimpses can still be seen, however; along the Duchy water-meadows cows graze in the tranquillity of an earlier age. Hedges become heavy with blackberries and snipe fly from the ditches where comfrey, great reedmace, water pepper, great hairy willow-herb and black horehound thrive. Salmon continue to run up the river to spawn and bare-footed boys search for crayfish among the stones. But even so the richness of the water-meadows has declined, for once the fields were regularly flooded, through a complex network of ditches and sluices, but now "efficient" drainage schemes help to keep the river strictly between its summer banks. What is left is also at risk, for like so many small attractive towns, Dorchester is being choked by the new twentieth-century flood – powered and polluted by internal combustion. Planners and engineers view the problem simplistically, in terms of traffic flow and feasibility, and see the water-meadows as an ideal site for a relief road. This tarmacadamed scar could also cut into more Duchy land to the west of Dorchester, threatening the remains of an old Roman aqueduct. Not only would that create an important archaeological loss, but some of the native downland flora would go too, for many of the chalk-loving plants associated with Dorset have colonised the ancient remains.

Much chalkland flora can be seen at Maiden Castle itself, where the steep defences dug out in ancient times to protect people, have, through hundreds of years, protected the downland grasses, flowers and butterflies from destruction. It is a most impressive, moving sight, for it is not a castle in the generally accepted term, but old earthworks that turned a whole hill into a fort. The earliest fortifications of Maiden Castle date back 4,000 years when ten to fifteen acres were enclosed behind a double ditch. Expansion took place steadily until during the Iron Age, about 150 BC; the whole forty-seven-acre hilltop was surrounded by a series of excavated ramparts, the largest having a steep face eighty feet high. It

Maiden Castle.

proved no barrier to the Roman legions, however, and was sacked in a single day.

Today it is still a place where its ancient past can be felt and heard in the wind. On the warm September day that I visited, the breeze carried the call of corn buntings and also small blue wings. They were common blue butterflies – several of them a deep violet-blue, being attracted to the flowers of devil's bit scabious and stemless thistles. Harebells and lesser knapweed, or "hard heads", also flowered, giving colour to grasses bleached by a long hot summer. The grazed sward was rich in chalkland plants, squinancywort, quaking grass or "maiden's hair", eyebright, fairy flax, meadow oat, salad burnet, tor grass, bird's-foot trefoil, horseshoe vetch, bee orchid, smooth hawksbeard, sticky mouse ear, wild thyme and many more.

For grassland today it is rich in butterflies, particularly blues, for in addition to the common blue, it has the small blue, the chalkhill blue, and the scarce and still dwindling adonis blue. The marbled white is another butterfly to have survived on the grasses of this island of old downland.

Clouded yellows on clover.

During the summer of 1983 one more striking and attractive butterfly was seen at Maiden Castle – the clouded yellow. It is a beautiful Mediterranean migrant that is unable to survive the British winter. Most years a few butterflies are seen in southern England, but about once in every seven years there is a great eruption and thousands arrive, turning it into a "clouded yellow year". One such year was 1983, for not only were clouded yellows seen at Maiden Castle, but they spread over much of England. Several were seen at Windsor, and many were attracted to fields of lucerne at Sandringham (they are also particularly fond of cultivated fields of clover). I saw my first clouded yellow too, during harvest on our farm; I was driving the tractor and grain trailer to the combine when deep yellow wings, edged in black, fluttered by at speed. By the time I had stopped and jumped down it had gone – lost in the glare of sun scorched stubble.

Leaving Maiden Castle and knowing I was in Thomas Hardy country I followed various signs leading to "Thomas Hardy's Monument"; it was a large tower on a hilltop, with grey squirrels climbing on the brickwork. I could not understand why a writer of Thomas Hardy's stature should require a memorial overlooking the sea. Then I read the inscription – it was Thomas Hardy – Vice-Admiral Sir Thomas Hardy, of "Kiss me Hardy" fame – Nelson's flag-captain during the battle of Trafalgar in 1805.

The coastline of Dorset, Devon and Cornwall is varied and beautiful; with pebble beaches, cliffs, coves, great sweeps of sand and broad estuaries. The wide river mouths and inlets of south Devon and Cornwall are "rias", drowned valleys, caused by the land falling, the sea rising, or a combination of the two; they form long arms of water winding inland between low, rounded hills, with muddy creeks branching from them, and old oak woods often reaching almost to the water's edge. The Duchy owns substantial areas of foreshore and fundus along three of the widest drowned valleys, all important to wildlife, especially in winter – the Kingsbridge estuary, and those of the Tamar and Helford rivers.

The Kingsbridge estuary is a most unusual area of shallow water, stretching from Salcombe to Kingsbridge, a distance of about four miles. Although the estuary runs north-south, long creeks branch off at right angles from it, giving acres of uncovered mud at low tide. In places small cliffs give shelter, and by foot or by boat it is possible to get away into a wilderness of water, rocks and mud. It is a large, shallow extension of the sea, for strangely no major river flows into it, simply a few insignificant streams. It is thought that at one time the estuary formed the outlet of the river Avon, but then streams cutting into softer rocks diverted the river several miles to the west. Because it is sea water and so sheltered, it provides unique conditions and is one of the richest areas for marine biology in the country, with various forms of specialised life, including numerous worms, molluscs and sea-squirts. It has sponges, sea-mats, sea-firs, tube-worms, flat-worms, fan-worms, rag-worms, sea anemones (including the burrowing anemone), starfish, butterfish, brittle-stars, sea-cucumbers, corals (including Devonshire cup coral), sea-gherkin, peppery furrow shells, Baltic tellins, laver spire shells, oysters and many other plants, creatures and algae. The fan-worm is one of the most unusual species; it builds a small mud tube in which to live, and when covered in water, a fan of tentacles extends from the top like a net to obtain minute particles of food.

Because of the estuary's abundant and varied marine life, Colonel George Montagu became extremely interested in its natural history, and after leaving the army and spending some time in Wiltshire, he moved to Kingsbridge. There he studied the worlds of sea, shore and mud, and as a result, in addition to the Montagu's harrier being named after him, there is a Montagu's sea-snail, a Montagu's blenny – a small fish that lives in rock pools and eats acorn barnacles – and Montagu's plated lobster, a green lobster just one and a half inches long. Others, too, find the richness of the sea attractive, and wildfowl, waders and fish all arrive for the comparatively easy feeding.

I walked along miles of the shore in summer, as harvest was about to begin and the holiday season had already started. My first glimpse of wildlife took me by surprise; a pair of shining white bodies, at first entangled, but then a flapping heap of arms and legs. It was evidently the mating season of homo sapiens – the male in panic draped a green towel over the most conspicuous parts of pale, pre-holiday skin and sat bolt upright, looking over the water with a fixed stare; it was obviously some sort of camouflage behaviour – an attempt to merge into the background, or even disappear completely. Perhaps those interested in the fauna and flora of the area should whistle or wear wellington boots with rattling buckles. Tourists, whether clothed or unclothed, are known as "grockles" throughout the region, although "emmets" is also a popular term – the West Country word for "ants".

Mute swans and shelducks had young and a heron fished. There were many shoals of grey mullet close to the shore, far too large for the heron; bass, plaice, mackerel and flounders are among the other fish to be found. Already many curlews were feeding in the mud, as from autumn until the spring, the estuary is an important feeding area for waders of all kinds.

In winter it is a bleak place, with the cold grey mud matching the weather. Well over eighty species of gulls, terns, water birds and waders have been identified, either stopping off briefly on migration, or wintering to take advantage of the plentiful supply of food. There can be up to 2,000 wigeon, 1,000 golden plovers, 700 dunlin, 350 redshank, 350 shelduck, 300 curlew and smaller numbers of many other species. Some call in every winter, while others appear infrequently; visitors include

An immature spotted redshank.

grey plovers, spotted redshank, greenshank, goldeneye, red-breasted mergansers, Bewick's swans, long-tailed ducks and both the bar-tailed and the black-tailed godwits. The godwits are distinctive and attractive birds, and like the avocet the black-tailed godwit has re-established itself as a breeding bird in Britain. Alarmingly for some ornithologists, the name "godwit" comes from two Anglo-Saxon words, "god" – good, and "wihta" – an animal – and literally means "good eating".

About twenty miles along the coast from Kingsbridge, avocets can sometimes be seen, for each year a small flock winters in and around the Tamar estuary. The Tamar is a fine, clean river, with tidal mud flats that stretch up to twelve miles above Plymouth. At low tide food is again plentiful with cockles, rag-worms, lug-worms, sand-hoppers and many more. As a result, curlew, dunlin, golden plovers, knot and redshank are all regularly attracted, in addition to the avocets.

I trudged along the edge of the mud on a freezing February day, yet despite the cold, violets were already flowering in the shelter of a small stone wall. As the tide quickly ebbed, exposing still more glutinous ooze, several curlews stood at the water's edge, with mud clinging to their feet. Finally I saw the avocets, far off on the other side of the river, about thirty of them feeding through their long upturned bills. They showed up clearly through binoculars, as did their unmistakable black and white wing patterns when they briefly flew.

Avocets have wintered on the Tamar for several years; some are continental birds, and it is thought that a few were hatched and ringed at Minsmere, a reserve of the Royal Society for the Protection of Birds, in Suffolk. Although there is a growing tendency for English avocets to remain on the coast throughout the year, most European birds spend their winters well away from the mud of the Tamar, spreading southwards from Brittany to East Africa.

The avocet is Britain's most striking and graceful wader and its return was most welcome. In the early nineteenth century it was wiped out as a breeding bird through drainage, egg collecting (both for eating and oology*) and shooting – for taxidermy, and for their feathers, which were popular for making fishing flies. Recolonisation began in the nineteen forties and their comeback was accelerated by the RSPB's work at Minsmere and Havergate Island. Now as the avocet's summer population steadily increases, so pairs are spreading to Norfolk. Soon they could even start breeding away from special reserves in several parts of East Anglia, where foxes are controlled and disturbance is kept to a minimum. Sandringham is one possible area.

The Tamar is significant for more than its wintering waders, for it also has salmon and sea trout, and during the summer its marshes have many salt-loving plants; sea-purslane, sea aster, sea-lavender and samphire. In

Avocet.

* The correct name for egg collecting as a hobby.

A grey dawn on the Tamar.

Devon and Cornwall samphire is often known as "glasswort", a name derived from the fact that it was once collected in large quantities and burnt to produce soda for glass-making. In some places it is also known as "pickle plant". More importantly, the Tamar, with its unpolluted water and bankside cover, is one of the rivers that help to make the South-West the most important remaining stronghold of the otter in England.

It was in the spring, hoping to see otters by the Tamar, that I experienced one of the most beautiful dawns that I have ever seen. It was a morning with the valley filled by mist; hedgerows swathed in white

and a late frost turning the dew crisp and white; and then the river —
fringed with tasselled reeds, and the sun rising in many shades of
shifting grey. Grey light, grey mist and grey water, all shimmering,
glowing, moving and changing gently, as the day gained in clarity. The
river steamed, rippled and reflected as the light increased; it was like
being part of a landscape painting — remote, detached and locked in time.
The mood changed and the mist melted away, restoring the fresh greens
to the bursting buds and giving depth to the rising bird song. Salmon
fishermen took their nets to the water and far off a curlew called.

Higher, and further inland, the mist still had not cleared, filling the
valleys with banks of soft rolling white, half-hiding the trees and houses
on the hilltops, and making them appear to float beneath a clear blue sky;
it resembled a soothing, surrealistic dream. I wanted to visit more land
owned by the Duchy containing a "butterfly wood", which meant
travelling along narrow country roads with their sides covered with
early spring flowers — primroses, lesser celandines, stitchwort and
violets.

The wood lies on a high bank of the Tamar Valley, adjoining the river
and surrounded by rolling farmland and wooded coombs; it is a 135-acre
haven of sheltered peace and seclusion. There are plantations of conifers,
as well as old indigenous trees — oak, ash, hazel and rowan; it lies around
two small tributary streams, with steep wooded sides to their own small
valleys. They flow parallel to each other, separated by a high ridge
covered with trees, woodland rides and open glades. Key areas for
wildlife are managed by the Cornwall Trust for Nature Conservation and
the Nature Conservancy Council, for it is one of the last British sites of
the heath fritillary butterfly — a beautiful butterfly with dark wings,
copper-brown and black. It loves woodlands with clearings and recently
cut wood, and was once common when valley sides were coppiced to
provide firewood and wood for tools, carts and buildings. Now the
conditions it prefers have become scarce, so the heath fritillary has
suffered a sharp decline, and like several other British butterflies its
future hangs in the balance.

For years the Cornwall Trust has managed part of the wood as a nature
reserve; but then after the Duchy planted an area outside the reserve
with conifers, more heath fritillaries were found among the new trees in
even larger numbers than on the reserve. Instead of simply mourning
the loss, the trees were removed and re-planted elsewhere. As a result
the colony of heath fritillaries is not only surviving but increasing.

It is a practical example of what can happen, with a combination of
sympathy, knowledge and proper concern. Prince Charles is pleased that
the butterflies have been saved:

The Duchy is not in the business of encouraging extinction and it was possible to sacrifice an area of commercial forestry for the heath fritillary. There are only a few areas left where they survive and it was important to make a contribution to their conservation. As I see how wonderful they are, I am becoming increasingly interested in butter-flies – they are like mobile flowers.

But at the same time Prince Charles plays down the importance of what he has done, saying: "It is not something we could afford to do every day." Yet the action was taken, the butterfly has been saved, at least for the present, and the continuing survival of the heath fritillary in Cornwall is an example to all those who own or manage land.

The wood itself is a place of total tranquillity, with the breeze in the branches and the musical flow of the streams and bird song. When the mist had cleared the trees dripped and the grasses shone with liquid crystal. Down by the river, flowers carpeted the ground: wood ane-mones, lesser celandines, marsh marigolds and freshly flowering wild daffodils. Ramsons were also bursting into flower – they made a beauti-ful floor covering, with leaves like those of lily of the valley and balls of small white flowers on slender stems; the overall shape of the plants gives them the country name of "brandy bottles". To bruise or sit among them is to understand how they came to be known most commonly as "stinking lillies", for instead of having a lily-like fragrance to match their appearance, they smell overpoweringly of onions. The tang is so strong that the leaves can be made into a fish sauce, of which Gerard wrote, it "maye very well be eaten in April and Maie with butter, of such as are of a strong constitution, and labouring men".

As the sun grew warmer, survivors of the winter flew – the first butterflies of the year, yellow brimstones in good condition and tattered peacocks. When resting with their wings closed, brimstones look re-markably similar to ivy leaves, and as a result they often hibernate in thick ivy. Wrens, blackbirds, thrushes, robins and a blackcap were singing loudly and the wood reverberated with birdsong. Goldcrests, coal tits and marsh or willow tits were feeding and a treecreeper was busy on an old ash tree. A buzzard drifted out high over the valley to be worried by a ragged gang of about thirty rooks.

By one of the streams, pussy willow shone in the sun and the leaves of bramble and honeysuckle were well forward. Hazel catkins were loose, their usefulness over, and it occurred to me that the wood was ideal for dormice, with both honeysuckle, which they use in their nests, and hazel which provides a much loved food. So far most of the attention in the wood has focused on the butterflies, and whether the dormouse is resident is unknown, although it is found elsewhere in Cornwall. Several nests of harvest mice have been found, however, and conditions in and around the wood are perfect for them too.

By the beginning of June the oaks and ashes had burst into full foliage and below, red campion, herb bennet and herb robert were flowering. The leaves of hart's tongue ferns had unfurled and maidenhair spleenwort grew between stones in an old wall; above, the buzzard still circled, unmolested on this occasion, and from high among oaks came a slowly accelerating melodic trill, for wood warblers also nest in the wood. Along a path much ribwort-plantain grew and on several plants small dark caterpillars were feeding, looking almost exactly like the plantain flowerheads themselves; they were the caterpillars of the heath fritillary. This form of camouflage, or mimicry is one of the great mysteries of nature – the brimstone butterfly and the ivy leaf, the caterpillar of the heath fritillary and the plantain flower, and even the bee orchid and the bee. Which came first? Was one modified by the other? And why have other vulnerable creatures and plants not adopted the same techniques? So far scientists and the theory of evolution do not give complete or convincing answers.

The caterpillars were eating well and numbers were high. Elsewhere their food plant is often cow-wheat, but although that also grows in the wood, they seem to prefer plantain. Under a holly leaf one had already turned into a chrysalis and soon the rest would begin their change, from rather ugly caterpillars, into attractive butterflies. Other butterflies had already completed their mysterious metamorphosis and several pearl bordered fritillaries were flying strongly. Over thirty species of butterfly have been recorded in the wood, including six of the ten British fritillaries, and both the purple and the green hairstreaks.

After only another fortnight, many heath fritillaries were already flying over the land cleared of planted conifers – they were darker and more beautiful than I had expected. There were many of them, showing that the woodland management suited them perfectly. Among grasses were several lesser butterfly orchids with very pale yellow petals. Other orchids have also been found in the wood including the early purple, heath spotted, marsh, fragrant and bird's nest. Other unusual plants are bastard balm, pink purslane, yellow bartsia and the rare, but very ordinary, Cornish bladder-seed. Adjoining the wood the Duchy recently purchased a small grassy field, as it gives the heath fritillaries more space to fly. It is also important in its own right for it has many heath spotted orchids, as well as a population of marsh fritillary butterflies; their caterpillars feed on Devil's bit scabious and various plantains which are plentiful. Like the heath fritillary, numbers of the marsh have fallen steadily, but they have not yet reached the same dangerously low level.

A cuckoo called as a buzzard swung into the small valley to perch in a tree; magpies and jays were searching for food and there was the strong, unmistakable odour of fox. High above, a tree pipit parachuted down to land on the very top of a tall conifer, and below, marsh tits were busy feeding their young in a tiny nest of moss and hair, built into a small

A heath fritillary butterfly on the
Duchy butterfly reserve.

A coal tit and a marsh tit.

natural crevice at the base of an oak. It is easier to tell the difference between a marsh tit and a willow tit during the breeding season — the marsh tit uses a natural hole for its nest, while the willow tit chips out its own hole in decaying wood.

On my return in mid-July the young birds had flown but the buzzards were still busy feeding their young; the fledged chicks had already left the nest in a high oak and were waiting in nearby trees for their parents to bring food. The wood itself was lush with the undergrowth and rides being at their full summer height — tall grasses, clumps of rosebay willow-herb and many foxgloves. At one of the streams a hard shingle bed showed where a ford had once crossed and damselflies flew with dazzling brilliance. They were one of Britain's most attractive damsel-flies, the "beautiful demoiselle"; a damselfly that loves clear, fast-flowing streams with pebble bottoms. One burned with colour as it flew, its rich sheen of emerald green changing with every turn. The colours of the male also seemed to glow through light and shade from deep purple to an incandescent metallic turquoise, that shone with such intensity in sunlight that the colours flowed into its wings. Strangely, as soon as they settled on leaves, the lace-like wings drained back to an ordinary dull brown. Normally the large golden-ringed dragonflies that also droned around the ford, with bodies of gold and black, would have caught the eye and held attention, but they were completely over-shadowed by the beautiful demoiselles. It was a morning of extravagant colours as the brilliant red, white and black of the large scarlet tiger moth flew dizzily in full daylight.

In the large clearing only a few ragged heath fritillaries flew; their brief butterfly lives were almost over, but the eggs ensuring the next generation had already been laid in large clusters on the leaves of the foodplant. They would hatch after a fortnight with the tiny caterpillars hibernating through the winter under lightly woven webs of silk. Enchanter's nightshade and wood sage showed that the open area had once been part of the covered woodland floor.

Along a ride of seeding grasses one of my favourite butterflies fluttered by, with slow almost lethargic wingbeats. The marbled white is a large butterfly of grassland, downland and woodland edges. I first saw it flying in a rich area of grasses and wildflowers on Salisbury Plain and now I always associate it with space and wide open skies. With the marbled white the scientists have again excelled, for although it is a striking black and white, it belongs to a family known collectively as the "browns". It is unusual as well as beautiful; most butterflies lay their eggs carefully on the caterpillars' foodplant, but the female marbled white scatters her eggs at random while flying. The only other British butterfly to rely on such a haphazard method is the ringlet. The wood has ringlets too and one had got things slightly wrong – it was trying to mate with a gatekeeper.

I left the dappled light and dancing wings with regret, for the wood is a unique place and I will always remember it with pleasure; its streams, its trees, the springtime flowers, the buzzards and the butterflies.

Dartmoor overlooks the Tamar valley, and dominates much Duchy land, as well as Devon itself. I first visited the moor for this book immediately after a trip to Balmoral, and by comparison it seemed rather tame and unspectacular, with little notable wildlife. But gradually its mists and moods began to attract, and by the end of a year of regular visits, after much walking and watching, I had come to look forward to its remoteness, its fast-flowing streams, the rolling, rounded moorland and the grey, granite tors.

The tors add an air of ancient mystery to the moor, great natural slabs and mounds of weathered rock that protrude from the high moorland tops of short grazed grass. Man has added to this feeling of antiquity, for Dartmoor has been occupied for at least 8,000 years, and as if to match the old natural altars of granite, early man left stone circles and great "clapper" bridges.

I saw the moor in all its seasons; mist rising in twisted pillars from dark plantations in autumn; the moors and mires locked in the ice of winter; the release of spring, with the gorse blooming, the skylarks singing, and the old grasses almost white in sunlight, looking like the plains of Africa; then full summer, with sheep resting in the shade of an isolated rowan tree and the silhouette of buzzards for ever wheeling over the valleys. At that time too, horse flies bit with monotonous regularity;

I would never want to visit a reserve for a rare horse fly – my spontaneous reaction would speed it into extinction.

The moor itself is a great intrusion of igneous rock that hardened as it cooled into coarse grained granite. It pushed up into softer sedimentary rocks, changing some of them with its heat to form veins of tin, copper, lead, silver and even gold. It was not covered by the great glaciers and ice sheets that helped to shape and carve the rocks of Deeside, but nevertheless it experienced long, low temperatures that cracked and shattered its rocks, contributing to the "clitter fields" that can still be seen today. The jagged edges of exposed rocks were then weathered by wind and water to create the present gently rounded landscape.

It is thought that weathering also helped to form the exposed tors; as the granite cooled it developed joints and lines of weakness that became exaggerated as the weight of rock above them was eroded away. They divided the granite into large rectangular blocks, that on exposure to ground water near the surface were smoothed and rounded by chemical weathering. As a result, although the tors appear as great slabs of rock heaped on top of each other, in fact their shapes and profiles have been eaten and worn away, mainly by water, over thousands of years.

But although the tors give the moor an appearance of wildness, it would be wrong to call Dartmoor a wilderness, for the hand of man has marked it for too long and too clearly. All British landscapes contain the imprint of man and that is why management, conservation and preservation are so important, for they retain, or restore, those areas where richness remains.

At one time Dartmoor was probably largely wooded, with small oaks, stunted by cold and wet. With their removal for fuel, both domestic and for the smelting of tin, came grazing, with livestock, and the moor became an area of grassland and heather. Land improvement and over-grazing have since hit the heather, with cultivated grasses taking over much of the low-lying land and purple moor grass invading the high open moor.

The present Duchy holding of 70,000 acres includes 50,000 of unenclosed moor, subject to common rights; it rises to 2,000 feet and is itself part of the Dartmoor National Park. There are just two places on Duchy land that give an indication of what the moor was once like: Black Tor Copse and Wistman's Wood which are ancient areas of aboriginal oak. They grow on valley sides overlooking moorland streams, with the copse covering a larger area than the wood. They are overlooked by tors, and the combination of old wood and exposed rocks emphasises the great age of the moor.

Each one is attractive and can only be reached by foot, but I prefer Wistman's Wood which is smaller and more compact. It is a remarkable place, that led the Reverend Samuel Ward to write in 1848: "The whole world cannot boast, probably, a greater curiosity in sylvan archaeology than this solitary grove in the Devonshire wilderness." Another clergy-man, Canon Ellacombe, considered it to be: "The most weird and curious wood in England if not in Europe."

The reason the wood remains is possibly caused by the trees having grown in an area of "clitter", where those wanting firewood, or smelting fuel, would have experienced great difficulties in moving timber over the clefts and holes of frost scattered rock. It is still difficult to walk through the wood because of the irregular jumble of plant-covered granite and it would be easy to slip and suffer injury if trying to carry a load. The trees themselves are gnarled, twisted, stunted and spread-eagled, with their trunks and branches covered with luxuriant life. Even when leafless they retain a covering of different greens and browns from the numerous mosses, lichens, liverworts and ferns that thrive in Dartmoor's dampness. During the course of this century twenty-six types of moss, twenty-one liverworts and about seventy lichens have been recorded in the wood. Lichens develop from an intimate part-nership between fungi and algae, and they are very intolerant of air pollution. Their abundance in Devon and Cornwall shows how much of the air in south-west England is still clean.

The shapes, angles and airborne fronds on the branches give the wood a unique and ancient beauty, exaggerated by the damp smell and the trunks themselves which appear to be growing out of solid rock. In places the trunks of rowan and oak grow so tightly together, before splitting away at the top, that one tree appears to have two varieties of leaves and fruit. In this high, harsh land the English name of "mountain ash" seems far more descriptive and appropriate than the Scottish "rowan", as it does in Scotland itself. The oaks are the native "English" or "pedunculate" variety, distinguished from the other indigenous oak, the "sessile", by stalks on the acorns; indeed the word "sessile" means stalkless. The pedunculate oak is most common in southern England, while the sessile oak is more numerous in the north and north-west. Children who grow up in areas of sessile oak miss a small pleasure of childhood, for an empty acorn cup, with stalk, makes an imitation miniature pipe.

The wood was at its most attractive in autumn with the mosses, lichens and ferns still green and the golden light striking the copper of leaves and dying bracken. Acorns had fallen, but the bright orange berries of mountain ash still held. Once ripe they quickly vanished, for fieldfares and redwings arrived on Dartmoor just a few days after I had seen them passing through Balmoral, and they ate the English berries as greedily as the Scottish, regardless of the name. One of the West Country names for the redwing is "wind thrush", for it usually arrives with the winds of late autumn, which help its journey from northern Europe. It is smaller than the fieldfare, but just as attractive, with the typical spotted chest of most members of the thrush family, together

Wren.

The old oaks of Wistman's Wood.

with distinctive rufous-red flanks and underwings, and a white eye-stripe. Two woodcocks were also autumn visitors, flying low between the twisted trunks before dropping down into bracken. The wood has its own resident population of much smaller birds, for wrens appear to be always present, flitting into cracks between moss-covered boulders. For once they match their Latin name of *Troglodytes troglodytes* – ''a cave or hole dweller'', which for most parts of Britain does not suit the bird, its habits or its haunts.

Simply by walking to and from the wood it is possible to sense the flavour of the moor. Crows mobbing buzzards, relentlessly driving them away, and jackdaws tumbling for joy in the air currents of a windy day. In the spring a pair of buzzards tumbled together, actually clutching talons as they flew in their courtship display. It was pleasing to see them so numerous, for with the introduction of myxomatosis in the fifties and the disappearance of West Country rabbits, hundreds of buzzards slowly starved and there were fears for their future. But some struggled on, the rabbits returned, although not in their former numbers, and the buzzard is again a common and welcome sight overhead. On a hot day I saw a strange reversal of habits; a buzzard was hovering over a hill, occasion-ally fluttering its wings, held aloft by a ridge of rising air, while a kestrel was being carried in wide open circles by a thermal, hunting in the usual way of a buzzard.

The remains of moles are regularly found in the nests of buzzards and I have often wondered how a buzzard would set about catching a mole. Once on Dartmoor, and again in a field on a Duchy farm, I saw a buzzard standing next to a group of molehills, and these fleeting glimpses only added to the mystery. Do they wait until they see or hear movement, just underground, before striking, or does the mole actually come to the surface? When crane-flies are emerging in the grass, moles sometimes leave the safety of their subterranean passages, but the two buzzards I saw were studying mole hills well before the crane-fly season.

Around the wood there is moor, mire, bog, and by the stream, in June, oozing areas with so many tiny frogs that each footstep had to be taken with great care. A heron landed and it too seemed as if it had come to find frogs. The common toad is another creature to be found on the moor, as is the palmate newt; it is small, light brown and smooth-skinned, with a spotted pale orange underside. In addition there are common lizards, adders and slow worms, as well as a few grass snakes.

The wet flushes had more than small frogs, for the water squelched through thick layers of sphagnum mosses, together with pennywort, tufted forget-me-nots, pondweed and spearwort – recognised from the buttercup by its pointed spear-like leaves. Among longer grasses and rushes taller plants flowered, foxgloves, ragged robin and marsh thistles.

On higher moor, bog asphodel and tormentil flowered and there were also patches of an attractive little lichen with small erect stems and red tips; the scientific name is *Cladonia floerkeana* – the locals call them "Dartmoor matches". The shorter grasses with small outcrops of rock were also preferred by wheatears, meadow pipits and skylarks. An estimated 20,000 pairs of meadow pipits nest on the moor as well as 15,000 skylarks and over 1,000 wheatears. Apart from the heron, the largest breeding bird is the raven.

All over Dartmoor the streams, bogs, rocks, moors, valleys and plantations of pines give so many varied sights and sounds, that when pieced together, they show the whole moor, its appeal, its wildlife, and its problems. I particularly enjoyed an area of old heather moorland near the Warren Inn; the heather is old, bedraggled and unmanaged, and covers open country, as well as the steep sides of long abandoned tin workings. On a cold February day streams had falls and fingers of hanging ice, and where water oozed from warmer depths, great sheets of ice crept imperceptibly forward. The wind was bitter, whipping up the light covering of powdered snow into small white wisps, and causing ponies to huddle behind walls. As I walked, three grouse burst into reluctant flight; I had heard of red grouse on the moor before, but had never actually seen one.

About fifty pairs nest each year, but they have great problems; the heather, their main source of food, is old and receding, there is disturbance from visitors during the breeding season, and losses occur because of foxes and crows. They are not natives of the area, but were reintroduced before the First World War by the then Prince of Wales, later the Duke of Windsor. One old man who lives on the edge of the moor recalls the arrival of the birds: "There were between forty and fifty pairs in all; some were released at Fernworthy and the others behind the Warren Inn. They came down from Scotland on the passenger train in specially made wooden boxes, divided by partitions for each grouse. They were collected from Moretonhampstead railway station by my father and released in mid-summer. Strict instructions were given to prevent them being shot. They have not had an easy time. During the cold weather of 1947 they flew off the moor and roosted under corn ricks. Since then the moor has changed, there is over-grazing now, with too many black cattle. When I was a boy all the cattle were red." He is a knowledgeable, understanding old man, a "country gentleman", who touches his cap and retains the manners and habits of an earlier time. He is unassuming too, for he said: "Oh no, I don't want my name in a book, that would never do." He, and people like him, are now under more pressure than the Dartmoor grouse, almost obsolete in a brash and more abrasive age; the countryside is a poorer place because of it.

At one time black grouse also bred on the moor, but now only an occasional bird is seen. The last known lek was abandoned in the 1950s, but a pair are thought to have bred in 1968 and two separate sightings were reported in 1978. Because the red grouse were introduced, some people believe that black grouse were also brought in and released, but the old gentleman of the moor disagrees: "When I was a boy, blackcock were around, long before the red grouse arrived. They were genuine wild birds, indigenous to the area, but they gradually died out. Their disappearance is very sad – they were beautiful birds."

Not wanting to disturb the grouse again I dropped down into a small valley out of the wind. Even the shafts of sunlight felt warm as they shone through patches of thin dark cloud. It was comparatively mild and green, with ice dripping and water flowing – in one valley, arctic ice and in the next, melting spring. The warmth and shelter surprised me still more, for clumps of frog spawn were in the stream. Some were white and milky, killed by frost, but others had been protected from the cold by the flowing water. Since frogs disappeared from our farm, due to the local Water Authority draining their spawning pond, I always feel pleased after finding frogs or spawn; it means that "improvements" have not yet improved them into oblivion.

So far the water on the moor is good and salmon and sea trout also spawn in some of the streams, but another elderly man who has spent most of his working life on the moor sees clear warning signs: "Salmon come right up here to breed, but there has been much poaching and disease and their numbers have fallen. I blame the Forestry Commission most of all, for they dig their culverts in such a way that after rain the water simply flushes from the moor. It is made worse too by water draining from the roads. It gouges out the beds, plucking away weed, and there is no depth of water for any length of time, making it difficult for the fish to move upstream. This flushing has also made conditions bad for the brown trout.'' If true, then it seems that lessons from the past have not been learnt, and the future of the otter could be put at risk as well as the salmon.

I returned to the small stream in June, the tadpoles had gone and the edges of the water were white with water crowfoot. Meadow pipits flew and a monotonous call came from a ring ouzel on the hillside. It is a summer visitor and resembles a highland blackbird, with a broad white crescent on its chest, that in sunlight is edged with a rich chestnut-brown. The bird was finally silenced by a squall of cold rain.

It was convenient having the Warren Inn so near, for one of its boasts is that its fire never goes out, although some locals hint otherwise; as a result, in cold weather, whatever the season, it is always warm and welcoming. Inner warmth can be obtained too, as it sells a range of real country wines as well as mead. The Dartmoor Inn is another famous stopping place, just off Duchy land, at Merrivale – its wine list includes dandelion, cowslip, birch, damson and redcurrant; the cowslip gives as much pleasure and happiness as the flower itself.

Vixen Tor lies close to the Dartmoor Inn, again just off Duchy land, but nevertheless it is a most impressive remnant of old rock. It was in late April, at the tor, that I had both a pleasant and a disturbing experience. As I walked over the moorland towards the pile of smooth, divided granite, a small flock of golden plovers flew over fast, flying towards higher ground. Each year a few pairs breed, as well as a few pairs of dunlin, both at the southernmost edge of their range. Dusk was approaching and several new lambs were suckling, their tails wagging enthusiastically. One ewe was wild eyed and worried; it had given birth to twins, but one of its lambs was already dead and it was ignoring the other, leaving it to bleat in hunger and confusion. In the morning both lambs were dead and their eyes had been pecked out by crows. I felt an irrational anger, and can well understand how hill farmers feel when they suffer losses through foxes and crows. Seen as a whole the casualties are few, but emotion, and often the genuine affection of a shepherd for his flock, can magnify the damage and the suffering. Magpies too loiter around dead and dying lambs, and magpies, crows and foxes are all numerous on the moor. The old man who mourned the decline of the salmon believes that all three are increasing because fewer people are interested in game, and the cost of cartridges is so high: ''I have noticed something else too – as their numbers have gone up, so the number of curlews, snipe and golden plovers breeding on the moor have gone down.'' The pressure from predators could also be one of the reasons for the disappearance of the black grouse.

The tor is well named, for one of the great slabs of rock looks exactly like a vixen, crouching or resting. But in addition to Vixen Tor the moor also has Foxtor Mire, a large area of genuine mire, that a fox could cross quite easily, but which can give great problems to a walker. After a heavy shower of summer rain I had to make a long detour, despite many attempts to get over. Where firm ground seemed to be indicated the sphagnum mosses seeped water and my stick broke through into bottomless mud. I have never seen such luxuriant beds of sphagnum, and in addition there were rushes, pond weeds, more bog asphodel, sundew, flowering cotton grass and a clump of heath spotted orchids, all separated by pools and rivulets of black mud and water. In days gone by the ladies of Princetown collected sphagnum; it was washed and dried and used for medical dressings, up to and including the First World War. At that time too the nearby prison, which is also in Duchy ownership, held conscientious objectors, many of whom were well-to-do Quakers.

The use of sphagnum is not as primitive as it seems, for it does have extremely good absorptive properties and it also contains a micro-organism, a species of penicillium, that could actually assist recovery. Indeed some doctors believe that it could have medical uses today in preference to several of the synthetic substances currently preferred.

There is a growing belief that many of our wild plants still hold valuable chemicals that could be of long-term value to man; this takes the importance of conservation beyond aesthetic considerations and the responsibility of man towards the world and the creatures that share it with him, for it means saving renewable natural resources which may be of later medical, industrial or agricultural importance. At the moment one of Britain's largest chemical companies is carrying out tests on bog asphodel, as it is believed that it may be important in the fight against cancer.

One of my favourite places on the moor is a small valley and stream with alders and sallow growing from its banks. When I saw it first, yellow "flags" were flowering and nearby pools held hundreds of tadpoles. Where the stream joined a wider river, the water murmured and rushed over and around stones and boulders. Chaffinches were singing and feeding; they are birds that I have come to associate with Devon. In my own parish the house sparrow is most numerous. In Britain and Ireland as a whole, it has been estimated that there are five million pairs of house sparrows, but seven million pairs of chaffinches.

A redstart flew to perch on a branch and from a group of old pines a green woodpecker called. Most appropriately, a willow warbler sang from an overhanging willow, occasionally flying out after insects. On stepping stones, a grey wagtail also flitted in pursuit of food. A dipper landed on a rock in mid-stream, briefly pausing to "dip"; it is one of the most beautiful and characteristic of moorland birds. Previously I had seen dippers picking up insects from stones, swimming buoyantly on fast

A dipper with a beak full of food for its young.

streams, and at Balmoral I saw one plunge completely in; this one simply walked into the water and disappeared from sight. It was quite astonishing to see, and it is easy to understand why the idea of a dipper walking under water was once ridiculed. It is now generally accepted that the force of water on the bird's back or wings keeps it submerged, until it changes direction and floats up again. Soon it popped to the surface with several water beetles in its beak.

The name "dipper" comes from the bird's habit of bobbing and bowing while standing on rocks. Because of its general shape and manner it is also known as the "water thrush", "water ouzel" and "water blackbird". They nest close to water; the domed nests are usually made from moss and lined with leaves, looking like miniature Masai huts. Deeper water rippled as trout rose after flies and large pond skaters moved easily over the water close to the bank. It was the first time I had noticed them on fast-flowing water.

As summer moved on, so several "beautiful demoiselles" appeared where the stream met the river. In the deeper flow, fish swam quickly away, with surface reflections concealing whether salmon or trout. Flowers gave varied colours to the lush greens by the water; the vivid yellow monkey flower, honeysuckle, sneezewort and betony. Sneezewort did not get its name as a cure for sneezes, instead, smelling the flowers is said to cause them. It did have one medical use, however, for it was once used to ease toothache.

Like the other Royal Estates, Dartmoor held a number of surprises and one of them came as I was walking by the small tributary stream. I looked up just as a peregrine passed almost overhead, which was unusual, for they do not breed on the moor. Pigeons also saw it and scattered in alarm.

The following morning I was up at dawn by another small stream where otters sometimes breed; when otter-hunting took place hounds would often flush three or four during the course of their hunt, but numbers have since declined. One farmer not noted for his conservation leanings, likes otters and is anxious to keep them on his land: "I want fewer 'yellow wellies' around – to prevent the otters being driven away."

The water flowed musically over stones and a family of grey wagtails moved with it, flitting lightly from rock to rock. Fingers of dark weed waved and trailed in the current and many trout darted for cover. Dragonflies were already patrolling their territories and a pair of green woodpeckers with three grown young were feeding on ants below gorse.

In places, large blocks of peat had fallen into the water and there were narrow shallows with shingle and large boulders, as well as wider, deeper pools where the surface was still. Along some sections, the bank created a small overhanging arch, ideal for cover and concealment. The overhangs of one small tributary almost gave it a roof where the stream flowed into dark water – my attention was higher, wandering in the grey sky where a lark was singing. By the far bank there was a sudden splash and a swirl, followed by stillness; it was certainly not a fish, but no more movement came. My lapse in watching the banks had cost me the sight of a mink or an otter. There are many mink on the moor, and in the rivers of Devon, but from the stream's past record, and its nature, it seemed to me that I had just missed seeing my first English otter.

As I returned, adult whinchats were busy, on gorse and broom, singing their grating song and feeding young. Suddenly they were silent and dropped into cover; again I was surprised – above was a small bird of prey flying fast. It saw me and veered away over the moor where it stooped into grass; two meadow pipits rose and fell, it had missed its quarry and flew on its way. The misty light helped to conceal its markings and it could have been a merlin; but from its scimitar wings and accelerating fall it was more probably a hobby; both are occasionally seen in the area. With its departure the whinchats immediately re-appeared and their song resumed.

In addition to the otter, Dartmoor and Duchy land in Cornwall have another animal, the greater horseshoe bat, that has disappeared from many of its former haunts. It is one of Britain's largest and most endangered bats, with a wingspan of fifteen and a half inches. At the turn of the century greater horseshoe bats were still common in southern England, with some colonies numbering several hundred. Their dis-appearance has followed a reduction in insect life through agricultural sprays, which to the bat means less food, and they have also suffered from the disturbance of caving and quarrying, for they are very shy animals. In winter they are particularly fond of caves and derelict mine shafts and passages, where they hibernate in groups, hanging upside down from the ceilings. During the summer they prefer old barns and attics where the females give birth to their young. Around Cornwall and the edges of the moor they are lucky, for there are many disused mines which suit them perfectly; the food supply is still quite plentiful, with large insects such as cockchafers and moths, which they prefer. They can easily fly ten miles to feed and will travel up to thirty miles to get to a roost. This means that bats will regularly fly across the lower parts of the moor and at times may pass right over it.

At one time local authorities in Cornwall were capping mines for safety, but when colonies of bats were found, the work stopped to allow a survey to be undertaken. Those mines with bats were then given grilles, rather than caps, to allow continued access.

The greater horsehose bat is a very peculiar bat, for mating takes place in September, with the females searching out the males, who often lead solitary lives. The sperm is then stored in the uterus until fertilisation occurs in April. The females give birth to single young in June, and they start flying about twenty-two days later.

A few old hay meadows were other elements of the moor that I found appealing; they were natural mixtures of grasses and wild flowers that have remained the same for generations. Sadly only a few are left, for when tenancies are given up, the new tenants often want to "improve" their primitive fields. It is a great pity, and again Prince Charles has set an example. At his Highgrove home, in Gloucestershire, he has kept a small meadow of five acres for wild flowers, which are not cut or grazed until seeding has taken place.

I saw one field in peak bloom, with heath bedstraw, ox-eye daisies, yellow rattle, sheeps sorrel, foxgloves, self heal, tufted vetch and many more; orchids grow too, the heath spotted and the greater butterfly. Just as the chaffinch is the bird of Devon, so the foxglove is the flower – almost to match the number of foxes. The meaning of the name is simple, for foxes were said to wear a flower on each paw, to help them go about their work more silently.

Dartmoor can be a wild and beautiful place, but it is under great pressure and in places over-grazing is obvious. It is simple for those in soft jobs, with annual increments to their assured salaries, to criticise, but moorland farming is far from easy and the farmer's income is often hard earned and still dictated by the weather, disease and political whims. As a result the problem of a decent living for hill farmers, while respecting and preserving the moor, is not easy. The other great difficulty is caused by mass use, for understandably thousands of people want to visit the moor each year. Because of this wildlife is disturbed and numerous feet erode peat and the fragile moorland soils. The Ten Tors walk encourages many to tramp across the moor in the spring, a vital time for golden plovers, grouse and other ground nesting birds. Yet if the event was held in late summer, after the young have flown and the wild flowers and grasses seeded, there would be little cause for concern. Although Dartmoor is a National Park, there may well come a time when limits to access may be required – to safeguard what remains – the moor, its wildlife and the local people. Fortunately both the Duchy of Cornwall and the National Park officers are aware of the problems and are watching them closely.

The most spectacular part of the Duchy is undoubtedly along the coast of North Cornwall where it owns a small amount of land as well as lengths of foreshore. It is where great cliffs and the Atlantic Ocean meet, sometimes in the spectacular fury of onshore gales. At other times the foreshore makes a complete contrast, a quiet world of rock pools, barnacles, sea shells and straggling weed, with oyster-catchers scolding intruders. Caves too have been tunnelled out of the rock by the power of the sea, where in the autumn, grey seals have their young.

High up in the cliffs ravens and peregrines breed; rocky coasts were always a favourite haunt of the peregrine, but during the Second World War many birds were shot, to prevent them killing carrier pigeons, released during times of radio silence. After the war numbers recovered, until by 1956 there were over 650 pairs throughout the country. The unfortunate peregrine was then hit by pesticide sprays and numbers plummeted again, to just sixty-eight known breeding birds. Despite thefts by egg collectors and those illegally wanting young birds for falconry, numbers are slowly improving and a few of the old coastal sites have been re-colonised.

Persecution has been the cause of the raven's demise, but the Cornish coast remains a stronghold. They are large members of the crow family, and are acrobatic fliers for their size; they even manage to loop the loop and fly upside down when courting or playing in the air currents.

They are great scavengers, but will also take eggs, small animals and birds. Inevitably the Reverend Samuel Ward knew all about the feeding habits of the raven: "The raven, in its wild state, is a voracious plunderer. He is not delicate in the choice of his food, but whether his prey be living, or dead and putrid, he greedily falls to; and, after having sufficiently gorged himself, flies to acquaint his companions so that they may participate in the spoil." But once again the reverend gentleman's knowledge was not exhausted, for the raven "may be instructed in the art of fowling like a hawk; and, like a spaniel, he may be taught to fetch and carry. He may indeed be taught to speak like a parrot; and Dr. Goldsmith assures us he can be taught to sing like a man."

The cliff tops are not strictly Duchy land, but they do give superb views of the coast. There too are the typical plants of Cornwall's cliffs and coastal grasslands; sea carrot, spring squill, Cornish gentian, dainty hairy greenweed, burnet rose, silvery hairgrass and numerous others. Unfortunately, in late summer the area looks weary through its annual pounding from innumerable feet and it is worsened by the discarded litter of those unable to appreciate beauty – incredibly somebody had even abandoned an old refrigerator.

Not all the northern coast is high and the Duchy owns sand dunes and foreshore at the estuary of the river Camel. It is another area of importance for wintering birds, because of its acres of glistening mud and sand. In addition to the usual waders it gets visits from a flock of white-fronted geese, and, like the Isles of Scilly, because of its position, it regularly gets birds blown in from America. Most autumns pectoral sandpipers are seen, and other rarities from America have included the lesser yellow legs, the American stint, and the belted kingfisher; ospreys also visit as they move south at the end of each summer. The Camel as a whole is another of Cornwall's river systems that still holds the otter.

Rock dunes lie towards the end of the estuary, next to the local golf course, also in Duchy ownership. Again they have suffered from visitor pressure, and some have been fenced off to allow the vegetation to recover and stabilise the sand. It is easy to see why people find dunes attractive, with their clumps of marram grass and free flowing sand;

A common blue on kidney vetch at Rock dunes.

even now I get the childhood urge to slide and jump, but sadly, all around our coast, dunes are being reduced in size and their flora and fauna damaged. Several times I walked over them however, with the highest dune giving a fine view of the estuary; it is a large natural wind-blown mound of sand made higher by its base, a small intrusion of volcanic rock.

The dunes in winter were cold, with the wind driving in from the sea, but in late spring they were transformed, with soft carpets of flowering kidney vetch, and many common blues seeking nectar. Their wings were a delicate blue, paler than those at Maiden Castle, but just as beautiful. Other flowers, bird's-foot trefoil, red and white valerian, yellow rattle, hop trefoil and ox-eye daisies, were all out of favour, for the butterflies all seemed to prefer the vetch. Dwarf blackthorn bushes had been stunted by the winds, and wild native privet thrived in sheltered valleys of sand; some bushes were covered with the trailing arms of traveller's joy – better known in the autumn as old man's beard because of their fluffy seed heads.

Even in mid-holiday season the dunes were full of life, as well as people. The flowers of kidney vetch had passed, as had most of the common blues, but there was lady's bedstraw, knapweed, eyebright, fading orchids and wild thyme. I always enjoy seeing the deep mauve flowers of wild thyme, for they give hope that the large blue butterfly may one day be reintroduced to Britain. Immediately after hatching the caterpillars eat the flowers, before progressing to the larvae of myrmica ants. Sadly the large blue disappeared from Cornwall, as well as a few secluded valleys of Dartmoor, in the early seventies.

Isolated evening primroses were also flowering on the dunes; a wild flower now grown commercially so that the oil from its seeds can be used in medicine. Like the flowers, the butterflies had changed with the passing of the season, to meadow browns, gatekeepers, small skippers and again, the superb marbled white. Linnets and wrens were busy feeding young as were a pair of stonechats. Magpies and crows varied their meals between the dunes and the sea-shore, as did holiday-makers, pink in the sun.

A favourite spot of mine is north-east of the Camel, at Tintagel; it is also owned by the Duchy but managed by the Department of the Environment under a Guardianship agreement. Some of the adjoining foreshore is also Duchy property. Tintagel itself is known as an "island", but it is still joined to the mainland by a thin high wall of resistant rock, across which a wooden bridge and steps give thousands of annual visitors access. To me, the island, and the view in both directions sums up the appeal of North Cornwall – dark towering cliffs of slate and hard volcanic rocks, the white spray of the ever moving sea, its smell and sound in the air, banks of flowers, and the cry of gulls. Its beauty is made greater by the secrets of its past, for although archaeologists know the origins of its ancient ruins, the romantic legend of King Arthur and Camelot still persists; a writer of graffiti almost agrees, for scratched on a seat was "Auther was here 350 AD." If true, then dyslexia was also at the Round Table.

A few fulmars nest on rock ledges and they can often be seen wheeling effortlessly on the slightest breeze. Jackdaws too love both the ledges and the open chasms of turbulent air where they ride and tumble in the wind; because of their ragged wings and love of flight, a local name for them is "rock choughs", for coastal jackdaws seem to adopt different habits from those inland, with their flight resembling that of the chough. Unfortunately the chough itself became extinct in Cornwall in the late 1960s but can still be seen on the county's coat of arms. Rock doves and feral pigeons are more residents of the cliffs, providing the coastal peregrines with a regular source of food.

It was by way of coincidence that I was at the very end of Tintagel on April 15th, simply sitting and watching, with the blue sea and sky giving a hint of purple to the rocks. By tradition, it is the day that swallows first arrive for the summer, and sure enough a small group of four passed by, over the sea, feeding as they flew. Their springtime journey seems enormous for birds so small, and several early naturalists, including Gilbert White, believed that they hibernated for the winter. The original *Cruden's Complete Concordance to the Old and New Testaments and the Apocrypha*, of 1737, does not quite agree, but makes an equally astonishing claim:

> The swallow is of a black colour, with some spots of a dirt black under her belly; its flight is very unequal, and its sight is very quick. It appears in spring and summer, and goes away in autumn. It is thought that it passes the sea, and withdraws into hotter climates, where it either hides itself in holes in the earth, or even in marshes, and under the water, wherein sometimes great lumps of swallows have been fished up, fixed one to another by the claws and beak; when they are laid in a warm place, they move and recover, though before they seemed to be dead.

The swallows were not the only heralds of true spring, for the buds of sea thrift and sea campion were about to burst into full flower.

Tintagel has abundant cliff-top flowers with the pink of thrift dominating the early summer. Among the most attractive are hottentot fig, English stonecrop, spring squill, sheepsbit scabious, wall pennywort, rocky spurrey, and the common red campion. As usual, where there are flowers, butterflies also appear, and I saw wall browns, small tortoiseshells, a fading painted lady, and to my surprise, in late October, a wind-buffeted small copper. The matted stems of grasses and flowers encourage mice and voles to breed, attracting kestrels to hover high over the cliff tops. In places rabbits graze the grasses low, and they too are sometimes hunted; one day as the ticket-collector stood silently watching the sea a family of stoats passed him on the bridge; they climbed the steps and disappeared on to the island.

Despite the high number of visitors each year, it is still a fascinating and attractive place, and there is always the chance of catching a fleeting glimpse of a peregrine. But above all, the memories of Tintagel are dominated by the sea – its sound, its smell, its ageless mystery and power.

It is the sea that dominates the richest part of the Duchy of Cornwall, for the Isles of Scilly are unique, beautiful and unspoilt, set well into the Atlantic Ocean. They lie twenty-eight miles south-west of Land's End, a collection of 145 low-lying islands and exposed rocks, of which only five are inhabited – St Mary's, Tresco, St Martin's, St Agnes and Bryher; they are separated from each other by shallow sounds and channels, and the sea itself is as full of wildlife as the land. In all, these islands comprise a rare concentration of vibrant life, on, over and around a mere 4,085 acres of island and rock – creating a naturalist's paradise.

They are remnants of hard granite, part of the same volcanic chain as Dartmoor and Bodmin Moor, and they are all that is left of land that is thought to have separated from Cornwall 300,000 years ago. Many islands are simply jagged stumps and pinnacles of bare rock, refuges for sea birds and a danger to those at sea. The most impressive is Men-a-vaur, three close turrets of fissured sea-battered granite, where kittiwakes, puffins, razorbills and guillemots breed. Others are larger and flatter, the biggest being St Mary's, with 1,554 acres, 1,500 inhabitants, and ten miles of road. The total population of all the islands is just under 2,000.

At first sight in summer, the Isles of Scilly are almost overwhelming and I envied the fate of John Biddle, a Unitarian dissenter in 1655; for Cromwell banished him to the Isles for "blasphemy" on an allowance of 100 crowns. Apparently, the unorthodox puritans could not cope with someone even more unorthodox; understandably, Biddle grew to enjoy his banishment and actually wrote letters to Cromwell thanking him.

The islands formed part of the original Duchy in 1337, when the Black Prince, as first Duke of Cornwall, could demand a rent of 6/8d (33½p) or 300 puffins a year. That continued without review until 1570, when the puffins gained reprieve. As Prince Charles says: "Perhaps even by the sixteenth century the Duchy was becoming conservation conscious. Sadly, the Scillies would be hard pushed to count 100 puffins today."

The appeal of the Isles of Scilly is not lost on Prince Charles:

The islands are extremely beautiful, although according to the EEC they make up a "less favoured area". The people are splendid, and

A typical coastal view from the
Isles of Scilly.

several families go back many generations – they are very traditional and conservative. The peace and pace of life in the islands are among its biggest attractions, for there are not too many people. At the moment there is a very precise and delicate balance and we must be sure not to disturb it. That is one of the problems in trying to create more wealth, to ensure that we do not damage what is already there.

It is difficult to manage the wildlife side; but again we want to conserve the islands' richness, without upsetting the islanders. We want to do it together, to set an example and preserve them in the best possible way.

The islands really are places of peace, where the pace of life matches the daily rhythms of nature. It is the deep blue of the sea, streaked with varying shades of marine turquoise that sets off the beauty, giving a background of movement to the white sand, boiling surf and the green tops of those islands with soil. The larger islands have the feeling of the Mediterranean, with boats and bays and small fields hemmed in by high hedges to keep out the wind. It is the wind that cools, but once in a sheltered cove, or hidden by a barrier of protective leaves, the climate is mild, bringing some types of daffodil on flower for Christmas.

I shall always remember my first walk shortly after arrival on St Mary's in early June, simply for the profusion of wild flowers, familiar natives of Britain, as well as exotic escapees from one of the islands' basic industries, the sale of bulbs and flowers; others have arrived too, carried in southerly currents or accidentally on boats.

Even the roadside walls had turned into wild gardens, with the attractive penny-like leaves and spiked flowers of wall pennywort, hottentot fig; the great flowering arrowheads of aeonium, from the Canary Isles, red campion, whistling jacks, fennel, alexanders, three cornered leeks, ivy, lichens and many more, all growing between stones. In places there is even a small ivy leaved toadflax with white flowers; on the mainland the flowers are purple. Then came roads and tracks with lush verges, winding between small fields and familiar trees – their shape, touch and even smell brought back instant and joyous recognition – elms; the tree that once dominated the landscape of my own parish, as they did over large parts of lowland Britain. Only odd "suckers" are left in most of England, as well as a few skeletal remains, constant reminders of what the countryside has lost. Indeed, it is one of my regrets that I failed to see Sandringham and Windsor before the death of their elms. The loss of the elm has been a tragedy, made worse by the knowledge that the arrival of Dutch elm disease came as a result of human carelessness. Its spread was also allowed by government and local authorities, who spent time arguing over the cost of its eradication; rather than actually doing the work required.

Seeing the trees was like meeting old friends, who in the past had shown me my first kestrel's nest, provided welcome shade around the edges of the harvest fields, and had even given me my first pet fox, for it came as a cub from a hole in the trunk of an old elm, at least eight feet from the ground. Fortunately the same south-westerly winds that helped to spread Dutch elm quickly across England, has kept the Scilly elms safe and they are free from disease.

More whistling jacks and three cornered leeks grew in fields and verges. Both are aliens; the three cornered leeks are like small white bluebells with three sided stems and "whistling jacks", from North Africa, are attractive red gladioli, grown originally as garden flowers. Tufted vetch, common vetch and honeysuckle hung their beauty among grasses and scrub and fuschias were also growing wild; the fuchsia is a flowering shrub that in the Scilly Isles grows to well over head height. Insects are fond of its nectar and nearly every summer humming-bird hawk-moths, migratory moths from southern Europe, are attracted to its flowers. They hover in front of each bloom, like miniature humming-birds, to feed, and despite their size, when they migrate they can travel up to 100 miles a day.

The bulb fields were full of "weeds", giving splashes of yellow and pink; the Bermuda buttercup, which is not a true buttercup, and comes from South Africa, pink oxalis, corn marigold, English catchfly, and fumitary. From a distance fumitary is supposed to look like smoke, and its original name *Fumus terrae* means "smoke of the earth". When pulled up its smell is said to resemble smoke and its sap makes the eyes water. To me it looked and smelt like a pleasant trailing plant, that at first glance, resembles a vetch, with delicate pink flowers.

The small hedged areas of bulbs seemed far too small for people to make a living but one old farmer put things in perspective: "We've got eight acres of bulbs on our farm. Do you know how many square inches to the acre? Six million. You can't grow a bulb in every square inch, but when you're working out there, it seems like it." He had a novel explanation for the world's problems: "It's all caused by electricity. People should get up when it gets light and go to bed when it gets dark." His wife had heard it before and was not impressed: "That would make you stay in bed rather a long time during the winter, wouldn't it, dear," she said ruefully. The family can trace its ancestry back to 1630, fishing and farming on the islands.

Most of the windbrake hedges are of New Zealand origin — pittosporum, coprosma and hedge veronica, or "hebes". They have strong wind resisting evergreen leaves, with the same texture as holly and ivy. Because of this the holly blue butterfly now breeds among them, the caterpillars having forsaken most of their traditional food.

A path led over marshy ground, where beds of yellow iris flowered: there was watercress, spearwort, ragged robin, clumps of tussock sedge and the large fronds of royal fern. A frog hopped from beneath long damp grasses — they are not found on all the islands and the toad appears to be completely absent. There were many common birds: thrushes, blackbirds, robins, linnets, hedgesparrows and wrens; most seemed more tame than their relatives on the mainland, with the cuckoo being the one exception. Walking through reeds, sallow and flowering irises, with songbirds singing it was even possible to forget the close proximity of the sea.

I was pleased to see both the wren and the hedge sparrow again. The hedge sparrow, or dunnock, is often overlooked, but in the early spring it sings vigorously, and its song almost matches that of the wren. It is found virtually from one end of Britain to the other, from the Isles of Scilly to the Orkneys, and most places in between. The wren does slightly better, reaching right up into Shetland, and surprisingly it is the most numerous of all our birds, with an estimated ten million pairs in Britain and Ireland — except following a hard winter.

After a small rise, the sea again dominated, with the long inlet of Porth Hellick Bay; it is the place where Rear-Admiral Sir Cloudesley Shovell met his death in 1707, either drowned, or murdered by a local for his rings, as he lay exhausted on the beach. In his flagship, the *Association*, he led the English fleet on to the Western Rocks; four ships were lost and well over a thousand men. The sea all round Scilly is treacherous, and numerous boats have gone down; the hazards are not restricted to those in wooden sailing ships, for it was on the Seven Stones reef in 1967, eight miles north-east of St Martin's, that the 61,000 oil tanker the *Torrey Canyon* went aground, warning the world of the dangers of oil pollution. On St Agnes, Beady Pool gets its name from a much earlier wreck; in the seventeenth century, a Venetian ship carrying a cargo of Dutch beads and trinkets sank, and they are still being washed up in the bay today.

Porth Hellick is a beautiful bay between headlands of dark rock; it has a sandy beach with small reefs of empty shells, a mixture of yellows, browns and creams, some with a touch of purple and others inlaid with mother-of-pearl. The water was clear and clean with waving trails of weed showing some of the luxuriant underwater life. Not to be outdone, on the higher levels of the beach itself were beds of hottentot fig, with succulent green stems and bright yellow flowers. It is another plant, now growing wild, that originated in South Africa and was given its name when the early Europeans of the Cape saw the Hottentots eating the ripe fruit, or "figs", after the flowers had faded. It was introduced into this country as long ago as 1690, and once had the botanical name of Mesembryanthemum; this was much too difficult for the Cornish, who adapted it to "Sally-my-handsome", a name still used today. Elsewhere

Hottentot figs on flower.

on the islands, hottentot figs cascade over walls and rocks giving large carpets of colour; in addition to yellow they have flowers of rose-red, pink and mauve. Other bays on St Mary's show a wide range of salt-loving plants – sea kale, sea beet, sea purslane, prickly saltwort, sea radish and sea spurge. The kale and beet look remarkably similar to the agricultural crops of the same name, and the flower of the sea radish resembles that of the garden radish.

At Old Town Bay, fennel grew thick and high, as did whistling jacks and clumps of tree mallow, with stems as thick as farmyard kale. In the small churchyard the gravestones told brief tragic stories, carved in stone, of young deaths and drownings at sea; but they revealed far more, for they were covered with rich colonies of lichens, showing the high quality of the clean air. In an adjoining bulb field was another escapee, rosy garlic, one of the prettiest alien wild flowers, with stiff upright stems, like those of bolted onions or leeks, with a cluster of long-stalked, fine pink flowers at the top.

By the breaking waves a herring gull stood on a boulder eating a starfish; gulping to accommodate all the arms of the star. No sooner had it succeeded, than it picked a squirming pipe fish from the surface of the sea. It swallowed that too, with difficulty, like wriggling spaghetti – the bird had obviously chosen two extremely uncomfortable titbits.

Beyond bracken, brambles, gorse and red campion was an area of heathland, with rabbit-grazed grass. Among the grasses were lousewort, eyebright, and broad yellow patches of bird's-foot trefoil, which attracted the fast dancing flight of more common blues. Thrift and sea campion thrived facing the sea, and over flat exposed rock the flowers of English stonecrop were beginning to show.

Great rocks like sea-washed tors marked the edge of the land, where waves crashed into granite with flying white spray and the sound of foaming water and surging tide. The headlands stood like ancient sculptures, fashioned, smoothed and polished by the combined efforts of wind, sand, sea and rain, with lichens adding to the appearance of extreme old age. Their lines of stress and weakness had been worn into finely finished curves and hollows, leaving rounded rock on rounded rock, sometimes balanced precariously. Below, the sea continued to pound, and above, a rock pipit parachuted down, for each small pipit, meadow, tree, and rock, has its own favourite haunt.

On a fine dawn the great boulders and monuments of rock seemed to absorb the first bronze rays of the early sun, standing above the dark sea, where each wave and ripple had a single silver side. Increasing light restored life to the landscape, with an early common blue already flying and a cuckoo being chased off by two rock pipits.

The widest blends of colour form at the end of the day, taking in the sky, the sea and the islands. Dusk is best seen from the old Garrison on St Mary's, with its fine stone walls, and bushes of straggling tamarisk.

Unusually for the islands, the walls are free from rock-loving wild flowers, for they are "maintained" by the inappropriately named Department of the Environment, who spray them with weedkiller, to attain an out of place mainland urban tidiness.

Watching the sun set is a fine way to finish a long summer day of flowers, sea and birds; gradually the Atlantic becomes a sheet of glittering gold, and the western sky is fired with an array of reds, pinks and mauves, one colour merging with another, causing the scattered needles of stark rock to stand out with greater harshness. As daylight falters and the sun falls beyond Samson and the furthest isles, so, on a still evening, the scent of honeysuckle hangs at its sweetest.

Among the flowers of the islands, two are found nowhere else in Britain, the dwarf pansy and the early adder's tongue. Each island has its own botanical specialities; on Bryher there are dunes bound tight by a thick covering of marram grass, in complete contrast to the over-used dunes at Rock. They have sea holly too, with leaves similar in shape and sharpness to the holly tree; the dunes on St Martin's are different, higher and looser, with trailing sea bindweed among the grasses. Tresco is the island for escapees, many of them originating from the Tresco Abbey Gardens, one of the best collections of plants in the British Isles. Several species grow outdoors nowhere else in the country, including plants from New Zealand, Burma, Australia and California; astonishingly, they even have outdoor bananas. The island is leased from the Duchy of Cornwall by the Dorrien Smith family, and the plant collection was started by Augustus Smith in 1834. At the northern end of Tresco on the high land overlooking the sea, the flora is entirely natural and indigenous – ling and bell heather, blown by the onshore winds into "waved heath"; ridges of heather with shallow eroded depressions between them.

It is while travelling between islands that the sea birds are first seen; guillemots washing in clouds of sparkling spray, razorbills paddling along the surface into flight and large flocks of shags, at a distance looking completely black. Gulls, kittiwakes, cormorants and small groups of waders can all be seen, as well as some of the most graceful seabirds of all – terns; common, sandwich and the rare roseate. They are delicate slender birds with finely forked tails, and their flight is dainty on white buoyant wings, sometimes skimming the surface to live up to their name of "sea swallows". Often they will pick small fish from the top of the water as they float lightly above it, but more often they will fly higher to hover, before tucking in their wings to plunge headlong at their prey, sometimes travelling several feet below the surface of the water.

They are masters of flight; one day a roseate tern flew by, scratching its head with its foot as it passed, and a common tern juggled with a fish, turning it and catching it in mid-air, in order to swallow. The common tern is the most numerous, white and grey with a black crown and a

Roseate tern incubating eggs.

matching black tip to the end of its dark red beak. It is a noisy bird, nesting on the ground in colonies that erupt with harsh cries of anger and hostile diving flight, when intruders approach too close. Often they nest in dunes near the Abbey Pool on Tresco, where the colony is roped off to prevent too much disturbance from visitors.

It is while there are many birds in the air that the few roseate terns can be seen most easily — their call gives them away, for it is distinctly lower and harsher than that of the common tern. Once the cry has been located, then the other differences become more obvious; from a distance the beak appears to be totally black, its tail streamers are longer than those of other terns and often there is a faint hint of pink on its breast.

Until the arrival of George Montagu, the roseate tern had not been recognised as a separate species, but just as he noticed the differences between harriers, so he was the first to recognise a new tern. It was from his home at Kingsbridge, too, that he realised that the cirl bunting and the yellowhammer were separate species. Today with fine reference books and high-powered binoculars, much is taken for granted; but natural history owes a great debt to the simple observations of people like George Montagu, Thomas Bewick and Gilbert White.

The roseate tern is an elegant bird, but its future in Britain is unsure; disturbance is the main risk in the breeding season, but during the winter it faces more problems. It migrates to the west coast of Africa where it is trapped by small boys with snares and bait. The birds are often eaten, but it is done mainly as a sport, to break monotony, as sea birds form an insignificant part of the local diet. Britain and Ireland attract most of Europe's breeding population, which has fluctuated between 3,500 pairs in the mid-sixties, to 600 pairs in 1977. At the moment about 1,000 are hoped for each summer.

From around 1927 roseate terns were thought to be extinct in Scilly, but then during the Second World War, in 1943, a young serviceman,

Humfrey Wakefield, spent part of his leave from the RAF photographing birds. He set up a hide to photograph common terns at the nest, but in one of the developed pictures he noticed a roseate tern in the background. How long they had been back is not known, but they are thought to have returned in small numbers every summer since. After the War, Humfrey set up permanent home in the Isles of Scilly, on the Garrison, where he now works as a potter, producing articles of the highest quality. Every morning I pour tea from one of his handmade, finely finished teapots: it does not leak or drip, and it is a pleasure to hold and touch.

The other tern, the sandwich, only started breeding among the islands in 1978, and a few continue to do so. It is the easiest of the three terns to identify, being slightly larger with a heavier, yellow-tipped bill. Its most distinctive feature, however, is its black crest on the back of its head. Some birds winter along the west coast of Africa, but others continue down, as far as South Africa, the Indian Ocean and the great rollers off the coast of Natal.

Thrift or "sea pink" on the island of Annet.

A gannet flying overhead.

Puffin.

The local boatmen run special evening boat trips to look at the sea birds. They are knowledgeable, amusing men, proud of their past and resistant to change. Their open boats are long and low and one bore a message accurately reflecting its owner's feelings: "If God had meant us to build fibre-glass boats, he would have grown fibre-glass trees." I went to look at the birds on a fine, clear evening, with John Hicks, whose family has been on the islands for many generations. His accent has the pleasant rolling ring of Devon and Cornwall, and his sun-bleached hair and beard match his profession. The most famous wildlife island is Annet, inhabited only by birds; it is run as a nature reserve by the Nature Conservancy Council, and landings are severely restricted, to prevent damage and disturbance. Even so the island still gives pleasure, for in early summer it is covered with acres of thrift – "sea pink". Throughout Scilly it can be seen, a floating carpet of soft, delicate pink, edged in by rocks and white breaking waves. Its thrift cannot be bettered, with great cushions five feet across, two feet deep, and hundreds of flower heads. It seems almost like a different plant from the small pink flowers protruding from a stone wall or struggling for survival on an exposed rock ledge. Thrift is found all around the coast of Britain, on islands and cliffs, and is so attractive that it can also be found in window boxes and garden rockeries. Apart from "sea pink" its most appropriate names both come from Devon, "pincushion" and "cliff rose".

Although the evening was fine, it was also rough, with a heavy swell and a strong wind. On the outer Western Rocks and the Norrard Rocks, huge waves were breaking, sending great spires of spume and spray, far higher than the islands themselves. As we passed St Agnes, three gannets flew over quite high, clearly looking for fish. Every three wingbeats was followed by an easy, open-winged glide, on a six-foot span; in the sunlight their plumage looked spotless white, making the black tips to their wings seem even blacker. One suddenly pulled in its wings and fell, beak spearing downwards to hit the dark moving water at speed, in a cloud of spray. It caught a fish, swallowed its victim head-first and again took to the air, shaking the water from its wings as it flew. With the great dark troughs between walls of rolling water, higher than the boat, and the strength of the wind, the accuracy of the aerial strike was quite remarkable. The others also met with success, and they continued searching for fish as they moved steadily north-west. At one time gannets bred on the Isles of Scilly, but now the nearest nesting site is the huge colony of Grassholm, off the Pembrokeshire coast. Despite this, solitary birds and small groups regularly pass by or fish in the waters around the islands.

Annet was spectacular, with late sun lighting its beds of thrift and its cliffs half hidden in sheets of silver spray. Puffins swam unconcerned by the swell, and some flew up to their cliff-top nests, made in holes, some of them deserted by rabbits. Unlike puffins in many other areas, the

Scilly puffins seldom seem to land outside their burrows, to stand and pass the time of day with their neighbours, instead they hurry inside. This is probably to reduce the danger from marauding great black-backed gulls. Kittiwakes sat comfortably on their nests of seaweed, built carefully on ledges; they are the most attractive of all our gulls in appearance, behaviour, and in their distinctive cry of "kitteeewake, kitteeewake". The black tips to their wings match their small dark eyes and black legs, and in flight they almost float above the water. They do not scavenge, steal and plunder, like most other members of their family, but live almost entirely on fish.

Where the island met the full force of the sea, on a ridge of pointed rocks, known as the "Haycocks" because of their shape, it was awesome – a cauldron of crashing waves and flying spray whipped higher by the wind; brilliant and diffuse light cut through the mist and reflected from the boiling water; it was a full raging sea, powerful, relentless, and above all, beautiful.

As the light began to fade we turned away, close to where a raft of almost fifty Manx shearwaters quietly floated. They were waiting for darkness, to avoid the black-backed gulls that prey on them when they fly in to take their turns incubating their underground eggs. They are endearing birds and their name comes from their gliding flight, "shearing" the water, just above the waves. At the end of each breeding season they head south; many British birds spend the winter along the coast of South America, while a few may even reach Australia. On the Isles of Scilly, the guillemots, razorbills, puffins and shearwaters are all just surviving at the southern edge of their range.

Every island has an appeal of its own. Annet has its thrift; Tresco its towering headlands; St Martin's, colonies of cliff nesting kittiwakes, and Bryher, wonderful views of the Norrard Rocks – fortresses and turrets of castellated tumbling rock, where great rollers bore in from the Atlantic, to break up in a frenzy of thunder and spray.

My own particular favourite is the uninhabited island of Samson, between St Mary's and Tresco. Two humps of granite, covered with gorse, grasses, bracken, brambles and red campion, and joined by a bar of sand; in all it totals ninety-five and a half acres. Its sand is fine, white and glittering, of the kind that helps to brighten the appearance of the sea, filling it with reflected colours and refracted light. From the top of South Hill the panorama of the islands can be seen – every island and the vivid patchwork of the sea – turquoise, metallic blue and aquamarine. In bright sunlight some shades match the brilliance of a kingfisher in flight and the sun drenched wings of the common blue. Terns often breed, and there is a huge colony of over 2,000 pairs of lesser black-backed gulls. As I walked by they clamoured in anger and hostility, and the rush of wind warned of airborne attack. Flapping wings were joined by screams of abuse and even droppings, fortunately directed with inaccurate aim. One hit me hard with its feet, on the back of my head, almost knocking me over, sending my hat flying and drawing blood. Once away from the nests, what passes for peace in a colony of gulls quickly returned. One unguarded chick was seized by a passing great black-backed gull, and swallowed whole, slowly and with great difficulty. They are large, ruthless gulls and their numbers are controlled, to prevent them from dominating the islands too completely. During the summer they steal eggs and chicks and kill other vulnerable birds. If left unhindered they could pose a threat to the small numbers of shearwaters and puffins. Lesser black-backs are other robbers of eggs and young, and to protect the terns, there is also a case for reducing their numbers. Over recent years they have experienced a population explosion, for they thrive on the discarded filth of man: offal and rubbish at sea and waste-tips on the mainland in Europe and even in Africa during their winter migration.

John Hicks has a simple way of telling a great black-backed gull from a lesser black-backed gull:

> The Greater black-back's back is
> blacker than a Lesser black-back's back,
> because a Lesser black-back's back isn't
> as black as a Greater black-back's back –
> it's lighter.

He claims that if said quickly it is clear and easy to remember.

Despite the raging sea on the outer rocks, one of Samson's bays was quiet and almost still; great trailing coils and strands of weed rippled in gentle movement and a seal's head appeared, resting and watching. The

Seaweed around the shore of Samson.

sea was completely clear showing a confusion of browns and watery
greens. The common names of the "weeds" completely matched their
waving nature – sea bootlaces, tangle, sea belt and thong weed. Rock
pools also held life, ferns, sponges, corals and sea anemones, in shades of
pink, brown, green and dark red. Shells showed the presence of limpets,
whelks, pod-razors and scallops, and the seal indicated that in deeper
water there were plenty of fish. The marine life is among the richest in
Britain, for the sea is clean and unpolluted and a place where waters from
the north and south meet, bringing a great variety of species. Some years
there are invasions of the small "by the wind sailor", which has tentacles
and a sail, and they are followed by purple sea snails, from the equatorial
Atlantic, that feed on them. Sunfish are sometimes seen, as well as an
occasional leatherback turtle.

Further along the shore, boulders and rocks gave way to more sand
where non-breeding turnstones and dunlin fed, at the water's edge, in
fine, full summer plumage. Ringed plovers also searched for food,
moving from pool to pool in short jerky runs, and as their parents
whistled in warning, two fluffy oyster-catcher chicks tried to hide among
a cluster of rocks. Smaller birds were present; stonechats among gorse,
wrens, rock pipits, and on shorter grass, a pair of wheatears. There were
butterflies too, red admirals and speckled woods, far from the woodland
rides they normally prefer. Being so far south, clouded yellows are
frequently seen on the islands and there are also records of the monarch,
possibly arriving on wind assisted passages over the Atlantic.

On Tresco I saw a most unusual butterfly; one of the first meadow
browns of the summer. It was so much brighter than those on the
mainland, an orange-yellow – it looked like a new species. Studies have
shown that not only do the meadow browns of the Isles of Scilly differ
from those on the mainland, they also vary from island to island. There
are several other evolutionary lessons to be learnt from the islands; the
beaks of the blackbirds are almost orange – a deeper shade than those in
the rest of Britain, where they are usually bright yellow; in addition
many house sparrows have reverted to their "weaver" origins and build
in trees; the wood mouse has a conspicuous light stripe, and house mice
live mainly outside. The islands also have their own shrew – the lesser
white-toothed, or Scilly shrew. It occurs nowhere else in the British
Isles, but in the same way as the dwarf pansy, it is found in Brittany.
Some common mainland creatures are absent, however, including the
fox, badger, hedgehog, hare, squirrel, mole, stoat, weasel, snake, newt,
lizard and horse fly.

Even some of the most barren islands have life, and one day I went
with wardens of the Nature Conservancy Council to the Western
Rocks – scattered remnants of bare rock and a place of great danger to
those unaware of the currents and hidden reefs. The NCC boatman is a
native Scillonian and knows the pattern of rocks and tides. I was

Young herring gull.

introduced to him as somebody "looking at Duchy properties". His eyes lit up: "Well if you've got time, come and look at my house, it's very damp."

The jutting rocks were home for cormorants, shags, great black-backed gulls and basking seals. There were a few guillemots and razorbills too, with their attractive young. Incubating shags threatened from beneath the natural arches among boulders, their open beaks showing a brilliant yellow gape. There were hundreds of them, giving an acrid smell to the air, and when first heard, their warning cry is startling, like a long, deep staccato belch. Some eggs had already hatched, with the young scrambling about beneath the rocks; their reptilian past could never be doubted, for they looked like miniature pterodactyls.

At close quarters the shag is remarkably attractive, for it has clear emerald eyes and its dark plumage shines with ever-changing green sheens. They are so numerous that only a few years ago "shag shoots" were held by the local people, both for amusement, and in the mistaken belief that fish stocks would improve as a result. The name shag comes from the Old Norse "skegg", or beard, which was first used to describe the shag's crest, during the breeding season. A few cormorants also breed on the islands in large open nests of sticks and weed.

The sea was flat-calm, but just on the point of dusk the glow of dying flame lit areas of broken cloud in the western sky, embroidering the steel grey water with pools, ripples and reflections of pink. We landed where a storm beach of boulders had been thrown high and dry, and deep down among the crevices and cracks came strange purring hiccoughs – the noise of incubating storm petrels. Several of the smaller islands have no rats, allowing the storm petrels, or "mother Carey's chickens", to breed in large numbers. A small mist net was erected, to allow homeward flying birds to be ringed, for there are still gaps to be filled in the life cycle of this mysterious little bird.

As soon as most of the light had gone they began fluttering in from the sea, with a dainty bat-like flight. They were far smaller and more beautiful than I had imagined – dark, with a vivid white tail bar, and only the size of a chaffinch. I was astonished too at their numbers, and soon half the net was removed to allow the ringer to keep pace with the arrival of the birds.

I have reservations about netting and ringing, but one bird caught was first ringed seventeen years ago, and had clearly been returning to the same island to breed ever since. They fly to land only during the breeding season, and for the rest of the year they stay far out to sea; it is almost beyond understanding how a bird so frail and small can withstand the great Atlantic storms; but the bird and its name are obviously well suited to its life on the ocean. Sometimes it flies and feeds with its feet pattering on the surface of the sea and the name "petrel" comes from "St Peter" after his effort at walking on the Sea of Galilee.

Storm petrel.

On the last day of my summer visit, I went to St Agnes; it is lower than many of the islands, being gently undulating, with fields and tracks where high hedges hold in the heat, and areas of heath go down to the sea. Above, larks sang, and their songs mingled easily with the sounds of the shore. Great rocks and boulders littered the headlands and bays, and again some had long lichens, which if left undisturbed, can live for hundreds of years. On one beach a ringed plover had a shallow scrape holding four eggs, and another bird was picking its way through pink thrift; they made a perfect combination. Ringed plovers no longer breed in Cornwall, but each year there are several nests on Scilly.

A fine day with the sun burning through the sea breeze made the island life of St Agnes seem idyllic. A small cottage just off the main road made it better still for there Suzy bakes and sells homemade cakes. After the bare uninhabited islands of the Western Rocks, it seemed very civilised to pause at midday for a pot of tea and a slice of "Suzy's sensation"; a mixture of plain chocolate, biscuit, fruit and nuts.

At low tide the island of Gugh is joined to St Agnes by a causeway of sand, given the delightful geographical name of a "tombolo". Two back-to-back bays of weaker rock had been eroded away, allowing the sea to break through. It is an island of interest in its own right, with a high heather top and more ancient slabs of exposed rock. Just over the sand bar was a fine clump of sea holly and several yellow horned poppies with paper-like petals. Among thrift were hundreds of six-spotted burnets, attractive day flying moths; some were just emerging from chrysalises and others had found the flowering plants of viper's bugloss.

It seemed a good island for beetles, as two shiny green tiger beetles were mating, in the middle of a path, oblivious to the world. They are aggressive creatures, as are their young, which have large jaws and dig burrows in the ground, up to a foot deep. When a smaller insect such as an ant passes by, it is seized and dragged downwards. They have a selection of eleven types of ant – in Britain as a whole there are over forty. A rose chafer droned by, before settling on heather; it had a light golden gloss to its shining green sheen. The name does not come from the colour, but from its habit of damaging roses.

One of the most peculiar beetles found on the Isles of Scilly is the oil beetle, a large black beetle with a life cycle as remarkable as that of the large blue. The female grows long and fat and if alarmed releases a foul smelling liquid. She lays thousands of eggs in holes and cracks in the ground, which hatch into long legged little larvae. During hot weather they climb on to flowers and a few successfully attach themselves to a particular type of hairy flower bee. Once in the bee's nest, the small oil beetle finds a bee larva still in its cell, eats it, and spends the rest of the summer eating the honey and pollen meant for its victim. By the winter it is a fat legless maggot, and in the spring it emerges as a fully adult oil beetle. Only about one in 5,000 oil beetle larvae reach adulthood.

The islands also have minotaur beetles; they too dig deep burrows, filling them with rabbit droppings or cow dung. The Isles of Scilly have no dog licences, and because of the number of dogs, some of the beetles have expanded their diet. One local man complained bitterly: "It's disgraceful, they don't pay anything for a dog here; I think it should cost three times as much." I could not quite follow his arithmetic; in East Anglia, nothing multiplied by three would still be very cheap. The indigenous insects have been joined by some aliens, probably brought in accidentally on some of the exotic trees and plants; there are spring tails and stick insects from New Zealand, as well as a flat-worm from Australia.

Away from the insects there were rock pipits, hedge sparrows, linnets, and at the edge of the sea, a turnstone. I was surprised to see so many turnstones, for they breed in the arctic tundra. A few common terns had nests among heather and when a male cuckoo ventured too close, to begin its song from a rock, it was mobbed; one tern actually knocked it from its perch and it was hustled away.

Soon after returning over the tombolo to St Agnes for the boat, Gugh became an island again with the waters of the rising tide meeting in turbulent eddies over the sand. But the islands still had one more surprise and pleasure, for halfway back to St Mary's the boatman suddenly shouted "Shark", and cut his engine. We drifted slowly alongside a huge thirty-foot basking shark, almost as long as the boat itself. The way in which the dorsal fin broke the surface looked menacing, but beneath the water the great marbled hulk of its body seemed unconcerned. It briefly slapped at the hull as we drifted too close, but they are harmless creatures, cruising slowly about the oceans, filtering plankton and small shrimps from the sea. I was without my underwater face mask, and so did not join it over the side – it was an excellent excuse.

The Isles of Scilly are attractive at all seasons, but they are particularly interesting in the autumn, when despite their small size, many migrants pass through, moving south; every year rarities also arrive, as a result of bad navigation, or after being blown off course, from eastern Europe, Asia, and America. Other strange creatures follow the birds – "twitchers", hordes of birdwatchers who physically "twitch" at the sound of passing wings, in the excitement and hope of seeing a new bird.

They arrive in the islands by the hundred, greeting each other with a hurried: "What's about then?" before rushing off to the latest rarity. Although they seem to be a strange raggle-taggle army, appearances are deceptive, for they wear expensive coats of oiled cotton, and good quality boots, and most of the binoculars are Zeiss or Leitz. The aim is to add new birds to their "life list", or "year list", and each new species receives a "tick"; over 300 is good, 350 is very good, and 400 is excellent. One factory worker reckoned he spent about forty pounds for every new bird, and the year before, other twitchers had left Scilly early, in a hurry, to fly up to Fair Isle to tick an even rarer rarity, at a cost of well over two hundred pounds.

They seem to hunt in packs, and some spend hours looking out to sea, "sea-watching". At the time of my arrival a black-throated thrush, from Asia or Russia, was the great attraction, and 250 twitchers were aiming telescopes, binoculars and telephoto lenses at a bush from behind a stone wall. Some, in their eagerness to obtain a better view, dislodged stones, but they paid no attention to the damage they were causing. As they watched, a merlin swept overhead – it was ignored: "Common stuff".

The next day it was like a military operation with camouflaged jackets and long lenses travelling at-the-double to the harbour, a Radde's warbler, another vagrant from Asia, was on St Agnes. One twitcher "borrowed" a local's bike, without the owner's consent, to avoid missing a boat. The occupants of three full boats were saturated by a rough sea, but they leapt ashore like invading marines and ran to a small orchard. Three hundred and fifty cramped twitchers had a few trees "staked out"; they formed a solid wall of people, ten deep in places, just standing and watching, and a few more stones were dislodged. Most of them failed to see the little brown bird, and appropriately, according to one bird book, the call of the Radde's warbler is a whistling "twit, twit".

During my week's stay, twitcher rarities to be seen were a wryneck, a red-breasted flycatcher, a scarlet tanager and various warblers including Pallas's and the yellow-browed. I found it all rather sad – an extension of train-spotting, and the behaviour of some did for wildlife and bird-watching what football hooligans do for football. Several were knowledgeable and knew long Latin names, and others called themselves "birders" to give themselves greater respectability, yet their contribution to conservation was not obvious. I enjoy seeing new birds, animals, butterflies and flowers, but watching small, lost, exhausted vagrants, almost certain to die, while standing in groups of hundreds, apparently oblivious to most other aspects of nature, seemed strangely perverse. Some twitchers have extended their twitching to birds at the nest, which for rare birds could be disastrous. The next stage could even be egg-collecting and a few minutes with a twitcher in the summer would give an egg-collector much useful information. Consequently, they have turned a worthwhile branch of natural history into a competitive sport; as one twitcher said: "This is essentially a male thing, akin to hunting and collecting – my life list is 330." The advent of twitching has meant an extension of the islands' holiday season, which is good for the islanders, and individually many of the twitchers are pleasant and likeable; but as so often is the case, once in a group their collective behaviour can become irrational, inconsiderate and offensive.

Away from the twitchers the islands retained their charm; at the water's edge sanderlings ran backwards and forwards with the wash of each wave and there were groups of turnstones and ringed plovers. From

Opposite page: Annet at dusk.

a hide overlooking a fresh water pool, a water rail skulked among reeds and greenshanks and pectoral sandpipers, from America, were probing and prodding their beaks in mud. An osprey glided into a tree, clutching a fish, to feed.

I had hoped to go to the Western Rocks to look for seals, but after a storm the swell was still too high; instead I went with John Hicks to the more sheltered Eastern Isles. From the boat it was possible to see the coast of Cornwall where many of the grey seals breed in caves, but on the Isles of Scilly they give birth to their pups above the high water mark, among rocks and boulders. There are thought to be over 100 around the islands, with about forty pups being born each year. During the winter numbers increase and there is considerable movement between the populations of Cornwall and the Pembrokeshire Islands, which are other areas favoured by seals.

As we approached the outer islands we passed close to a grey phalarope — a delicate little bird, with apparently hardly any fear of man. I had only seen red phalaropes before, breeding in the Shetlands — the grey breeds in Greenland, Siberia and Spitzbergen. With both species the female is the dominant partner, leaving the male to incubate eggs and rear the young. Every autumn some birds pass through the waters of the south-west on their way to their wintering quarters off the west coast of Africa. The name phalarope comes from the Greek for "coot-foot", because of their large strange shaped feet.

Two curlews flew over, with one cry of "curlew", and other ghost-like calls came from a large rocky outcrop — it was the mournful sound of seals. Hearing the soft, distant wailing, it was easy to understand how stories of ghosts and "seal women" became associated with remote islands in the sea. There were about forty seals, some of whom had eased themselves out of the water to bask in the weak sun. The cows were particularly beautiful, with wide doleful eyes, as if bearing great sadness, and several swam close to the boat to look at us enquiringly. The colour variations were wide, from almost black, to mottled white, the same pattern as the foam and restless water. Their calm, while watching, was deceptive, for when startled by sudden movement, they shot off underwater at great speed. A large old bull did not welcome our presence and watched with a mixture of boredom and contempt, before flopping ponderously into the water. We found no pups up in the boulders, although a two-year-old cow still had the light coat of youth as she swam. The recent wild seas had been higher than usual and many newly born young could have been swept away, or pounded against rocks. It is a sad fact that with many wild populations, nature sometimes takes its own very heavy toll. One old boatman was not surprised by our lack of success: "At one time they gave birth to their pups on sandy beaches, above the high water mark. Now for some reason, possibly because of more disturbance, they have them among the rocks; in bad weather they are in more danger there."

Grey phalarope swimming among weed.

A grey seal resting on a ledge.

Red admiral on blackberries.

The next day gales had returned with huge waves. I watched them coming in from the high northern headlands of Tresco; enormous Atlantic rollers, separated by deep dark troughs; they broke far out and rolled in, a thundering line of turquoise sea, surf and wind-whipped wave tops that were blown high and backwards in great sheets and plumes of spray. They rolled on relentlessly as if unable to reduce the momentum of their long ocean journey; where they met rock they crashed in a cauldron of noise and churning water. Those parts of the waves missing the land continued trekking along the narrow sounds, between the islands, leaving trails of foam and troubled water behind them. Out to sea gannets flew, cutting easily into the wind, completely at home in its wildness.

Almost as if to emphasise the contrasts of the islands, as I returned towards the quay I passed through a small valley; its sides gave complete shelter and warmth and a red admiral butterfly fed on over-ripe black-berries. In just a few yards fury had turned into complete peace.

It is the mixture of ancient beauty and simplicity that gives the Isles of Scilly their great attraction, for like so much royal land, they have not been developed for maximum commercial return, and both the islands and their people have been respected. With their clean air, rich wildlife, and surrounding sea, they are like a cluster of old and irreplaceable natural jewels; a collection to be treasured and protected.

The Duchy of Lancaster

Although the Duchy of Lancaster consists of about 50,000 acres, it is even more widely dispersed than the Duchy of Cornwall, with land in Lancashire, Yorkshire, Cheshire, Staffordshire, Derbyshire, Leicestershire, Northamptonshire, Glamorgan and London. Like other royal land, because of its spread and historical continuity it includes areas of great natural beauty and wildlife importance.

The base from which the Duchy grew was established in 1265 when King Henry III gave his younger son, Edmund, estates forfeited or surrendered by rebellious barons, including Simon de Montfort, Earl of Leicester, and later Robert Ferrers, Earl of Derby. The first link with the name Lancaster came in 1267 when Edmund was given the ''county, honor, and castle of Lancaster'', and the title Earl of Lancaster. The Duchy still possesses some of the original land.

As a result of deaths, both natural and un-natural, the title passed to Edmund's grandson Henry, who was then created Duke of Lancaster in 1351, for his ''astonishing deeds of prowess and feats of arms''. The County of Lancaster was made a ''County Palatine'', which gave the Duke certain rights and duties that elsewhere were the prerogative of the King. Because of this he also became the owner of all the foreshore in the county, that had not already been given to others, and was entitled to Treasure Trove.

In 1399 when Henry of Bolingbroke, the Duke of Lancaster, became Henry IV it was laid down that the Duchy of Lancaster be put under its own management and separated from all the other crown lands, for the benefit of succeeding monarchs.

Its size and value declined considerably at the beginning of the seventeenth century because of Charles I's need to raise money, and at the Restoration, most of the remainder was returned to Charles II and it has been the Sovereign's private estate ever since, with the net revenues going into the "Privy Purse". The Queen still receives this income today "in right of her Duchy", and in Lancashire she is toasted as "The Queen, Duke of Lancaster"; strict genealogists would disagree with the correctness of this term, and Prince Philip is certainly not the Duchess.

Henry IV found it impossible to run the Duchy personally because of his onerous duties and responsibilities as Monarch. Consequently he appointed a Chancellor to administer the estates for him; but for the last two hundred years the Chancellor of the Duchy of Lancaster has been a member of the Government, often inside the Cabinet. Through his, or her, ancient duties, the Chancellor still appoints justices of the peace for Lancashire, Merseyside and Greater Manchester, with the Queen herself appointing the High Sherriffs of the three counties, without reference to the Privy Council.

In a similar way to the Duchy of Cornwall, the size and shape of the Duchy of Lancaster continues to change, with land bought and sold to suit the requirements of the various estates. For the ease of management the land has been divided into four "Surveys", for Lancashire, Yorkshire, Crewe and the South, with each Survey being run by a resident "Surveyor of Lands". The South Survey has little of wildlife interest, but the other three all have important and surprising features, and each Surveyor of Lands takes an active interest in his region.

The Lancashire Survey retains areas of 1267 land, with some still being within the old county town of Lancaster. Resulting from its special status of 1351, it has great tracts of foreshore in the estuaries of the Ribble, Mersey and Morecambe Bay, which give wildlife sights that are among the most spectacular in Europe. All three areas are of great importance to wintering waders and wildfowl with Morecambe Bay containing as many as 250,000 individual wading birds at its peak, nearly 100,000 more than any other British estuary. The Ribble comes behind the Wash and the Cheshire/Clwyd Dee in importance, with about 120,000 birds. The Mersey comes fourteenth with up to 50,000 waders; in addition it holds 60,000 gulls and as many as 38,000 ducks.

The greatest areas of Duchy foreshore are to be found in the Bay. It is a low-lying part of the Lancashire coastline, with numerous inlets and creeks, made into a large basin by the intrusion of Cumbria. Five rivers flow into this long, wide, natural bay, the Lune, Wyre, Keer, Kent and Leven, and they, together with the work of the tides and the sea have built up a vast, changing world of sand and silt, that at the lowest tides stretches over 120 square miles. From the sea looking inland it is beautiful, for the bay is set within a backcloth of high hills belonging to the Lake District and the Forest of Bowland.

I first saw the bay in high summer, virtually deserted, shimmering in the heat, with the sea almost lost to view. A herring gull stood listlessly on one leg and two curlews fed at a shallow pool. But in late winter it had changed, to dull greys and browns, with the sea merging with the mist. The sand was rippled and in places glistening with moisture where shelducks searched for food; at the edge of the sea were lines of birds, thousands of them in all – dunlin, knot, bar-tailed godwits, redshank and curlew.

Peak numbers for individual species can be 100,000 knot, 50,000 dunlin, 45,000 oyster-catchers, 14,000 curlew, 12,000 redshank, and 7,000 bar-tailed godwits. In addition there are usually ringed plovers, turnstones, sanderlings, golden plovers and grey plovers as well as birds that only pass through on passage, such as curlew, sandpipers, little stints, whimbrel and greenshank. It is when high tides push these thousands of birds on to small ridges, banks and beaches of sand that the most astonishing sights can be observed, for similar masses will not be seen anywhere else around the coast of Britain.

Wintering wildfowl also frequent the estuary, with a mixture of sea ducks, diving for their food, and others that fly inland to feed in the fields and marshes. They include wigeon, pintail, teal, shoveler, scaup, golden-eye, common scoter, and eider, with occasional visits from long-tailed ducks and velvet scoters. There are often over 1,000 pintails and the drake is among the most handsome and easily identified of wildfowl, with a dark chocolate brown head above a clean white breast, and a distinctive "pin tail", often more than eight inches long. Because of its long tail, in Dorset it is known as the "sea pheasant", but in northern England it is called "thin neck"; from a distance the dark head on the light neck does make it appear to be thin, but overall it only adds to the duck's elegance. The common scoter is black and far more squat, however, and is a true sea-going duck. I am always pleased to see it, for it was a drake seen at close quarters, as a small boy, that helped show me the great appeal of birds. It arrived exhausted on a neighbour's lawn, blown inland by gales, and we restored it back to health with cups full of Scots Porridge Oats; for a northern duck it seemed most appropriate. The total winter population of shelducks exceeds 5,000; several pairs breed in the area during the summer, but unlike those at the Wash, most of the adults leave in late June and July to moult, possibly on the German coast. The return journey begins towards the end of September.

Geese too roost in the bay and well over 1,000 pink-footed stay during the winter; often numbers will increase to 4,000 with even more pausing as the migration begins. Three to four hundred greylags are usually present as well, forming the largest flock of genuinely wild greylags in England. A few white-fronted geese also frequent the area as well as occasional brent and barnacle geese.

During the course of a year, all the familiar gulls visit the bay – herring, black-headed, common, little, lesser black-backed and great black-backed, as well as irregular winter visits from glaucus and Iceland gulls. The summer sees an influx of terns, feeding on sand eels just off the shore, and several pairs breed; the common and sandwich terns are the most numerous, with smaller numbers of little and arctic. Cormorants, divers, red-breasted mergansers and herons, are still more that feed on the bay's rich harvest. Occasionally signs of otters and foxes are seen on the foreshore and peregrine falcons hunt silently over the great flocks of waders; they drift in from their nearby stronghold of the Lake District.

A walk on to the exposed silt and sand quickly reveals a surprising new and densely populated world, and it is immediately clear how so many birds can find food. The higher sand content of the shore makes it far firmer than the mud of Salcombe and the Wash, but the casts, holes and signs of disturbance show the abundant life. In fact the estuary is three times more fertile than top quality farm land because of all the nutrients carried in by the rivers and the sea.

In the wetter areas there are thousands of marine snails, which average about 3,000 per square yard. The smaller waders love them, as do shelducks, sieving them busily with their large scarlet bills; the snails are so small that it must take thousands to satisfy such a large duck. The Baltic tellin, a small shellfish with a beautiful rose-pink shell, averages in the region of 4,000 a square yard; the small tellins are taken by knot, while the larger ones are loved by oyster-catchers. At one time the oyster-catchers fed exclusively in the bay, but during the bad winter of 1962–3 they began searching inland. They have continued that habit, feeding on worms, but they use Morecambe Bay as well, to get the best of both worlds.

Curlew.

Most waders eat sandhoppers that live in small U-shaped burrows, 6,000 to the square yard. In addition there are mussels, a few cockles and various other molluscs and crustaceans that bolster the food supply still more. At the same time tens of thousands of worm casts reveal the presence of lug worms; rag worms are also quite plentiful, but they leave no tell-tale heaps of sand. The two larger worms live at greater depths, beyond the reach of knot, dunlin and redshank; instead they fall prey to the long curved beak of the curlew, and the slightly up-turned slender bill of the bar-tailed godwit.

As I walked over countless thousands of the sand's hidden residents, two huge flocks of knot flew in the distance; they resembled clouds of locusts wheeling and turning through the air in total unison, before flying down to resume feeding. They are pleasing little birds and soon they would be moving up to Greenland to breed, stopping briefly at Iceland on the way to feed and rest. The name "knot" is said to come from "Canute". They were known as King Canute's birds because of the way they feed along the sea shore, running backwards and forwards with the waves.

The name of the turnstone is much more simple and appropriate, but it

Turnstone.

Corn marigolds near Winmarleigh
Moss.

turns over not only stones, but also shells and weed, looking for insects and shrimps. A few mingled with other birds and they too would soon be heading north, to nest in tussocks and bare rock in the high arctic. Dunlin flew, several hundred of them, again twisting and turning together, first showing the light of their undersides and then their darker backs.

Near oyster-catcher droppings were small heaps of shattered mussel shells, having been passed right through the birds, or brought up in the same way that owls bring up pellets of indigestible material. A large flock of golden plovers rested at a shallow pool, a few already getting their summer plumage. Suddenly they flew, fast and high, before plunging down, and then straight up again; one minute they flew as a tight ball of birds, the next, strung out like long wisps of wind blown smoke, still in perfect unity, and holding their symmetry around the edges; it was like watching a newly formed cloud being pulled, sucked and pushed by the wind and eddies of restless air, at many times normal speed. Unlike a true cloud, the plovers swooped down again, as one, to settle in a field of grass.

At a creek, goldeneye were swimming and diving and the afternoon ended in a perfect way, with hundreds of pink-footed geese wheeling and calling in the air. A few made for the bay to roost, while most of the birds swung round to glide down into grass fields to graze. Now, whenever anybody mentions to me the beauties of Morecambe Bay, I shall not think of summer beauty queens, looking absurd in high-heeled shoes and bathing costumes, but clouds of waders, worms and flying geese.

Until quite recently a plan was being mooted to erect a barrage in the bay to store fresh water for the great industrial conurbations of the area. Such a scheme would have been disastrous for the wintering birds; fortunately, for the present, it has been dropped. In any case it would be far more sensible, and cheaper, to use the fresh water already available, more wisely and sparingly.

Some of the farmland just south of the bay is owned by the Duchy and one of the farmers gets much pleasure from the geese: "I love to see them; I grow no winter corn and they do no damage. Sometimes the fields are black with them. Even if you grow winter wheat, they only do harm in very wet weather because of the size of their big feet – they press the plants down into the water."

In July I arrived at his farmyard to walk to Winmarleigh Moss, which adjoins his fields and is in Duchy ownership. "I don't know about wild-life," he said, "but as you go down there mind you don't get dazzled by the corn marigolds." In many parts of the country the old corn-field flowers have almost disappeared – the cornflower, the corncockle and even the field scabious, but in Lancashire the corn marigold was surviv-ing too well. The fields and ditches were gold with them, as the cold wet spring had interfered with land work and spraying. Indeed, when I visited the Moss in May, apart from lapwings displaying and meadow pipits mobbing cuckoos, it had been like winter. Seeing wild flowers in large numbers is usually a pleasure, but so many corn marigolds in the farmer's spring barley would clearly and significantly affect his yield – a bad spring was being turned into a disappointing summer.

Winmarleigh Moss itself covers just over 147 acres, with almost all of it belonging to the Duchy. Technically it is an area of "lowland acid peat" – "a raised bog"; altogether there are 51,000 acres in Lancashire, most of which have been reclaimed for arable agriculture, and the process of improvement and reclamation is continuing. Winmarleigh is impor-tant, for although the drainage systems of the surrounding fields have made it drier than it would otherwise be, there are no plans to "improve" it, and it remains a relic of old Lancashire.

A "raised bog" forms in a natural basin where the soil becomes waterlogged. Gradually it fills up with plant remains to form peat, and at Winmarleigh the peat contains reeds, cotton grass, heather, birch, alder, oak and sphagnum mosses. Once the basin is full, the sphagnum continues to grow, above the water level creating a "raised bog".

Winmarleigh is flat and difficult to walk over, being spongy, with deep heather, purple moor grass and plenty of sphagnum. It creates ideal cover for voles and mice and the area is regularly hunted by kestrels, little owls and barn owls, that all breed in the nearby woodland. Sparrow-hawks too hunt, at all seasons, for there are plenty of meadow pipits, yellowhammers, linnets and reed buntings. In winter they are often joined by short-eared owls, merlins and hen harriers.

The dampness and thick vegetation is also ideal for snipe, lapwings, curlew and redshank, and they regularly rear young successfully, despite the presence of foxes. Several areas of birch scrub are encroaching on to the moss, but shelducks find them ideal for their nests, well away from the sea.

The seeding heads of hare's-tail cotton-grass were being combed out by the wind, with just a single white tuft on each slender stem. Pools of pink rosebay willow-herb attracted bees and their working hum could be heard well away from the flowers. The bitter-sweet scent of bog myrtle mingled with the damper smells of heather and old bog, and there were small clumps of flowering bog rosemary – their flowers looking exactly like small, pale pink berries.

Many meadow brown butterflies flopped lethargically; the male is much darker than the female, and the early naturalists decided that they were different species; seeing them together, it is easy to understand their mistake. Winmarleigh is also an important site for the large heath, a bog loving northern butterfly that is in general decline elsewhere, because of drainage and the development of land. During the summer of 1983 Winmarleigh and Morecambe Bay received large numbers of clouded yellows – a rare event so far north.

Another insect very local in the north and Midlands is the black darter dragonfly, which has long been established on the bog. The common darter is also found in good numbers, as well as the azure, large red and blue-tailed damselflies, and the brown and common hawker dragonflies. The bush cricket is another inhabitant: it is extremely rare in the north of England as a whole.

Day flying moths danced frenetically in the air and about 100 species of moth have been recorded. Again some have beautifully descriptive names such as the common lutestring, flame shoulder and the sad sounding, neglected rustic. The Mother Shipton actually has descriptive wings, for the pattern is supposed to resemble the facial profile of old Mother Shipton, the Yorkshire witch. Unfortunately, at times the descriptive powers of lepidopterists become repetitive, for Winmarleigh Moss has the least yellow underwing, the large yellow underwing, the beautiful yellow underwing and the lesser broad-bordered yellow underwing. Several of the moths are rare – the pebble hook tip, Manchester treble bar, purple bordered gold and the grass wave. Again as befitting royal land there are varieties of "ermines" and "emeralds", and the common footman is present once more. There are also a number of carpet moths including the common, green, flame and the dark-barred twin-spot; in the moth world there appears to be no red carpet, only a "red-green" carpet.

As I prepared to return waist deep in ditch-side corn marigolds, another male reed bunting perched at the top of a bramble bush, singing his chirping song and flicking his tail. They are handsome birds, with

A male tufted duck.

chestnut-brown wings and a black head and throat divided by a streak of vivid white; it has the appearance of a jaunty old fashioned country gentleman, with a dark moustache above a white-winged collar. It is another on the catalogue of once familiar birds that have recently ceased to breed in my own parish.

As it divides Lancashire, the M6 motorway cuts through countryside and conurbation alike, a harsh trail of noise, fumes and speed. Winmarleigh lies to the west, but just to the east is another small area of Duchy land of great interest, 100 acres, where deposits of gravel have been gouged from the old flood plain of the river Wyre. Gravel is still being dug next to the river, but exhausted pits have been left holding water. Their edges have been planted with trees and shrubs and already wild bird populations have moved in; for gravel extraction is one of the few industrial activities to benefit wildlife.

The resident and visiting bird populations of gravel pits have sparked off a natural history interest in many people, and their simple and maturing charm should never be under-rated. My early days included visits to gravel pits next to the old Cambridge sewage farm – giving me my first views of tufted ducks and great crested grebes, two birds which still give me much pleasure. Both may be found in the Duchy gravel pits.

The new lakes are already creating interest, and as I walked along a roadway between two great pools, the driver of a gravel truck halted after seeing my binoculars: "Do you know about birds? The other day one got up – it was green with a bright red head and a flight that went up and down. It was a bonny bird." He had seen his first green woodpecker, and both green woodpeckers and lesser spotted woodpeckers breed in the old trees on the site. He was pleased with his discovery: "There are lots of good birds here – down there an old coot's sitting on eggs."

He resumed his work and roared off; he was right – a coot was incubating eggs on her nest of reeds. They are argumentative birds, and because they are so common and aggressive, their appearance is often ignored. But they are most unusual, with red eyes and a large white shield above the beak. The feet are enormous; olive green, with long lobed toes to help swimming and diving. It is strange that a bird so dainty and different as the phalarope, should have feet so similar.

I enjoyed seeing tufted duck again, and the pits are already the second most important breeding site in Lancashire. Before the middle of the nineteenth century they were rare visitors to Britain, now they are Britain's most common diving duck, diving to feed on submerged water plants, insects, frogs and small fish. Their arrival and spread came with the construction of reservoirs, ornamental ponds and lakes, and the increased use of gravel. They are easily recognised, being dark with bright white flanks and a prominent feathery tuft. In sunlight the head has a fine purple sheen and both the duck and drake have conspicuous golden eyes. Perhaps "golden-eye" would make a more suitable name,

Sedge warbler – another bird expected to breed at the pits as the vegetation increases.

to include the more sombre female. Real goldeneyes visit the pits in winter; they too have eyes the colour of gold, but the most distinctive feature of the drake is the white spot below each eye. ''White spot'' would be more appropriate, or, because of its black and white plumage, ''pied wigeon'', which is one of its local names. Among other birds to have bred around the river and pits are the dabchick, dipper, curlew, redshank, Canada goose, ringed plover, oyster-catcher, grey wagtail, sand martin and sedge warbler.

There were several large broods of Canada geese, mallards and tufted on the day of my visit, and an oyster-catcher piped in warning, but any young remained well hidden. During the summer of 1983 a goosander also bred for the first time, and more arrive in the winter; it shows that the bird's steady spread southwards is continuing.

From autumn onwards the population of the pits increases during the cold weather, with the appearance of wigeon, shoveler, teal and pochard, and even three green sandpipers stayed one winter; for a wader the green sandpiper is unusual, as it usually nests above the ground, in trees, in northern Europe and Scandinavia. Over 100 species have been seen at the pits, including the kingfisher, little ringed plover, black tern, yellow wagtail and greenshank. Birds are not the only ones to benefit, for the brilliant yellow monkey flower has already established itself at the water's edge. It was a wild flower that caught the eye of travellers in Unalaska Island off the coast of Alaska, and it was then introduced into British gardens. It escaped and quickly spread along the wet banks of streams and water courses, which provide it with ideal conditions. On the island of its natural home it rains over 250 days a year, and so it has added colour to some of our wettest areas. In many instances it has survived drainage with greater tenacity than our own native wild flowers.

The name "monkey flower" does not do justice to its appearance, for it is said to resemble a grinning monkey-like face. Part of the plant's success has been caused by its efficient method of pollination. When a bee's tongue forces its way into the flower, seeking nectar, it has to push its way past the open stigma (the female part of the flower), which removes any pollen, and then closes. The tongue proceeds to the anthers (the male parts), where fresh pollen is dusted on to it. With the stigma still closed, the tongue and new pollen are withdrawn, to be carried to the next flower. In the absence of farm sprays, a few cowslips have also established themselves on the site, and conditions for the whole area look promising; when gravel extraction ceases, the mixture of pits, river and trees will become an increasingly important wildlife haven.

Further west still, the Forest of Bowland appears as a great block of dark, high land – a large plateau with steeply falling sides. The approach is along winding country roads, with small fields, stone walls and over-hanging trees. The visual warmth of small villages, farms and fields ends abruptly with open moor – heather clad hills and the call of grouse. As I approached for the first time in the spring, I stopped, for the mass of moorland seemed to be alive with grouse – the laughing, chuckling calls and the display flights of the cocks; they were doing far better than the birds of Dartmoor and Lochnagar.

The road wound up into the high moorland before dropping into a steep-sided valley by a boulder-strewn stream. It is a curious landscape – wild, yet gentle, with rounded hills and ridges, holding green valleys sprinkled with beech, mountain ash, sycamore and alder; it lacks the ruggedness of land dominated by crags and bare rock. The stream flowed into the River Hodder, where it meandered through fields of grass and sheep, with its valley floor spreading to sides that climbed to bracken and high heather; a few blocks of pines did not intrude unduly, but they confirmed the man-made nature of the scene.

It is along the Hodder valley, with river, meadow, woodland and moor, that the Duchy owns 5,500 acres; an unusual blend of highland and lowland, stretching from beyond Dunsop Bridge – Staple Oak Fell and Beatrix Fell, to well below Whitewell. The whole area of Bowland Forest covers over 310 square miles and was created an "Area of Outstanding Natural Beauty" in 1964. The Duchy's comparatively small holding of fell and valley is one of the most attractive parts of the "Forest".

Like most almost treeless "forests", Bowland once had much natural woodland, with deer, wild boar and wild cattle, making it ideal for hunting and the attractions of the "chase". The name of nearby Wolf Fell suggests that it once had even wilder residents. Deafforestation and farming gradually changed the landscape and the larger animals disappeared; the last fallow and red deer were killed at the beginning of the nineteenth century. But the new "forest" has its appeal, although its description as, "An Area of Great Natural Beauty" is not strictly true; it does contain great beauty, but it is not "natural", although it has rich veins of wildlife running through it.

The river is one of the richest veins and from a high fell-side in sunlight its reflecting surface winds like a flowing thread of silver. It is from high up too, that the valley takes on the appearance of a great "trough" that has cut its way into moorland, to be widened, smoothed and rounded by ice, which in its turn left a series of unusual ridges and knolls. Wind-bent bushes of hawthorn and trees of beech showed the strength of the prevailing wind, and a sudden spattering of ice cold rain reminded me of the harshness gained with height. The bubbling call of a curlew accompanied its gliding flight, and a meadow pipit parachuted down as if to emphasise the presence of moorland birds. Grass and heather rise to well over 1,000 feet; and other familiar birds also nest in the "forest" – dunlin, golden plovers, ring ouzels and short-eared owls. Whirring wingbeats sent a grouse gliding low, and at times other slower, silent wings carry talons to quarter the heather.

It was warm down in the valley, sheltered from the wind, with shallow water flowing fast over large pebbles and between small boulders; marsh marigolds grew in profusion, much larger than the flowers at Balmoral, but smaller than those of the Sandringham water-meadows. A plant missing at Sandringham was growing in abundance, however: female butterbur, with long bending stems and seeding heads.

Along the bank, beech roots had been washed free of soil by the river in spate, making ideal cover for otters. Sadly the Forest of Bowland is another place where otters are now seldom seen, as mink increase. Dippers and common sandpipers live well and perching kingfishers are often reflected in the clear pools. Red-breasted mergansers successfully rear their chicks in the fast swirling water and goosanders also breed. The river is well stocked with natural, native fish, including salmon, sea trout and brown trout.

The floor of one wooded river bank had a carpet of wood anemones, with feathery leaves and soft white flowers on frail, slender stems. It is a delightful flower that heralds the warmer days of summer; but its appearance often coincides with a brief return of cold winter wind – giving it the widely used name of "windflower". In damp weather the flowers close and droop, with the shape inviting more country names including "granny's nightcap" and "lady's milkcans". Another name which well suits the upright open flowers is "milkmaids". Once more John Parkinson caught their charm exactly:

> The anemones or Windeflowers are so full
> of variety and so dainty, so pleasant and so
> delightsome flowers, that the sight of them doth
> enforce an ernest longing desire in the minde of
> any one to be a possessour of some of them at least.

The best sight of them remains the natural one – on woodland floors and the banks of rivers, streams and country roads.

Along the roadsides were large clumps of white flowers above dense green leaves – it was like cow parsley, but with firmer, fuller flower heads. I picked a stem and my hands immediately took on a strong pleasant smell, which as the plant dried was like a mixture of newly made hay and aniseed. It was a plant new to me – sweet cicely – which is thought to be another old introduction to herb gardens; again it is a plant that has gone wild, flourishing in the higher and wetter parts of northern Britain. In the Lake District it has the name of "sweet bracken" and was used not only in cooking, but also as a polish for oak panels, for it made the wood "receive a fine polish and agreeable scent". Gerard considered that the raw leaves in salad, or the roots boiled with oil, pepper and vinegar, made an excellent "pick-me-up". If eaten by old people who were "dull and without courage", he claimed that it increased their "lust and strength".

In mid-July, the moors and meadows were at their most benevolent. Quiet, peaceful, hot and half hidden in a haze that gave the hills an even greater softness. The Hodder was low in water, and sea trout idled in its soothing, gentle flow. June, July and August are the main months when they move upstream to spawn. They are the same species as the brown trout, but a deep inner urge sends them down to the sea in the same way as the salmon. Perhaps the movement started in rivers where fresh water food became scarce and a pattern was established that genetics have reinforced from one generation to the next. However it started, the movement continues each year, with the fish swimming upstream when depth and flow permit.

At the water's edge, half in the shade of alders and ash, the marsh marigolds and butterbur had been replaced by flowers of equal beauty –

Opposite page:
Female butterbur on the Hodder river in the Forest of Bowland.

forget-me-nots, more monkey flowers, and giant bellflowers, well over three feet tall.

By an arched bridge sand martins had nested in holes excavated in the river bank, and a busy passage of birds fed their young. A common sandpiper flew low before landing on a rock in mid-stream and both pied and grey wagtails chased after insects over the water; a trout rose to take in a fly. Yellow wagtails are sometimes seen in the low grass meadows, while pied flycatchers also occasionally visit. Along the roadside clusters of meadow cranesbill shone a translucent blue; while in those fields empty of sheep, hay work was in full swing.

In the heat, it was hard climbing up to the high fell tops, but despite the dry weather, streams still murmured and wet flushes of sphagnum seemed bottomless. Gnats danced in the shade of pines and twigs snapped to the sound of running feet within the trees. Even in haze, the wide views of fells and valleys were a tribute to summer; bell heather and cross-leaved heath were beginning to flower, attracting bumble bees and a covey of grouse burst into the air, chattering as they flew. Briefly a small bird of prey rose, before falling back to perch on a tuft of grass – to keep me in view. From its behaviour it seemed that its nest was nearby, and I made a large detour to leave it in peace. The local gamekeeper confirmed that a merlin had young; he was a good naturalist, knowing and understanding the seasons, as well as the wildlife that goes with them: "It's a good little bird – it does no harm to us." The merlin is rather like a grey backed kestrel, flying down larks and meadow pipits, but quite capable of taking birds as large as a ring ouzel. Insects, lizards and voles will also be in danger if they remain away from cover for too long. At one time merlins were persecuted by keepers, but they take few chicks and the adult grouse are quite safe.

Unfortunately in some areas of Bowland, away from Royal land, birds of prey have been persecuted, particularly the hen harrier and peregrine. But some hen harriers do breed successfully and their numbers through-out the country are rising, enabling them to push slowly south. There is no doubt that they do take some grouse as they quarter the heather systematically; indeed their name suggests that they are quite capable of "harrying" far larger birds. Their overall impact on a grouse moor will be small, however, with most of the damage to nests, chicks and incubating birds coming from foxes and crows. The persecution of the peregrine is far more difficult to understand; for there are few of them and their effect is usually very slight. Their disappearance could be the work of gamekeepers, but pigeon fanciers and falconers must also come under suspicion.

Just as there is little doubt that hen harriers take grouse, there is also no doubt that well run grouse moors provide suitable habitat for a wide range of moorland plants, insects and birds. Without the grouse interest and the revenue it brings in, sheep densities would increase and excessive

Meadow pipit.

grazing would eventually kill the heather. Once that occurs the land owner has only two choices to get an income from his poor quality land; he can try to improve the grazing by applying fertilisers, harming the wild flora still more, or he can plant blocks of pines, which for most moorland life is a disaster.

The red grouse itself is a bird of great character and distinction. Once it was said to be unique to Britain, but now scientific twitchers have re-classified it as a sub-species of the willow grouse, which occurs over much of Europe, Asia and North America. The heather moors of Bowland are managed for grouse, being burnt in rotation, giving a patched and striped appearance; this provides plenty of short young shoots for adults and chicks alike, as well as leaving larger, older plants for cover. Consequently the surplus grouse that are shot can rightly be regarded as a harvest from the hills; they are very good to eat too. At their best they are served on fried bread, with bacon and redcurrant or rowan jelly and with port in the gravy.

Walking through the heather I flushed several more grouse, as well as the usual meadow pipits. One meadow pipit had fallen victim to the merlin, with its head and breast eaten, leaving just bones, legs and wing feathers. During the course of my visits to the Royal Estates, I became quite fond of this inconspicuous yet pretty little bird, for it is found at Balmoral, Sandringham, Windsor and the two Duchies. Throughout the natural world there is, in human terms, a great undercurrent of sadness, or even injustice, personified by the meadow pipit. It is harmless and inoffensive, yet it seems that its lot in life is to provide merlins, kestrels and even peregrines with food, and cuckoos with nests in which to lay their eggs. It is hard on the pipit, but that in turn eats numerous insects, and its demise ensures the survival of others. Despite the harassment, it has an estimated population of over three million pairs in Britain and Ireland, spreading from the Isles of Scilly to Shetland. Another moorland bird to be present on the Duchy estate is the black grouse, but throughout the Forest of Bowland its numbers are small.

Close to the unfortunate pipit I narrowly avoided treading on the caterpillar of one of our most typical moorland moths – the emperor. For a caterpillar it was enormous, over two inches long, bright green, with warty rings of yellow. Despite its gaudy colours, it merged well with the heather. The emperor moth is unmistakable; it is the only British member of the silk moth family, although its cocoons have no commercial value. The males fly in daylight during April and May, searching out the scent of un-mated females with their strange feathery antennae. The females fly at night and spend their days sitting in heather or scrub; they are larger than the males with a wingspan of three inches. Both sexes have prominent eye-spots on their wings.

Oyster-catchers watched uneasily through their crimson eyes as I sat in the shade of an alder by the river, cooling off after my climb; they

Emperor moth.

breed along the Hodder, and lesser black-backed gulls also nest well away from the sea, preferring areas of the high moors. I thought about the breaking twigs and running hooves within the pines as I had climbed the fell; it seemed likely that I had disturbed sika deer, for with Dorset and the New Forest, the Forest of Bowland is noted for their presence. Several early mornings I tried to see them grazing in the fields on the edge of the woodland, but on each occasion I was foiled by thick mist. They are not natives of Britain, coming from Japan and Siberia. The ancestors of the present Bowland deer were released between 1904–6 for sport, and some have cross bred with red deer moving down from the Lake District.

The sika is slightly larger than the fallow, but smaller than the red; if seen in the wild they cannot be mistaken for any other deer, although sightings are often brief as they like dense cover. In summer their coats are a rich chestnut brown, with many off-white spots, ideal for camouflage in dappled light, but by the autumn they become a uniform brown, which in turn is well suited for life in a winter wood. The stags have sharp antlers, but not so magnificent as those of the red, rarely exceeding four points. During the rut they make a noise resembling a whistle and the creaking hinge of a rusty gate.

Because of my failure to see them in the Forest of Bowland, I tried again as dusk approached in a private wood in the Midlands, with jays scolding and pheasants clattering up to roost. A small sapling had lost its bark, showing where a stag had been using its antlers at the start of the rut. The hawthorns and blackthorn were dense and dark, but suddenly there was the movement of a white tail – there were eight deer altogether, seven does and a stag, peering at me between the trees. They were darker and more beautiful than I had expected and when they ran they were fast and dainty on their feet for their size.

With Morecambe Bay, Winmarleigh Moss, the Wyre gravel pits and part of the Forest of Bowland, the Lancaster Survey is the richest part of the Duchy of Lancaster. The Crewe survey cannot boast such varied land, yet some of its holdings date back to 1265. It is mostly a mixture of woodland and farm fields, retaining a pleasant feeling of traditional rural England. It is an extension of the hunting landscape of the shires, for the pattern of hedgerow, copse and meadow still owes much to the early fox hunting boom, during and after the enclosures. Fox hunting still takes place, and although it does not dominate farming activities as it once did, it has left a countryside which favours many forms of wildlife in addition to the fox.

One of the oldest and most famous areas is Needwood Forest, part of the old Honor of Tutbury, which was taken into Duchy ownership in 1266. The history of the forest is linked closely to that of Tutbury castle, which also remains part of the estate. The castle is ideally positioned overlooking the valley of the River Dove. Its most famous resident was Mary Queen of Scots who was held there twice during the reign of Elizabeth I. To break the monotony the Chancellor of the Duchy provoked the anger of the Queen by going hawking and hunting in the forest with his prisoner. The forest was then rich in game and much valued for the "chase".

At that time the forest was described as having "huge oaks, limes, maples, wych-elms, holly and luxuriant underwood covering many square miles". In 1656 it covered 9,229 acres of land and contained "47,150 trees and 10,000 cord hollies and underwood", and before it was "disafforested" "20,000 deer and wild cattle roamed at large in its glades".

Most of the old land was "disafforested" and enclosed by two awards in 1805 and 1811 under George III. Then the Needwood estate covered about 8,000 acres; today 7,140 acres remain of which 1,200 acres are still woodland. The bulk of the present forest lies at the top of a steep escarpment overlooking Draycott in the Clay, in Staffordshire, and forms a plateau of red and green marls. Through the changing fashions of forestry much soft wood was planted in the twenties and thirties, based on a plan of planting and clear-felling. But now a more sympathetic view is taken; little clear-felling is done, with the emphasis being on the removal of selected timber, and much hardwood is being restored through planting and natural regeneration, particularly oak, ash and chestnut. Some firs and pines are also being planted and the future of Needwood Forest as an area of attractive mixed woodland seems secure.

Despite all the changes within the forest, there are a few areas where its old character can still be seen and the feel of a unique medieval woodland lingers in the air – it is a peculiar mixture of holly and oak, both native trees. The large oaks are in many instances surrounded by clusters of holly, not bushes, but large trees in their own right, for holly can reach sixty-five feet and at Needwood many grow to their full height. There are several explanations for this mixture; some assume it to be natural, for both the oak and the holly grow extremely well on the marl, which obviously suits them. A retired woodman can remember old forestry workers telling him as a boy that the hollies had been deliberately planted around the oaks to make the oak wood darker, and more attractive when used. Another possible explanation also involves the planting of holly around the young oaks to prevent them from being browsed by cattle and deer, for holly was once used as a natural forerunner to barbed wire – and that seems the most likely suggestion. Because of their spines, holly leaves were also sown with peas to prevent mice taking them, and were put on to maturing hams and cheeses to cover them for protection.

Holly trees are instantly recognisable with their evergreen, prickly leaves and bright red winter fruit. The berries are very popular with birds. From very early times, because of its long-lasting foliage and

Sika stag.

Fallow buck.

berries, holly was thought to represent immortality and to be able to ward off evil. Similarly it was said to be a protection against lightning and witches, and later, holly trees were planted close to houses to keep them safe. Because of its pagan popularity, churchmen then linked it to the story of Jesus, claiming that the leaves were made into the crown of thorns; the red berries were coloured by Christ's blood; the white flowers showed his purity and the bitter bark represented the passion. Consequently a tree popular with ancient beliefs was incorporated into the Christian tradition and turned into a Christmas decoration.

In the ground beneath the trees were many slot marks of deer, and during the course of my visits I had several sightings; they were fallow, again with a wide range of colour from almost black to white. On the whole they were much darker than the deer of Sandringham. Fallow deer make a fine addition to any wood, and it is good that the remnants of this ancient forest still echo with autumnal groanings, as arrogant bucks breathe out mist on cold autumn dawns.

Deer have been in Needwood Forest since at least 1313. The present population could be the survivors of these early deer, or they could have come from older stock, for fallow deer have been recorded at nearby Cannock Chase since 1271. Even before the official enclosures, the old deer parks became farms, but the deer did not disappear overnight, and venison from Needwood was sent to Buckingham Palace as late as the reign of Queen Victoria. The movements of deer are very secretive and difficult to follow, but it would be a romantic story if the original deer dispersed, only to move slowly back into their traditional woodland home.

Another old resident of the forest is the attractive holly blue butterfly, the only British blue to prefer trees and shrubs to grassland. Like all the blues it makes a welcome sight, particularly as it is one of the earliest to fly in the spring, often appearing on warm days in late March. It is distinguished from the common blue by simply having a few black spots on the underwings – none of them ringed, and without any orange markings. Normally, during the course of a summer there will be two populations, but in a long hot season there may even be three. It is an unusual butterfly in that it is the only British species to change its food plant according to the season. In the spring the eggs are laid on the flower buds of holly, but during the summer, ivy is the favourite plant. A much more recent inhabitant, much disliked by woodmen, is the grey squirrel. Strangely and most inappropriately the last recorded introduction of grey squirrels into Britain took place at Needwood in 1929* – unfortunately the Duchy has no records showing who was responsible or why the release took place.

The retired woodman who had heard of the link between dark oak and holly, knew of other plants in the wood belonging to the old forest, and they include spurge laurel, wood spurge, bitter-cress and coral root, an

* *The Naturalised Animals of the British Isles* by Christopher Lever (Hutchinson).

inconspicuous plant whose underground stems look similar to coral. He showed me a variety of trees and flowers; pines, field maples, Douglas firs, bluebells, dog's mercury, red campion and yellow archangel, resembling a flowering yellow nettle. Up in a Douglas fir he pointed to a sparrowhawk's nest, with the birds using their preferred tree, and he too looked for down caught up in the high-up webs of working spiders, to confirm the presence of young. Nearby he picked up a pheasant feather and put it in his pocket – he regards them as free pipe cleaners. We came to a well used badger's sett overlooking a small valley, lit by a pool of sunlight; with shafts of sunlight on the leaves and flowers on the woodland floor; it was the ideal place in which to have a forest home.

Across grass meadows with cuckoo flowers and hares he took me to another small part of the forest where just within the shade of trees was a fine collection of woodland flowers; wood anemones, wood sorrel, woodruff, red campion and early purple orchids. The small white flowers and ruffs of long narrow leaves are not the woodruff's only attraction, for when picked and dried, its smell of newly mown hay lingers long, and it was once widely used as a sweet smelling herb. Because of the shape of their tubers, early purple orchids were used as an aphrodisiac, to be eaten raw or added to love potions. Culpeper claimed that they "provoke venery, strengthen the genital parts, and help conception", they also "kill worms in children". Fortunately the law now prevents their removal, and in any case Culpeper's assessment was probably based on wishful thinking and superstition.

Another area of ancient forest had one more native survivor among bluebells – the beautiful but scarce small-leaved lime. It is given beauty by its shape, for its downward arching branches help it to form a smoothly rounded dome, which when on flower hums with working insects and radiates sweetness. The wood is as pleasing as the tree and was once loved by craftsmen; one of them was Grinling Gibbons who preferred to work in lime. It is also the ideal wood for piano keys and artists' charcoal. It was near a small-leaved lime in July that I came across a solitary wych-elm in full, fine leaf. Dutch elm disease has reached Needwood and most of the elms have gone, but for some strange and fortunate reason the tree stood completely unblemished. There are large-leaved limes in the wood, but few grow as genuinely wild trees in Britain, and most have been planted.

The forest is not the only part of the Crewe Survey to have flowers, for there are nearly 4,000 acres close to Crewe itself that have surprising plant life. Again the area is a mixture of undulating farms and woods, and it is refreshingly rural. The land extends to the very outskirts of Crewe, and where town turns into country the Crewe woodman has named it "the sanity line".

Through his work in the Duchy woods he has become a good and

Early purple orchids.

Elephant hawk moth.

enthusiastic naturalist and has several favourite areas. One is the marshy bed of what was once the lake of Crewe Hall; in the forties the dam was breached leaving fifty-seven acres of wild wetland. In the spring it was full of marsh marigolds, straggling willows, red campion and stitchwort, and willow warblers filled the air with falling song. By full summer it had turned into an almost impenetrable jungle, of nettles, reed canary-grass and tussock sedge, a breeding ground for vigorous mosquitoes, but visited too by snipe and mallard. It provides good breeding cover for sedge warblers, blackcaps, willow tits and willow warblers. Around the edges were sycamore, alder and rhododendrons, as well as fine yews and many wild raspberries. Recently planted woodland flowered with rosebay willowherb and broom, and there too were more badgers and signs of foxes. One small tree he claimed was suffering from "Sheffield blight" – he had accidentally hit it with a sickle while clearing weeds.

A less inhospitable area had some unexpected flowers of wetland; bogbean, marsh cinquefoil, yellow iris and marsh speedwell, with snipe breeding among them. Where the sides of a small valley dropped down to a stream were banks of greater richness, for the grasses shared their land with the unspoilt flowers of a wild northern meadow, including pignut, yellow rattle, greater bird's-foot trefoil, germander speedwell, zigzag clover, adder's tongue, common spotted orchid, bugle, cuckoo flower and field woodrush. At the water's edge they were joined by tall clumps of hemp agrimony and Himalayan balsam, and many butterflies flew – skippers, small tortoiseshells and a ragged winged comma. Common blues were also present and in direct contrast, small day-flying moths were being attracted to the brightest flowers; they were the aptly named chimney sweeper – small, dark and dapper, looking almost like a butterfly and very active in sunshine.

It was on a hot sunny day that I visited one of the smallest and most unusual Duchy holdings, just over 300 acres in the middle of the Derbyshire Peak District at Castleton, for the Peak Cavern, and, high above it, Peveril Castle, were both given to John of Gaunt. The cave entrance is set into a vertical limestone cliff that rises 250 feet to the castle, built by William Peveril, an illegitimate son of William the Conqueror. Because of its position, going deep into the earth, it had the coarse but descriptive name of "Divill's arse" in the seventeenth century. For many years rope-makers worked in the first part of the cavern, a traditional skill that finally ended in 1974; the old hand-worked machines are still there and the Duchy Custodian sometimes demonstrates the ancient craft. The Cavern is an oddity rather than an important area for wildlife, yet ash trees cling to life on the cliff face, and many jackdaws are able to nest in complete safety. When the Cavern is opened at Easter, after its winter closure, tawny owls and occasionally a barn owl have to seek shelter elsewhere. Below the high cliff, the stream whose

Pyramidal orchid.

work created the cavern has a number of very large trout, with an overhang of rock protecting them from fishermen; once inside the system of caves there are strange freshwater shrimps made colourless by the lack of light.

Of all the Surveys, it is hardest to do justice to Yorkshire, for its 21,556 acres are fragmented, with the boundaries cutting through moorland and valley sides, leaving some inside the North York Moors National Park and some outside. Much of the Yorkshire property was owned by the Duchy long before the houses of York and Lancaster were united under Henry VII, and the estates at Pickering, Goathland and Cloughton all date back to 1267; by coincidence they are the three most important areas for wildlife, and they encompass woodland, dale, moor and coastal cliffs, as well as foreshore.

Because of the variety of its countryside the Survey covers a wide range of wildlife; some is specialised and restricted in area and other branches are found throughout the region. Six sites in the Duchy have been surveyed for butterflies and moths, revealing 24 butterflies and an astonishing minimum number of 216 moths. They are a complete cross-section; the scarce small eggar, the migratory silvery Y, that arrives each spring to produce a second generation for the autumn, the large elephant hawk moth, as well as the scorched carpet and the muslin footman.

Similarly the changing landscapes and soil types have led to a diverse floral interest, with at least nine types of orchid. They are flowers that always attract me, possibly because they seem so few and far between in East Anglia, yet in Yorkshire they grow in woodland, along the cliff-tops and even by the roadside. Among the orchids to be found are the fragrant, burnt, bird's nest, frog, early purple, spotted, pyramidal, fly and greater butterfly.

The greatest wealth of wild flowers is in the Duchy woodland north of Pickering, and at its entrance in high summer was another wild field full of flowers that flourish on limestone, including the pyramidal orchid. The name perfectly describes the shape of the pink flowering head, with each small flower in the cluster being identical to that of its neighbour. They have such a plentiful supply of nectar that they attract butterflies and moths during both daylight and darkness. Another flower with an appropriate name was the ox-eye daisy – a relation of the corn marigold. The small rock rose, which looks nothing like a rose, was a lighter shade of corn marigold yellow, and among the other host of flowers was lady's bedstraw, St John's-wort, hawkweed, knapweed, great burnet, hogweed, valerian, various plantains, wild roses, rest harrow, self heal, red and white clover, and still the list was not exhausted. To see such a field of wild flowers is to echo the words of William Wordsworth:

> To me the meanest flower that blows can give
> Thoughts that do often lie too deep for tears.

Ox-eye daisies.

The seed heads of others showed what flowers had already passed, including many cowslips. Wild daffodils, violets and primroses are other flowers of spring as well as the false oxlip; it is not a true oxlip, but a hybrid cross between a cowslip and a primrose. When trees are felled the increase in light carpets the ground with primroses the following spring. At one time the flowers were so common throughout the country they were given the ugly Latin appendage "vulgaris". The word "primrose" is far better – coming from the medieval Latin "prima rosa" – the first rose – meaning the first flower of spring. Each plant has several pale yellow flowers, with a delicate scent, and towards the base of each petal there is a patch and line of darker yellow – "honey guides", to direct the bees towards the nectar. Culpeper advocated the use of primroses in medicine: "A dram and a half of the dried roots taken in the autumn, is a strong but safe emetic". For a herbalist his early demise was unfortunate – he died at the age of thirty-eight.

The presence of cowslips and primroses is important, for the rides and clearings of the woods have a good butterfly population, including the scarce and decreasing Duke of Burgundy fritillary, at one of its most northern British sites. The favourite food of the caterpillar is the leaf of cowslip, but if they are not available then primroses make an acceptable substitute. Although it looks similar to a fritillary it is in fact a different family, and is the only representative of its kind in Britain. As a result those with tidy scientific minds have recently begun to call it the Duke of Burgundy butterfly.

There are twenty-two types of butterfly at Pickering including the brown argus, the dark-green fritillary and the green hairstreak. The white-letter hairstreak is also present, possibly at its northern limit. It is a butterfly that has suffered considerably through Dutch elm disease as the leaves of elm form the foodplant. So far there are still many healthy wych-elms in the area enabling the caterpillars to feed.

Other plants in the wood include lily of the valley, globe flower and the scarce herb paris. There is much hardwood resulting from natural regeneration, particularly ash, sycamore and beech. Although many foresters and naturalists have little time for sycamore, its root system on a river bank makes an ideal holt for an otter. The retired Surveyor of Lands has a different view, however. "They are beautiful trees and can be worth a lot of money if they have a curl in the wood, for making violins. When you run your hand over it you can feel the ripple. We call it fiddle sycamore."

The best butterfly land lies just outside the North York Moors National Park, but a large block of Duchy moorland, at Goathland, is well within the Park boundary, including part of the head of Newton Dale. The National Park itself covers 553 square miles of upland, a mixture of limestones, sandstones and shales that have been folded and eroded and further confused by glacial deposits. As the last ice age retreated, melt-water was held back by ice near Goathland. It built up, before cascading over the barrier, gouging out Newton Dale as it went. The overall appearance of the area is unusual, for although much of the land rises to over 1,000 feet, there is no great feeling of height; it resembles a gently rising and falling plateau, until the land suddenly drops away into deep, wide dales – like miniature canyons, with steep sides and broad flat bottoms.

The National Park was created in 1952 and in 1950, forty-seven per cent of the area was moorland and rough pasture. Despite its special status, by 1980 this had been reduced to thirty-five per cent, due to the encroachment of improved agriculture and forestry. It is only where the grouse interest remains strong that the heather has been left untouched. Because of the threats, the National Park itself bought the 2,000 acres of Levisham Moor in 1976 to safeguard its future, and it is let for shooting and limited grazing.

The Duchy land too has grouse, as well as merlins, meadow pipits, fox and emperor moths, ling, bell heather and cross-leaved heath. It is heathermoor at the head of Newton Dale, and from the Duchy side, high up, it is a remarkable view. On the steep limestone side, birch, hawthorn and ash seem to grow from bare rock, as do guelder rose and spurge laurel. At the foot of the almost vertical wall was bog – water squelching sphagnum, with cotton grass, pennywort, bog asphodel, sundew, butter-wort, marsh violet, bogbean and pond weed. There was much bog myrtle too, although in Yorkshire it is commonly called sweet gale.

In a small moorland valley leading to an old oak wood, the bog myrtle grew even more profusely, scenting the air and making a suitable perch for a fine male stonechat, warning its fledglings, in gorse, of an intruder. A toad plodded across the path and the area also has common lizards, adders and slow worms. In the wood, dappled light played on bracken and long grasses, and as well as oak there were ancient mountain ashes, more twisted and gnarled than I had ever seen before. In the days of real horse-power mountain ash was an important tree to country people, for they believed that it kept off evil spirits and the work of witches. Horsekeepers had their whip handles made from the wood, and wore sprigs in their hats, and plough handles too were often made of mountain ash. It was included in butter churns to make the butter turn more quickly and sometimes it was even built into chimneys to keep the house safe from fires and bad luck.

Near one old tree a woodcock suddenly fluttered up, followed by three more. They flew briefly, before dropping down into high bracken. I had disturbed a mother and her almost full-grown brood – I was sorry to see them all fly unaided. The wood somehow seemed unusual, and by a stream, flowing smoothly over rocks, it suddenly struck me – for the bank-side birches and alders were almost entirely free from lichens; it showed that the air was not as clean as it seemed.

Woodcock.

Fulmar in flight.

Driving from Goathland to the coast, more Duchy woodland stands back from the road, where roe deer rest up during the day. Many of the trees are larch, planted both for the wood and their appearance – unlike most conifers they shed their leaves in winter, and in late autumn their branches hung like layered fronds of newly cast copper.

The land within the sound of the sea is undulating, with hedges and, during the summer, fields of hay and grazing dairy cattle. Larks sang high above corn, and red campion and tufted vetch filled the verges. Where the road stopped and a path ran down to the sea there was high hogweed, bracken, meadow vetchling and beds of a light, luxuriant vetch coloured with a soft hint of lilac – it was wood vetch, well away from any woodland. A whitethroat and linnet sang from brambles and then came the sea itself, with waves breaking over great slabs of eroded rock. The Duchy land spreads from just north of Scarborough, four miles along the coast, taking in a number of high cliffs and bays of crumbling clays and shales as well as solid ironstone. Spotted orchids, harebells, meadowsweet, centaury, crosswort and kidney vetch grew in profusion, and more chimney sweeper moths competed with butterflies for nectar. Many spotted burnet moths were also busy, the narrow-bordered five-spot burnet, a sub-species restricted to Yorkshire. Despite being day-flying moths and coloured with bright red spots, the burnets are safe, for their taste is quite unpalatable to birds, who quickly learn to leave them alone.

Tucked into some of the cliff ledges, kittiwakes and fulmars breed, and the long wheeling glide of the fulmar, on updrafts of air, is one of the several pleasing features of the coast. They could be overspill birds, for south of Scarborough are the spectacular 400 feet high Bempton Cliffs, with large numbers of breeding seabirds, including the only gannet colony in England – which is also the only mainland site in Britain. Consequently a long stretch of the Yorkshire coast can give sightings of sea-going birds. In the spring and autumn, terns too will fly by in large numbers, just out to sea.

Almost my last visit to royal land was to the Scarborough coast on a bleak overcast autumn day. As I arrived a woman asked: ''Have you seen the dinosaur's foot-prints? I heard about them on the television.'' Whether they were fossilised or recently arrived she did not say.

The colour of the water matched the dark bed of rock covered with weed and barnacles and showing many ammonites and other ancient remains. Because of the angle of the coast to the sea, great black rollers were pounding in, with the offshore wind lifting the crests of the waves into high clouds of spin-drift, white above the surging dark troughs. It was a fine way to finish, once more with a roaring, powerful sea.

The rough North Sea.

Opposite page:
Moorland stream near Goathland.

Reflections

I almost regretted reaching the end of this book, for it represents two years of travelling and writing, during which time the Royal Estates and their wildlife dominated my life. They have given me memories and images that I shall never forget, and I can understand why the Royal Family regards them with such affection.

To recall the ancient areas of Caledonian pine forest on the banks of the Dee; the wild seas crashing into the Isles of Scilly, and the rides and glades of Windsor with their woodland birds and glimpses of deer, will always give me pleasure. Sandringham too made an impact, where efforts have been made for farming and wildlife to coexist. To see barn owls, frogs, green woodpeckers, hares and butterflies on and over ordinary farmland was particularly pleasing, for they were once common parts of my own parish, but in the course of just over two decades they have disappeared.

It confirmed how fragile and vulnerable nature can be and that without care, as well as practical help, the countryside and the wildlife within it can be eroded away. Trees are chopped down, brooks and meadows are improved and drained, and monoculture replaces once rich and varied land. But changes are accepted and come sufficiently slowly for some people not even to notice; gradually the scales are tipped and birds, animals and flowers are lost into local, or even national extinction. Yet although modern agriculture has arrived at Sandringham barn owls and butterflies can still be seen.

To run an estate is costly, with people to employ, buildings to maintain and animals to feed, and so a financial return is essential. As a result of this pressure the estates have to be run commercially and Sandringham and the two Duchies are successful. However, on all the Royal Estates real efforts have been made to give the helping hand that nature needs; the areas of regeneration at Balmoral, the wetland and water meadows at Sandringham, and the butterfly wood in the Duchy of Cornwall are the most obvious examples. By their efforts the Royal Family has not only shown that wildlife and conservation can be encouraged, but they have also tried to set an example for other landowners and institutions to follow.

In any big organisation things can go wrong and faults can be found, and this is particularly true when dealing with farming and the land. Animals, the weather, and even farm workers can be fickle, and through them the best of intentions can be spoiled. Consequently at Balmoral cattle in a small field had barked birch trees, some old reeds at Sandringham were burnt out of rotation and on Dartmoor there had been some over-grazing by sheep. But overall the Royal Estates were well run and managed sensibly, with sympathy for the land.

In the management of its estates the Royal Family is fortunate, however, for it does not pay tax, particularly the crippling capital transfer tax; for taxation is one of the prime reasons for the over-intensification of British agriculture. Although it is fashionable to talk about "wealthy farmers" and their subsidies, the fact is that many of them are driven to obtain as much out of their land as possible. They want to hand their farms on to their children, but to do so they have to make provision for the huge tax demands on death, calculated on the "paper" value of their holdings. In order to pay this artificially created debt efforts are made to become even more productive; water-meadows are drained and old parkland is ploughed. For those that fail, large old houses are sold off separately from their land, and part of our rural heritage is destroyed. Consequently some farmers regard wildlife and conservation as an economic liability.

Surprisingly, there is no need for land to be nationalised in Britain, for the agricultural policies of successive governments have already dictated the type of farming carried out, and nationalised land would not yield the easy money that the government collects from the negative and destructive capital transfer tax. Apart from the raising of funds it is claimed that capital transfer tax is designed to force land on to the market so that newcomers can enter agriculture. Unfortunately these newcomers are often institutions that see land only as an investment; if there really was a wish to encourage newcomers into farming, then it could be achieved easily, as in France, with a limit set on the size of new holdings.

A few people have also suggested that if land was taken out of private hands, conservation would be treated more seriously. The evidence already available does not support this. Many local authorities actually have land, yet they rip out roadside hedges, they destroy wild flowers in the verges, and those with smallholdings have few stipulations about landscaping and planting trees. Even in city and country parks over-active "tree surgeons" are kept busy removing old branches and rotting wood, ensuring that there are few places suitable for woodland birds.

They have a mania for tidiness which is totally alien to the encouragement of wildlife.

Water authorities are also supposed to be "public bodies", although most are authoritarian in outlook and hostile to conservation. Their work has led to the transformation of countless once rich rivers and streams into barren drainage channels, and they have enabled thousands of acres of water meadows to be drained and ploughed. Because of the disturbance they cause and the quality of the water they discharge their activities have been one of the major reasons for the decline of the otter; this is acknowledged by many conservation bodies, but they remain quiet as they have to maintain a "working relationship" with some of the worst offenders.

Other national organisations show an equal indifference to environmental matters. One worrying aspect of my visits to Balmoral was the information already available on the damage being done by acid rain. Yet acid rain is caused mainly by the combined efforts of two nationalised British industries – coal and electricity; they appear to be doing little to curb the problem and both are supposed to be under the control of parliament. One spokesman has asked: "Is it worth spending a lot of money for the sake of a few fish?" It demonstrated his apparently limited vision, as acid rain threatens far more than fish; their plight is just a preliminary warning. It is slightly reassuring to know that when the lobbying started for the cleaning up of the air in our towns and cities, many politicians and bureaucrats were opposed on the grounds of cost; few, however, would now advocate a return to London smog.

Sadly, not all my memories of the Royal Estates are pleasant. Although the estates are beautiful, and the Queen and Prince Charles have opened up large areas for the general public to enjoy, a small minority of visitors have responded in a way that I found incomprehensible, and which offends most of those who enjoy and appreciate the countryside. As I travelled from the top of the country to the bottom, everywhere I came across litter, including a half full container of Banana Milk Shake at Loch Muick; a Beef Risotto wrapper at Wistman's Wood, and even an empty Guinness can on one of the deserted Western Rocks of the Scilly Isles. It seems incredible that an unconcerned minority should be so keen to foul the whole of their planet, even those parts set aside for beauty and wildlife. Worse still, half way up Lochnagar, on land designated as a nature reserve, was a broken bottle, left exposed and capable of crippling an otter, hare or deer.

At Balmoral others have also failed to distinguish themselves. The outbuildings of two remote houses on the estate have been made into "botheys" where climbers can rest, or seek shelter, in bad weather. The graffiti and general filth in one of them was so bad that on one occasion the Queen herself helped to clean it out. A lady-in-waiting signed the visitors' book and added the comment "The Queen swept here".

I had a saddening experience on Deeside that seemed to sum up the lack of care of some people. One evening I passed a young hedgehog rootling on the side of the road for insects. I stopped and moved him further into the verge for his own safety. The next morning he was still there – a flattened heap of prickles. Someone had been too idle or incompetent to slow down to avoid him.

Another unfortunate aspect, that came to light while writing this book, was that I have not been able to give the locations of all the species I saw and enjoyed for fear of egg collectors, twitchers and careless wildlife photographers. Even during the course of my travels I heard of twitchers on the Cairngorms walking across the high tops, like a line of pheasant beaters, trying to flush dotterel during the nesting season. At Windsor I was told of twitchers lingering around the hornbeams, so stopping the hawfinches from feeding during the short days of winter. Also at Windsor there was evidence of an egg collector living in the area who goes on highly planned egg collecting trips all over the country. Yet despite this, calls and campaigns are still being made for greater access to the countryside, while the amount of access already available is putting some wildlife at risk.

Inevitably during the last two years, the familiar calls were heard condemning the deerstalking, and pheasant shooting that takes place on royal land. I do not hunt, shoot or fish, and a few years ago wrote a book entitled *The Hunter and the Hunted* that examines the issues and the exaggerations in great detail. However, it should be said that without deerstalking at Balmoral, and in the absence of predators, there would be over-population, over-grazing, starvation and frequent bouts of disease. Even now during a hard winter the weaker deer will be lost; if deer were not shot for venison it would be a long annual season of slow death and suffering.

Pheasants and fox hunting, as well as a real and practical commitment to conservation have also led to the retention of grassland, woods and hedgerows, rich in flora and fauna. Confirmation of this comes from the remarkable fact that on the Royal Estates I saw or heard no fewer than sixteen species of birds of prey. For land outside specially managed nature reserves this is almost unheard of and reflects the health and the variety of the habitat.

Unfortunately a tremendous gap has developed between city and country. It began many years ago when people first drifted into the towns and it was even revealed by Samuel Pepys. After a visit to Windsor he wrote of it: "A very melancholy place, and little variety only trees." In many cases the urban mind simply does not see or understand the natural cycles, including life and death, that are essential for healthy wildlife populations. In a country such as Britain, over-populated and short of land, there is no such thing as a "natural balance", for many of the large predators that helped to create a balance were exterminated many years ago. In the same way there is no natural cycle in the land, with marshes, moors and forests unable to renew themselves, consequently man must manage both wildlife populations and the countryside they require as part of his responsibility towards them. Without the control of predators the avocet would not have come back to Britain. Without the management of land many wild flowers would have disappeared. During the summer of 1983 a pair of black-winged stilts nested in England, the first for many years; they received insufficient help and their eggs were taken by foxes.

It is control that allows wild pheasants to thrive at Sandringham and without the removal of great black-backed gulls on the Isles of Scilly, the tern and shearwater populations would be threatened. The fact that surplus pheasants are shot is not a contradiction; it is part of a natural harvest – man the hunter/gatherer at his most sophisticated.

An ancient Buddhist poet wrote:

> The fowl in the coop has food but will soon
> be boiled in the pot.
> No provisions are given to the wild crane
>   but the heaven and earth are his.

To me it is far easier to justify the eating of surplus wild birds and animals, that have enjoyed freedom in healthy surroundings, than to eat the meat of creatures raised intensively indoors, on monoculture wheat.

Without an interest in red deer and grouse, vast tracts of heather moor would be lost to pine plantations and more intensive sheep grazing. Much of our wildlife, typified by that at Balmoral and the Forest of Bowland would disappear, a fact confirmed by various conservation organisations. Without an interest in foxes, such as on the Duchy of Lancaster, or pheasants at Sandringham, even more areas of Britain would lose hedges and copses to arable agriculture. To know these facts and to ignore them, like some pressure groups and politicians, is both an evasion and a distortion. Unfortunately, too many people allow their judgments to be dictated by sentiment, which can be dangerous. It was uninformed sentiment that introduced the grey squirrel to Britain.

I hope that the contents of this book will have shown the true wealth of wildlife on the Royal Estates. I hope too that many people will visit those areas open to the public to see and experience them for themselves. The way in which the Royal Family manages its land and cares for its wildlife sets a great example; if others followed, then the British countryside would become a much greener and more pleasant place.

A Guide to the Royal Estates and their Wildlife

Balmoral
Balmoral Castle and grounds are open to the public from May 1st until July 31st from 10.00 a.m. to 5.00 p.m. except Sundays and when members of the Royal Family are in residence. A large car park is nearby, run by the local Regional Council. The Castle is situated close to the main A93 road between Ballater and Braemar.

A wide selection of the estate's wildlife can be seen on the Glen Muick and Lochnagar Wildlife Reserve. It consists of 6,350 acres of the estate, including Lochnagar and Loch Muick, and is run as a nature reserve by the Scottish Wildlife Trust. It is reached along the public road from Ballater into Glen Muick; at the end of the road there is a large free car park and a Visitors' Centre. The reserve offers a good chance of seeing red deer, red grouse, ptarmigan and golden eagles, as well as rarer species, depending on luck and the season.

Salmon can best be seen away from the estate at the Falls of Feugh at Banchory. The Banchory Lodge Hotel also has a fine stretch of river, with fishing available. Those wanting to see old Caledonian pine forest with public access should travel the short distance to Speyside and the Glen More Forest Park near Aviemore; the adjoining National Nature Reserve covers a large area of the Cairngorms. More superb old forest can be seen at the RSPB's Loch Garten Reserve, which in summer can give good views of ospreys, crested tits, red squirrels, and roe deer. Access is signposted from the Boat of Garten – Nethy Bridge road. A wide selection of native highland wildlife, in good surroundings, can be seen at the Highland Wildlife Park, Kincraig, Kingussie, again near Aviemore.

Sandringham

Sandringham House and Grounds are open from Easter until the end of September, except when members of the Royal Family are in residence. The grounds are usually open from 10.30 a.m. until 5.00 p.m. every Monday, Tuesday, Wednesday and Thursday, as well as from 11.30 a.m. to 5.00 p.m. every Sunday. There are ample free parking facilities. The House lies just off the main A149 Kings Lynn to Hunstanton road.

The Sandringham Country Park, Nature Trails and Picnic Areas are also open from Easter until the end of September; there is no admission charge for the Country Park. Enquiries concerning visiting dates should be made to the Estate Office, Sandringham, Norfolk, by letter or telephone.

Views of the Wash's wildlife can best be obtained at the RSPB's Snettisham Reserve – the beach is signposted in the village. Those wanting to see marsh harriers should proceed to the RSPB's Titchwell Reserve and Visitor Centre, near Hunstanton, or the Minsmere Reserve in Suffolk; details of visiting can be obtained from the RSPB, The Lodge, Sandy, Beds.

Buckingham Palace Garden

Visiting is by invitation only. Each year several thousand people from all walks of life attend the summer garden parties.

Windsor

The Great Park is open throughout the year from sunrise until sunset, as are the Valley Gardens. There is no admission charge.

The Savill Garden is open all the year, including Sundays, from 10.00 a.m. to 6.00 p.m. – extended until 7.00 p.m. at weekends during the summer. A self-service restaurant is available from March 1st to October 31st. The car parks and entrance are well signposted along the A30. Enquiries to: The Keeper of the Gardens, Crown Estate Office, Windsor, Berks.

Visits to Windsor Castle depend on its use as one of the Queen's official residences. The Precincts are open from 10 a.m. The State Apartments, however, are open only when the Queen is not in residence. Details of visiting can be obtained by writing or telephoning to: The Windsor Tourist Information Centre, Windsor, Berkshire.

The Duchy of Cornwall

Many parts of the Duchy of Cornwall are open to the public, or have roads slicing through them.

Maiden Castle is open throughout the year, with no admission charge.

There is a car park at the end of the road to the castle, off the A354 south of Dorchester.

The great drowned valley between Salcombe and Kingsbridge can be seen at both towns and there are regular boat trips between the two during the summer. Similarly, many fine sights of the Tamar estuary and valley can be obtained from the roads and villages around it. Cargreen gives views of the exposed mud-flats at low tide, while further up river, Halton Quay is particularly attractive. The nearby National Trust properties of Cothele Quay and Cothele House are also well worth a visit.

A good cross-section of Duchy land on Dartmoor is within walking distance of the B3212 road from Moretonhampstead, leading to Princetown and on to Tavistock. There are many parking places, picnic areas, and footpaths, as well as both the Warren Inn and the Dartmoor Inn. The National Park Office is situated at Parke, Haytor Road, Bovey Tracey, Newton Abbot, Devon.

Tintagel is open the whole year except Christmas Day and Boxing Day. From March 15th to October 15th it is open every day from 9.30 a.m. to 6.30 p.m. From October 16th to March 14th it is open on weekdays from 9.30 a.m. to 4.00 p.m. and from 2.00 p.m. to 4.00 p.m. on Sundays.

The Isles of Scilly can be reached by boat or air. British Airways helicopters fly regularly from the Penzance Heliport to St Mary's: information from British Airways Helicopters, Eastern Green, Penzance, Cornwall. Bryman Air Services fly from Newquay and Exeter. Details from Bryman Air Services, Roborough Airport, Plymouth.

The Isles of Scilly Steamship Company sails regularly from Penzance, including day trips. The voyage takes about two and a half hours. Booking from the Isles of Scilly Steamship Co., 16 Quay Street, Penzance, Cornwall. Information on accommodation can be obtained from The Tourist Information Centre, Town Hall, St Mary's, Isles of Scilly. A choice of accommodation is also available from Taylor Lane and Creber, The Estate Offices, Morrab Road, Penzance.

Boats of the St Mary's Boatmen's Association leave for the other major islands on most days from the spring until autumn.

Duchy of Lancaster
Various parts of the Duchy of Lancaster have public access. A large area of Duchy foreshore between the rivers Wyre and Lune, at Morecambe Bay has been made into a sanctuary, and good views of waders can be obtained at high tide during the winter. The RSPB's Morecambe Bay reserve is near Carnforth. The reserve at Leighton Moss is close by – it is away from Duchy land, but well worth a visit; I saw my first English otters there. Details of visiting from the RSPB.

For the Forest of Bowland the M6 should be left at Junctions 32 or 33 and signposts followed to the Trough of Bowland. The road passes through Dunsop Bridge and Whitewell, the centre of the Duchy holding.

The Crewe Survey has Tutbury Castle on the edge of Needwood Forest, open to visitors. It lies four miles north-west of Burton-on-Trent, close to the A50. From April until October it is open daily from 10.00 a.m. until 6.00 p.m. Arrangements for parties should be made with: The Custodian, Tutbury Castle, Tutbury, Near Burton-on-Trent.

The Peak Cavern is open each day from Easter until mid-September from 10.00 a.m. until 5.00 p.m. There are special rates for parties booked in advance. Information from: The Custodian, Peak Cavern House, Castleton, via Sheffield s30 2ws.

Information on visiting the North York Moors National Park can be obtained from the Park's Information Service at The Old Vicarage, Bondgate, Helmsley, York. The main A169 road between Pickering and Whitby passes close to the Duchy's Goathland estate, near the Ministry of Defence's early warning system at Fylingdales Moor. From car parks the moorland can be seen as well as Newton Dale. The North Yorkshire Moors Railway runs through Newton Dale from Pickering Station.
The old steam engines and the spectacular views make a pleasant combination.

Just north of Scarborough, the Cleveland Way Footpath passes along the cliff tops of Duchy land. The whole length of coastline is worth visiting and leads to Robin Hood's Bay. Details of the complete Cleveland Way can be obtained from The Countryside Commission, John Dower House, Crescent Place, Cheltenham, Gloucestershire.

HM The Queen is Patron of the Royal Society for the Protection of Birds. Details of membership and reserve visiting from: The RSPB, The Lodge, Sandy, Beds.
HRH The Duke of Edinburgh is President of the World Wildlife Fund-International. Information concerning activities, fund raising and membership from The World Wildlife Fund – UK, 11–13 Ockford Road, Godalming, Surrey.
HRH The Prince of Wales is Patron of the Royal Society for Nature Conservation. Details of local Naturalists' Trusts, membership and nature reserves from the RSNC, The Green, Nettleham, Lincoln LN2 2NR.

Acknowledgments

There are numerous people who made this book possible and many of them gave friendship as well as help, which made it such a pleasure to write. Firstly I would like to thank HRH The Duke of Edinburgh for giving permission for the book to be written and for giving up his time to talk to me, read the manuscript and write the Foreword. I am also very grateful to HRH The Prince of Wales, again for giving up time to see me and for his help and interest with the chapter on the Duchy of Cornwall.

The book would not have been possible without the assistance and encouragement of my family — my mother and father for taking in Bramble on the numerous occasions that he was unable to travel with me; my sister Rachael and sister-in-law Ellen for checking the manuscript and proofs, and my brother John for working on the farm for seven days a week, for so long, without complaint, while the book was actually being written; he showed that I am completely dispensable. Fiona Silver's contribution was also much valued, not only for her beautiful drawings and photographs, but also for her numerous helpful suggestions and aid in trying to identify various plants and flowers; one day perhaps she may even overcome her other art of falling into bogs while trying to draw.

My thanks are also due to Sir Laurens van der Post for his encouragement and interest from the book's birth until its completion; William Deedes also helped at its beginning, and Tony Littlechild and Colin Walsh of Book Production Consultants at Cambridge, who inadvertently inspired the original idea. I am grateful too, to Teresa Brown for typing the final draft so cheerfully, although various deadlines were bearing down on her.

Once the book was under way Mr John Haslam, the Queen's Assistant Press Secretary was always helpful, as was Jean Ross of the Nature

Conservancy Council and John Parslow of the Royal Society for the Protection of Birds. Gordon Beningfield was always pleased to help and advise and I would also like to thank Roger Tidman for his excellent photographs and wildlife knowledge.

At Balmoral thanks are due to the Factor, Mr M.R.M. Leslie, Sandy Masson the Head Keeper and his wife June, Betty and Charlie Wright and Nan and Alex Bain. I am particularly grateful to Neil Cook the Countryside Ranger for the benefit of all his help and knowledge, as well as for some of his superb photographs – also to his wife Lotte and daughter Denise, for her coffee on cold days. To Peggy and Dod Fraser for always making me so comfortable on each one of my visits to Scotland. To Dr Derek Mills of Edinburgh University for his advice on salmon and sea trout, Mike Everett of the RSPB, David Hay of the Freshwater Fisheries Laboratory, Pitlochry, Mr Bernard Gilchrist of the Scottish Wildlife Trust, Dr M. Young of Aberdeen University, Dr D. Jenkins of the Institute of Terrestrial Ecology at Banchory, and Mr and Mrs D. Jaffray of the Banchory Lodge Hotel.

At Sandringham my thanks to the Agent, Mr Julian Lloyd, the Head Keeper, Mr Bill Meldrum, Richard Cross and his son Edward, Jack Godfrey and George Godfrey. My special thanks to the Country Park Ranger, David Thorne, and his wife Daphne, and also the retired Head Keeper, Mont Christopher and his wife Zipha – for their knowledge, help and humour, which were always welcome. In addition, John Day, Jeremy Sorensen, and Peter Gotham of the RSPB, Dr Tim Sharrock of the Rare Breeding Birds Panel, Dick Jones of the Kings Lynn Museum, Mr J. P. Morley of the NCC, Richard Prior and Dr Stephen Tapper of the Game Conservancy, Mr John Marchant of the British Trust for Ornithology, Dr Max Walters, John Kemp and John Baxter. Help and advice on otters came from the Otter Trust, and from the Hon. Vincent Weir and Libby Andrews of the Otter Haven Project – part of the Vincent Wildlife Trust. Information on East Anglian red squirrels came from Rex Whitta of the Forestry Commission, Ian Keymer of the Ministry of Agriculture Veterinary Investigation Centre and Judith Rowe of the Forest Research Station at Farnham.

For Buckingham Palace Garden help came from the former Head Gardener Mr David Mitchell, Mr Fred Kemp, Mr David McClintock and Dr J. Bradley of the Natural History Museum.

At Windsor I received much help from the Deputy Ranger Mr A. R. Wiseman, the former Head Keeper Mr Bill Fenwick, Mr R. Taylor, Mr Graham Bish and Mr John Bond, Keeper of the Savill Gardens, as well as his predecessor Mr H. Findlay. Special thanks must go to Ted Green and Bert Winchester, as well as his wife Doris, for all their help and many excursions into the forest. Additional help came from Mr Peter Tinning and Dr Chris Smith of the NCC, the Rev. A. Harbottle, Dr Pat Morris, Sir Christopher Lever, Ian Walker, John Hooper, Jeff Bates, John

Chapell, Peter Standley and Brian Whyer. Also thanks to Mr W.P.K. Findlay author of *Fungi – Folklore, Fiction and Fact* (Richmond Publishing), for his information on fungi and lightning, and to "BB" – Denys Pitchford-Watkins – for telling me about the life cycle of his beloved purple emperor butterflies.

Help for the Duchy of Cornwall came from many people; Mr John Higgs, the Secretary and Keeper of the Records, and Land Stewards for the different sections of the Duchy; Mr M.S. Argles of the Eastern District, Mr J.O. Hitchings of the Central District, Mr J.R. Hickish of the Western District, and Lt.-Col. Ian Robertson of the Isles of Scilly. Officers of the NCC were particularly helpful, Russell Gomm, Pat Sargeant and Karen Jefferies, as well as Dr Martin Warren and Dr Bob Stebbings of the Institute of Terrestrial Ecology, Sheila Gowers of the Dorset Environmental Records Centre, Messrs J.H. Hemsley, J. Longworth-Krafft and T.W. Wright of the National Trust, Michael Chandler, Chairman of the Dorset Farming and Wildlife Advisory Group, Angela Brassley, formerly of the Devon Trust for Nature Conservation, Mr W. Arnoll, Caroline Rigby and Charles Robbins of the Cornwall Trust for Nature Conservation, and Elizabeth Lenton of the Vincent Wildlife Trust. For information on Dartmoor I am grateful to the National Park Officer, Ian Mercer, and Sue Goodfellow. Also on Dartmoor, Mr Leslie Mutton, Mr Martin Spiller and Miss Calmady-Hamlyn gave me the benefit of their many years on the moor. I am also grateful to Lyn Carr for letting me use her house on my visits to the West Country.

For the Isles of Scilly thanks to Ray Lawman of the NCC, the NCC boatman Cyril Nicholas, Prof. and Mrs L.A. Harvey, Humfrey Wakefield, John Hicks, David Knight, David Hunt, Francis Hicks, Peter Clough and Sheila Anderson of the Sea Mammal Research Unit.

In the Duchy of Lancaster I am grateful to the Clerk of the Council Mr M.K. Ridley, as well as the Surveyors of Lands, Mr J. Bailey, Mr D.J. Claxton, and Mr I. Parsons. In addition I received much valuable help from John Wilson and Dr Andre Farrar of the RSPB, and Mr N.A. Robinson, Mr J.A. Thompson and Mr M.J. D'Oyly of the NCC. In the Lancashire Survey, Owen Roberts supplied much invaluable information; more help came from Joe Pye, Malcolm Evans, Derek and Jeremy Sneeden, Gordon Stead of the Lancashire Trust for Nature Conservation, Terry Pickford, and Dr Dick Potts of the Game Conservancy. Help from the Crewe Survey came from Tom Glossop, Ray Davies, Bill Tipper, Tony Harrowsmith, Barry Vallans, and Gilbert Keaton, the Duchy Custodian at the Peak Cavern. In the Yorkshire Survey I am grateful to Harold Whitfield, Mr R.H.B. Hammersley, the former Surveyor of Lands, Philip Winter, Dr J.R. Lewis, and Mr A.J. Wallace. Also to Mr D.C. Statham and Nick Pennington of the North York Moors National Park. I would also like to thank Miriam Rothschild for allowing me to see her sika deer.

Others who have helped in various ways are Joy Greenall of the Cambridgeshire and Isle of Ely Naturalists' Trust, Claire Tidman, Melvin Allison, Paul and Ashley Barnwell, Steve Beal, Bernard Bishop, Bryan Bland, Rob Chadwick, Peter Clarke, Ray Fryatt, Alan Hale, Nicholas Huntes Ltd, Chris and Jo Knights, Paul Lee, Alan Lambert, Sara and Brian Lightfoot, Eddie Myers, Paul Pratley, Malcolm Rains, Brian Clapp, Caroline Jackson, Joe and Janet Reed, Roy Robinson, Di Rusling, Richard Waddingham, Harold Hems and Dave Horsley. Also to Ken Brett of the Dennett Engineering Co., for advice and provision of tripods, monopod and macro flash brackets.

Finally, thanks to Vivienne Schuster my agent and also to Ion Trewin, Christine Medcalf and Sharyn Troughton at Hodder and Stoughton for their enthusiasm and great patience. For all those I have temporarily forgotten while compiling this monumental list – I am sorry.

ILLUSTRATIONS
All line drawings are by Fiona Silver

Photographs
Roger Tidman – short-eared owl, p.16; a ptarmigan, p.18; the Linn of Muick, p.31; flowering chickweed wintergreen, p.47; adder, p.47; dwarf mountain azalea, p. 51; male redstart, p.54; cock pheasant, p.61; common snipe, p.63; black bryony berries, p.63; fly agaric, p.66; butterbur, p.70; Daubenton's bat, p.79; common frog, p.81; a dotterel, p.82; water avens, p.82; a pair of shelduck, p.83; a reed warbler, p.87; Buckingham Palace garden, p.94; peacock butterfly, p.99; adder's tongue, p.99; dabchick on nest, p.111; great spotted woodpecker, p.119; heron, p.123; kingfisher, p.123; fox, p.127; white admiral, p.131; hawfinch, p.138; jay with acorn, p.139; spotted redshank, p.150; coal tit and marsh tit, p.155; dipper with full beak, p.163; common blue, p.167; hottentot fig, p.174; gannet, p.179; puffin, p.179; young herring gull, p.183; grey phalarope, p.188; turnstone, p.195; sedge warbler, p.199; emperor moth, p.206; early purple orchids, p.210; elephant hawk moth, p.210; fulmar in flight, p.215.

Fiona Silver – Balmoral, p.14; Loch Muick, p.46; marsh pennywort, p.89; cotton grass, p.90; red-breasted geese, p.98; Windsor, p.102; bluebell wood, p.115; ancient oak, p.119; beef steak fungus, p.135; Tintagel, p.142; Maiden Castle, p.147; dawn on the Tamar, p.151; heath fritillary, p.154; old oaks, p.159; coastal view, p.171; thrift, p.178; seaweed, p.181; Annet, p.187; pyramidal orchid, p.211; moorland stream, p.214; the North Sea, p.215; Balmoral, p.222.

Neil Cook – Loch Muick, p.19; red deer stag, p.27; Lochnagar in snow, p.35; mountain hare, p.36; golden eagle with mountain hare (Aquila), p.38; rogue cock capercaillie, p.39; Balmoral Castle, p.43; harebells, p.55; p.216.

Tim Graham – the Queen at Balmoral, p.57; the Queen Mother at Sandringham, p.75; Prince Philip on the Long Walk at Windsor, p.105.

Robin Page – Scotch argus, p.23; pair of mandarins, p.140; grey seal, p.189; p.190; corn marigolds, p.195; female butterbur, p.202.

David Thorne – Sandringham, p.58.

Bob Scott – young marsh harrier, p.83.

Philippa Scoones – badger cub, p.118.

Frank V Blackburn – hobby, p.129.

The Western Morning News Co. Ltd. – Prince Charles on a Duchy Farm, p.145.

Index